CHAMPIONSHIP MOCK TRIAL

The Guide for Students and Coaches

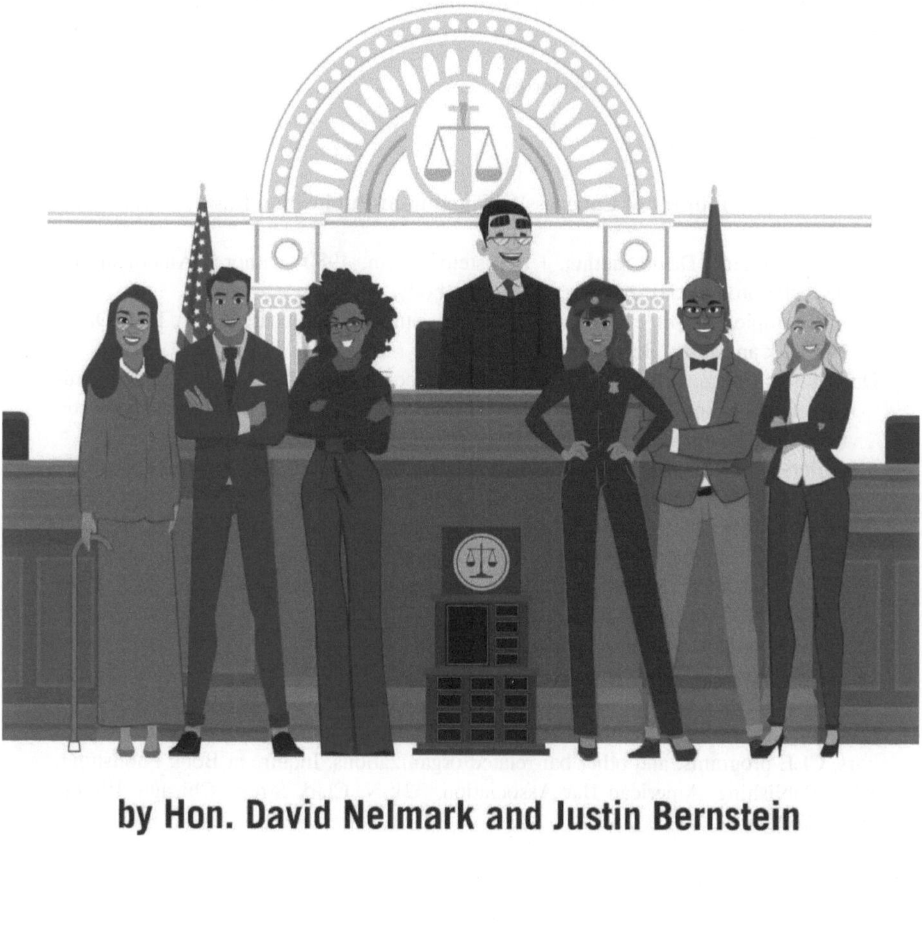

by Hon. David Nelmark and Justin Bernstein

Cover design by Sara Wadford/ABA Design

Printed in the United States of America.

26 25 24 23 22   5 4 3 2 1

Library of Congress Cataloging-in-Publication Data

Names: Nelmark, David, author. | Bernstein, Justin, 1980- author. | American Bar Association. Judicial Division, sponsoring body.
Title: Championship mock trial : the guide for students and coaches / by Hon. David Nelmark and Justin Bernstein.
Description: Chicago, Illinois : American Bar Association, [2022] | Includes bibliographical references and index. | Summary: "This book will teach you the nuts and bolts you need to be competitive in Mock Trial"—Provided by publisher.
Identifiers: LCCN 2022012424 (print) | LCCN 2022012425 (ebook) | ISBN 9781639050925 (paperback) | ISBN 9781639050932 (epub)
Subjects: LCSH: Mock trials. | Law—Study and teaching—United States. | Law—Study and teaching (Secondary)—United States.
Classification: LCC KF8918.N45 2022 (print) | LCC KF8918 (ebook) | DDC 340.071/173—dc23/eng/20220526
LC record available at https://lccn.loc.gov/2022012424
LC ebook record available at https://lccn.loc.gov/2022012425

Contents

Foreword

I am 46 years old, and I've been competing in or coaching trial advocacy competitions for exactly half my life. That's not because I come from a family of attorneys. (I didn't know any lawyers growing up.) It's not because I became a trial lawyer. (I didn't do my first trial until I was more than two decades out of law school). And it's not for the money or the class credit. (I've never gotten either of them for doing mock trial.) So why do I tell anyone who asks—students, parents, teachers, other lawyers—that they should compete in, coach, or help judge trial advocacy competitions?

The first reason is simple: *It's fun*. Mock trial combines the best of debate, forensics, and theater. You get to compete with your teammates but also against an opponent who is fighting back in real time. It allows you to build a case and create memorable characters, and then forces you to adapt when things don't go as planned. Even though mock trial is obviously fake, the adrenaline rush is every bit as real as those I've had in actual courtrooms.

The second is obvious: *You'll learn a ton*. There are the obvious things—the rules of evidence, courtroom procedure, and even a decent chunk of "substantive" law. But the most important lessons mock trial has to teach are just as valuable regardless of whether you have any interest in becoming a "real" lawyer. How to be a clear, confident, and persuasive public speaker. How to quickly absorb new material and then explain it to someone who has no idea what you're talking about. How to work as part of a team and alongside people with different backgrounds, perspectives, experience, and interest levels. I've learned more from mock trial than any class I've ever taken, and I've seen it help dozens of students become better versions of themselves no matter what they end up doing with their lives.

The last reason may be the most important: *It builds communities*. Two of our most dedicated volunteer judges are one of my high school teammates and a person whose team beat our team at the state competition 30 years ago. The students I've coached have become roommates in college, in law school, and for years beyond, and some have even gotten married. (Truth be told, I'm also married to someone with whom

I competed.) There's nothing quite like sustained hard work towards a shared goal—including periodic tensions and stress, the thrill of victory, and, yes, even the sting of defeat—to form lasting bonds and bring people together.

Anything worth doing is worth doing well. And no matter how good you are, there's always more to learn and room to get better. That's where this book comes in. Professor Justin Bernstein and Judge David Nelmark are two of the smartest and most thoughtful people I've ever met. I've learned a ton from them, and I'm sure you will too.

Toby J. Heytens
American Mock Trial Association Coaches Hall of Fame
All-American Attorney and National Champion Coach

About the Authors

Hon. David Nelmark

Judge Nelmark graduated first in his class from Drake University, where he earned two bachelor's degrees from the College of Liberal Arts and the College of Journalism and Mass Communication. After earning a perfect score on the Law School Admissions Test (LSAT), he enrolled at Stanford Law School where he served on Law Review and graduated Order of the Coif (top 10 percent of the class).

After clerking for the Honorable Michael J. Melloy on the Eighth Circuit Court of Appeals, he worked in private practice in Des Moines, Iowa, at the firms of Belin McCormick and Gislason & Hunter. His broad litigation practice resulted in significant jury verdicts representing both plaintiffs and defendants. He was elected as a shareholder in both firms and as President of the Polk County Bar Association. In July 2019, Iowa Governor Kim Reynolds appointed him as a District Court Judge.

Very few people have devoted more years of their life to Mock Trial than Judge Nelmark. He is so deep into the activity that when his wife's pregnancy was announced on social media, the first comment on the post was "I assume the name will be gender neutral." (If you're new to Mock Trial, that joke will make sense by the end of the book.)

The nation's first Middle School Mock Trial tournament occurred in Iowa in 1984. Judge Nelmark started competing in that program in 1988. As a high school competitor, he helped coach a middle school team. While in college, he helped coach a high school team. Prior to law school, he was the head coach of the Drake University Mock Trial program, which had two teams ranked in the top 25 nationally. He co-founded the Stanford Law School Mock Trial team and was a competitor and coach on the team, which qualified for a national championship tournament in its second year of existence.

In addition to competing and coaching, Judge Nelmark has been involved in multiple aspects of tournament administration. He was on the Board of Directors of the American Mock Trial Association (AMTA) and also served as its Tabulation Director. He hosted two AMTA National

Championship Tournaments in his hometown of Des Moines, Iowa. In 2010, Judge Nelmark became the first former competitor to be elected as President of AMTA. In 2014, he became the youngest recipient of AMTA's Neal Smith Award, which recognized his contributions to legal education. He also had the distinction of being the youngest AMTA President until his record was broken by . . . Justin Bernstein.

Justin Bernstein

Justin Bernstein is a professor and the director of trial advocacy at UCLA School of Law. He is a former president of the American Mock Trial Association and, in 2014, became the youngest person inducted into its Coaches Hall of Fame, at age 33. He is the only coach who has won national championships at the high school, college, *and* law school levels.

Professor Bernstein grew up in San Diego. After earning a perfect score on the SAT, he enrolled at UC Berkeley and joined the Mock Trial team. He earned three All-American Attorney Awards, the highest accolade available to collegiate competitors. At New York University School of Law, he was the first student in school history to win the fall and spring closing argument competitions. He also coached NYU's undergraduate team to its first appearance at the National Championship Tournament—and, eventually, its first national title.

After law school, Professor Bernstein worked for global law firms—O'Melveny & Myers and Haynes and Boone—where he represented Fortune 500 companies in large, sometimes high-profile, lawsuits. While practicing law, he taught at the University of California, Irvine, for nine years and coached its undergraduate team to back-to-back #1 national rankings.

Professor Bernstein has consulted with dozens of High School Mock Trial teams across the country. More than half the schools that hired him to assist with preparing for the Empire competitions went on to win a national or world championship.

Professor Bernstein has written more than 20 Mock Trial cases and hosted more than 30 Mock Trial competitions. He created Gladiator and Trial by Combat (the first one-on-one Mock Trial tournaments in high school and college history, respectively), the Beach Party tournament (the first bracket style competition in college Mock Trial history), and The Verdict (the first jury trial competition in law school history).

Professor Bernstein's law school teams have won all three of the most prestigious national tournaments: Tournament of Champions, the National Trial Competition, and the Student Trial Advocacy Competition.

In 2020–21, his UCLA teams became the first to win all three in the same season. He was the first coach to win Top Gun (the law school one-on-one national championship) twice. At the time of publication, UCLA Law's trial team was ranked #1 for the third consecutive season.

Acknowledgments

Only a small portion of the content in this book represents my original thought. Many of the tips and tricks were shared with me when I was a competitor or coach. Accordingly, the book is dedicated to everyone who has ever judged one of my teams' rounds and given feedback.

Special thanks to the attorney and educator coaches I had in middle school and high school (especially Beverly Ellis, Harvey Kimble, Kris Ensign, and Julie Kaercher.) Thanks to Alan Olson who taught many of my college teammates, and to Mary Lynn Neuhaus who brought me into the leadership of the American Mock Trial Association. Finally, deepest thanks to my own college coach Brad Reich, who is in the coaching tree of the Honorable Robert Blink and Jeff Noble. Professor Reich changed the way I thought about Mock Trial and influenced my life well beyond the activity.

Hon. David Nelmark

My mother, Anita Charney, has always been my biggest cheerleader—in Mock Trial and everything else. When I competed in college, she came to watch, no matter how far she had to fly. When my students compete within driving distance of her home in San Diego, she comes to watch. And when they compete farther away, she sends care packages to their hotels. This book is dedicated to her.

I thank Gonzalo Freixes, the coach who happened to judge my first round of collegiate Mock Trial. His encouragement—to a rival team—helped spur my success. I thank my friend Toby Heytens. Speaking with him and facing his teams has made me a better coach. I thank Mary Lynn Neuhaus for nominating me to the American Mock Trial Association board of directors—without asking me first!

Finally, I thank my students, who have made Mock Trial so fun and rewarding.

Justin Bernstein

We also thank everyone who reviewed this book and offered feedback: Vicki Drake, Matthew Eslick, Carl Gebo, Amber Haberl, Brandon Harper, Sue Johnson, Kaden Koch, Tim Semelroth, Anna Smith, William Warihay, Julie Warner, and Melissa Watt. It is a better book because of your help.

1

Introduction

Mock Trial is the greatest extracurricular activity ever created. Go ahead and argue with us about that. But you'll lose. Because we did Mock Trial.

If you think you might want to be a lawyer, Mock Trial is unparalleled training. Even if you don't want to be a lawyer, Mock Trial provides invaluable professional and life skills:

- Acting
- Adaptability
- Civility
- Confidence
- Creativity
- Critical Thinking
- Listening
- Memorization Persuasiveness
- Preparation Public Speaking
- Teamwork
- Thinking on Your Feet
- Time Management
- Work Ethic

But don't do Mock Trial merely because it's good for you. Join Mock Trial because it's fun, exciting, and creates lifelong friendships.

If you're a beginner, this book will teach you the nuts and bolts you need to be competitive. If you're experienced, this book's advanced advice will take you from good to great.

If you are new to the activity, the next four sections will give you a basic understanding of how it works. For those of you already familiar with the competition and its benefits, skip ahead to Section 1.5.

1.1 What Is a Trial?

People have disagreements all the time. They disagree about who was supposed to wash the dishes, whether an essay deserved a B+ or an A–, and whether LeBron is better than Jordan (he isn't). Most disagreements are resolved without going to court. But sometimes people need the legal system to help resolve their differences. The process can involve criminal law—when the government accuses someone of an illegal activity, such as theft. Or it can involve civil law—when people or companies sue each other, such as a pedestrian suing the driver who hit her or a man suing the pharmaceutical company whose medication made him sick.

When those disputes end up in a courtroom so a judge or jury can decide who is right, we call that a trial. But most people don't have the legal knowledge or skills to represent themselves in court. So they have lawyers to advocate for them. The lawyers offer exhibits, such as videos, emails, and physical evidence. The lawyers have witnesses come to court and tell the judge and the jury what they know. And the lawyers argue that the evidence—the exhibits and the witnesses—proves that their side is correct. Once the lawyers finish their presentations, the jury discusses the evidence and announces their decision as to which side prevailed; this is called a "verdict."

1.2 What Is Mock Trial?

A "mock trial" is what it sounds like: a "mock" or pretend version of a real trial. Mock trials occur in a variety of contexts—for example, some lawyers will use mock trials to prepare for real ones—but this book focuses on competitive "Mock Trial" where students play the roles of attorneys and witnesses, and the win is awarded to the team that scores the most points.

Each season, teams are given a "closed universe" case packet that includes everything needed to prepare for competition: witness statements, exhibits, and legal documents. Two opposing teams represent the two sides of the case during a trial or "round." A tournament typically lasts three to five rounds. In some rounds, the team represents the defense. In other rounds, the team represents the plaintiff (in a civil case) or the prosecution (in a criminal case).

Whether the case is civil or criminal, it is designed to be evenly balanced with facts helpful to both sides. The goal of the competition is to determine which team puts on the better performance. If a case were one-sided, the winner of the round could be determined by which team was lucky and drew the better side.

The judge and jurors are generally real attorneys, and they score each part of the trial. The winner is the team that receives the higher scores, not the team that wins the verdict. In fact, in most instances, the verdict is not even announced. Why? Because in real life the jury's goal is to reach the correct result, but in Mock Trial the scorers' goal is to identify the stronger team.

1.3 Overview of a Mock Trial Round

In the real world, lots of things happen prior to trial, including the filing of the lawsuit or the pressing of criminal charges and discovery (where parties ask questions and get documents from the other side). Mock Trial hits fast forward on all that and jumps to the juicy part.

1.3.1 Getting Started

Your team gets to the courthouse and learns that you'll be representing the defense in your first trial. You head to your assigned courtroom. This is where you will battle for the first round. You say hello to the opposing team and wish them good luck.

You find the appropriate counsel table. Witnesses and coaches sit in the gallery. You wait for the judges.

The judges enter the courtroom. Everyone stands. The presiding judge sits on the bench, at the front of the courtroom. The other judges—also known as scoring judges, scorers, raters, or evaluators—sit in the jury box. The presiding judge tells everyone they may be seated.

1.3.2 Preliminary Matters

The attorneys introduce themselves. Your opponent says: "Good morning, Your Honor. My name is Maxine Gomez, and I represent the State." You provide your own introduction. In some competitions, it's also customary for witnesses and coaches to introduce themselves, but in others, including college Mock Trial, only the lawyers introduce themselves at the start of trial.

Trial usually begins with some preliminary matters, sometimes called "housekeeping." This is procedural and can include learning the judge's preferences—for example, whether attorneys may move around while speaking or whether they must remain at a podium. Some competitions also include substantive arguments at the start of trial, called "motions in limine" or "pretrial arguments." These usually relate to whether a key piece of evidence will be permitted during trial.

1.3.3 Opening Statements

The "opening statement" is a speech at the beginning of trial. It is not evidence; instead, it is a preview of the evidence the jury will hear during the course of the trial. In a criminal trial, the prosecuting attorney goes first, explaining what the case is about and summarizing the evidence she will present to prove the defendant's guilt. She tells the jury this is a murder trial, and the defendant had the means, motive, and opportunity to commit the crime. She summarizes her case theory into a catchy theme the jury will remember. You're on next. You explain what evidence will be missing and why the prosecution will not be able to prove its case.

1.3.4 Witness Examination

The prosecution calls its first witness: an eyewitness who says he saw the defendant pull the trigger. The witness walks to the "witness stand," a seat at the front of the courtroom. The lawyer who called the witness asks questions to highlight the key facts in the case, and the witness answers. They're teammates from the same school. This is called "direct examination." When the opposing attorney asks a question that your team thinks is inappropriate, one of your lawyers can object. "Objection, speculation!" The judge acts as referee, deciding which questions and answers are okay for the jury to hear. When the evidence is permitted, the objection is "overruled." If the evidence is excluded, the objection is "sustained."

Once the prosecution is done questioning the eyewitness, your defense team gets a chance to question the witness. This is called "cross-examination." Your goal is to undermine the witness's testimony. You establish that the witness didn't have a clear view of the murder and can't be sure it was the defendant who fired the gun.

The prosecution calls more witnesses—say, a police officer and a forensics expert. They show some exhibits to the jury. Each time a witness takes the stand, the prosecution asks questions first to build their case, and then you ask questions to tear it down.

After the prosecution finishes calling their witnesses (usually three or four), the prosecution "rests." That means they will not be calling any more witnesses. The court takes a short break (known as a "recess").

Now you get to present your case. You call the same number of witnesses. Your attorneys perform the direct examination of each witness, asking questions that allow the witness to tell their story. One witness provides an alibi for your client. Another presents evidence that maybe it was someone else who killed the victim. But each time you finish questioning a witness, the prosecution gets their chance to cross-examine. They show that the first witness was biased, and the second has a history of dishonesty. Notice that the witnesses play a huge role in the trial.

After the defense finishes calling its witnesses, the defense announces that it "rests" its case. The court takes another short break.

1.3.5 Closing Argument

Each team gives a speech about why their side is right. We call this a "closing argument." The prosecution goes first. The attorney explains why the evidence proves the defense is guilty. Then the defense gives its closing argument. Your attorney explains that the prosecution has not met its burden of proof because there is reasonable doubt about who killed the victim. Then the prosecution gives a "rebuttal," a short final argument.

1.3.6 After the Trial

The judges fill out a "ballot," a sheet where they write scores for each part of trial (or a computer version of the same). Each trial function is scored, generally on a 1–5 or 1–10 point scale. Those ballots are collected by the tournament organizers, who calculate results (usually in another room called the Tab Room). Meanwhile, the judges provide feedback to the teams on what they did well and what they can improve. Take notes, so you can later discuss with your teammates and coaches which aspects of the feedback to incorporate.

You shake hands with the other team, pack up your exhibits and legal pads, and get ready for the next trial. You're about to do it all again, this time representing the prosecution.

***

That was one trial. A Mock Trial competition usually gives each school about four trials. You will represent both sides: the prosecution/plaintiff[1] and the defense. Each trial has a different presiding judge, different scoring judges, and a different opponent.

If you're lucky, the competition will take place in an actual courthouse where you can argue your case in real courtrooms. Some competitions take place on campus, where classrooms or conference rooms are rearranged to resemble courtrooms.

1. "Plaintiff" and "prosecution" are often used interchangeably in this book. In any tournament, the case has a plaintiff (in a civil case) or a prosecution (in a criminal case) but not both.

Competitions usually occur either over a single weekend with trials back to back or over a series of weeknights. Trials are rarely held during normal weekday work hours because that's when lawyers and judges—the volunteers who preside over and score your trials—are working and when courthouses are busy with real cases.

The cumulative results from all of the trials determine which teams advance to the next stage of competition.

1.4 The Five Obstacles

In Mock Trial, there are five obstacles standing between you and victory. This book will help you navigate them.

Your first obstacle is the fact pattern. It is supposed to be written so both sides have equally strong positions. Each party has to deal with some really bad facts—witnesses who aren't credible, investigators who were sloppy, or defendants who said incriminating things. When you represent the prosecution, you need to find a way to make it sound like the prosecution has the better argument. Then when you represent the defense, you need to flip it and make it sound like the defense is right. And whichever side you're on, you need to find a way to address the bad facts.

Your second obstacle is time. Mock Trial has strict time limits for your opening statement, witness examinations, and closing argument. The cases are complicated. You might be arguing a murder case that, in real life, would take weeks. But you have only two or three hours. How will you take a case that real lawyers spend weeks presenting and package it in a way that's persuasive in two to three hours?

Your third obstacle is the rules of evidence. These are the rules that limit which questions your attorneys are allowed to ask, what answers your witnesses are allowed to give, and what exhibits you're allowed to show to the jury. For example, attorneys can't ask leading questions on direct examination ("The person you saw commit the crime was the defendant, wasn't it?") because we don't want lawyers putting words in the witness's mouth. Witnesses can't guess or "speculate." They need to stick to what they *know*. And you can't show the jury the murder weapon unless a witness testifies that it is authentic—that it's actually the knife recovered at the scene. If you don't know the rules of evidence, your opponents will object and prevent you from proving your case.

The fourth obstacle is the judges. Every presiding judge interprets the rules of evidence a little differently. But you won't know your presiding judge's approach until the trial gets underway. You have to evaluate a presiding judge the way a batter evaluates a pitcher. You look for tendencies and preferences. That way you can win objections, which will allow you to present all of your desired evidence and prevent the other side from presenting all of theirs. You also need to think about your scoring judges. Every scoring judge, like every person, comes to a trial with their own opinions, biases, and life experiences. How can you present the case in a way that appeals universally so that people who normally hold very different views all agree with you?

Notice that, so far, all of the obstacles are also opportunities. It's hard to present a balanced fact pattern in a way that makes your side look like it's on the side of justice—but if you do, you will look more persuasive than your opponent. It's hard to present a complicated fact pattern in a tight time limit—but if you do, your position will be clearer than your opponent's. It's hard to learn the rules of evidence, and harder still to adapt your understanding to the interpretations of a particular judge—but if you do, you will control the courtroom. It's hard to craft a trial strategy that will appeal to a diverse set of strangers—but if you do, you will be in a position to win no matter which judges are assigned to your round.

Your final obstacle is the opposing team. You will face smart, talented, hardworking people who want to succeed just as much as you do. They will try at every chance to show why your theory of the case is wrong. They will object to your evidence. Their witnesses will argue with your questions. They will be fighting for the same thing you are: points.

1.5 It's All About Points!

Dick Calkins, the founder of the American Mock Trial Association (AMTA), loves to say: "All are winners in Mock Trial!" That's true. If you work hard at this activity, you will reap great rewards, whether by ultimately becoming a lawyer or by doing something else entirely. The benefits are both personal and professional.

The goals of Mock Trial teams vary widely. Whatever your goals, the strategies in this book will help you reach them. Some new teams are just trying to win a ballot. Some experienced teams will be disappointed with anything less than a national championship. Some new teams and some experienced teams just want to have fun. While it's appropriate for the competitors, captains, and coaches to put their heads together and select a reasonable goal, the authors would like to remind everyone that having fun and winning are not mutually exclusive. Quite the contrary. Winning is fun!

So how do you win? How do you advance to the playoff rounds? How do you win your county and then your state? By remembering that the goal of Mock Trial is to score points.

This is the mantra that drives every piece of advice in this book. *The goal is to score points.* More specifically, the goal is to consistently score more points than your opponent. The goal isn't to win the verdict. The goal isn't to win more objections than the other side. The goal isn't to have better witnesses or better lawyers. These are all useful goals, of course. But they are useful because they help you score more points than the other team.

Mock Trial is part art. There is some amount of subjectivity. Not all scoring judges like the same things. The "best" team does not always win. That can be extremely frustrating. If you can't deal with that, take up bowling.

But Mock Trial is also part science. The strongest Mock Trial teams find ways to be universally appealing—to find success regardless of who is judging them. The strongest teams win year after year. Since 1999, Tim Semelroth's teams have won nine Iowa High School Mock Trial Championships, and from 2013 to 2019 the Central Carolina Homeschoolers won the North Carolina competition every season. Rhodes College qualified for the collegiate national championship tournament 33 years in a row. Professor Bernstein has coached three different schools to #1 national rankings. That's not luck. These teams have figured out how to maximize their chances of outscoring other teams regardless of who is scoring their rounds or what side of the case they are arguing.

There is a reason we say "how to maximize their chances of outscoring other teams" instead of "how to win every time." No trial strategy can guarantee victory. Even Central Carolina Homeschoolers, Rhodes College and UCLA Law lose trials. But the best trial strategy will help you win the most competitions.

As you make decisions about how to organize your practices and how to present your case, keep coming back to the goal: *It's All About Points!* Should we create a timeline on a whiteboard to help the jury follow the sequence of events? Should we mention any of the bad facts in our opening statement? You make those decisions by asking whether it will help you score points. Should I object to my opponent's question as irrelevant? Should I try to impeach the witness because she said "possibly" when her witness statement says "probably"? Again, you make those decisions by asking what will help you score points.

Okay, you're thinking, *but how do I know what will help me score points?*

Step one: Keep reading.

2

Building Your Case

2.1 The Case

Real attorneys often have to find their evidence. Prosecutors rely on police officers. Criminal defense lawyers often hire investigators. Civil attorneys use a process called "discovery," which allows them to demand documents from the other party ("requests for production") and question witnesses under oath before trial ("depositions").

Let's Get Real: In real life, the process of finding evidence is so lengthy that cases often take years to reach trial.

In Mock Trial, your life is much easier. All of the information gathering has already been done for you! That's the "fact pattern"[1]: a collection of all the evidence that each side can choose from in presenting their case. The components of a fact pattern typically include:

- **Witness Statements.**[2] This category includes affidavits (fact summaries prepared by witnesses), depositions (transcripts of witnesses answering questions under oath), and police reports and expert reports (witnesses' summaries of methods, evidence, and conclusions).
- **Exhibits**. This includes charts, maps, ransom notes, photographs, emails, etc.

1. Sometimes it's called a "case packet," "case problem," "fact situation," etc.

2. Although this book will generally refer to "affidavits," the techniques are equally applicable to depositions, "witness statements," or wherever content for the characters is derived from.

- **Stipulations**. These are the facts agreed to by both parties. For example, the parties might agree that a person was left-handed or that a certain witness is unavailable to testify.
- **Governing Law**. These are the legal rules that govern the trial. They can include statutes (codified legal rules, such as the definition of murder), case law (also known as "precedent," case law is past decisions by judges in similar circumstances), pretrial orders (rulings that will dictate how the trial will operate), and jury instructions (which, in real life, are read by the judge at the close of evidence before the jury deliberates to reach a verdict).

Sometimes the case packet also includes competition rules or the rules of evidence, though often those are separate documents. In high school competitions, the rules of evidence and governing law may be simpler than their real-world counterparts for two reasons. First, the competitors have not graduated from law school. Second, a Mock Trial is typically completed in three hours or less, whereas a real-world trial may last days, weeks, or even months. Most college and law school competitions use the Federal Rules of Evidence (or a slightly modified version of them).

The length of the case packet varies widely by competition. We've seen everything from 25 pages to 300 pages. Interestingly, most law school case packets are shorter than the average college case (because college cases have more witnesses).

Every team member should read the *entire* case packet. Although specialization happens over the course of the season, and different team members will focus on certain parts of the case (a witness might read her statement hundreds of times in order to memorize it), it's imperative that every member of the team has a working knowledge of everyone else's parts and roles. Without knowing how things fit together, it's impossible to contribute meaningfully to discussions about theme and theory.

2.2 The Law

So what's the best way to read the case? Start by understanding the law—specifically, figure out what the prosecution has to prove for each charged crime or what the plaintiff has to prove to hold the defendant liable. Sometimes you learn this from a statute. Other times it's part of the jury instructions. Each fact that a party has to prove in order to establish a crime, claim, or affirmative defense is called an "element." The elements become a checklist for each side.

Let's Get Real: While Mock Trials usually have one charge or claim that must be proven, real trials often feature a lot more. Judge Nelmark and Professor Bernstein have both litigated cases where the plaintiff alleged more than a dozen separate causes of action—and that's not unusual.

For example, suppose in a civil case, the plaintiff Julia has sued a parasailing company after her husband Ethan was seriously injured in a crash when the boat failed to go the proper speed. Julia sues the company for negligence. This means Julia must prove (1) the company owed a duty to Ethan, (2) the company breached that duty by acting carelessly, and (3) the company's carelessness caused Ethan's injuries. Each of those three facts is an element of the plaintiff's claim.

That legal information tells you what you have to prove during trial. If you are the plaintiff, you win the verdict by proving all three elements of your claim for negligence. If you are the defense, you win the verdict if the plaintiff fails to prove any of its three elements. Now when you read the witness statements and exhibits, you will understand which facts of the case are most important—because those are the facts that help prove or disprove one or more of the elements.

After you read the prosecution's charges (or plaintiff's claims), see if there are any affirmative defenses. An affirmative defense is an argument that the defense can prove to defeat the prosecution's charge. Not all cases involve affirmative defenses. Going back to our parasailing example, suppose the company raises an affirmative defense of assumption of risk, which requires the company to prove Ethan (1) understood the risk that sometimes parasailers crash and (2) chose to participate in the activity anyway. Both of those facts are elements of the company's affirmative defense. If the plaintiff proves the company was negligent, the defense still wins the verdict if it proves Ethan was properly informed and assumed the risks of parasailing. Again, understanding the affirmative defense will help you recognize which facts are important as you read the witness statements. Legal elements in a Mock Trial often vary slightly from those in the real-world location where the tournament is held. So, it's important to focus on your case packet.

You might ask, "Why does proving your case matter? You're the ones who said it's all about scoring points!" True. But judges are more likely to score you highly if it's clear that you know the elements you need to prove and if you introduce facts to prove those elements.

2.3 The Facts

There is no "right way" to read a Mock Trial case. Some people read it slowly the first time, trying to absorb as much as possible. Judge Nelmark likes to read it through quickly to see the big picture and then go back through and take notes on the details. Professor Bernstein reads it once, identifies every possible theory for each side, and then reads the case again to see which facts support each theory.

But no matter how you read the case, you will need to organize the information. It will help you discover connections, patterns, missing facts, and more. The following sections offer some effective methods for organizing the information.

2.3.1 T-Charts

For each witness, make a "T-Chart," listing the character's name at the top, with a line down the middle of the page. On one side, write all the things that are good for the plaintiff, and, on the other side, write down everything that is good for the defense. In a well-written case, there should be plenty of material on both sides. At the bottom of the page, you can note facts that might be useful to both teams. These T-Charts can serve as the building block for initial direct and cross-examinations.

Here is an example T-Chart from the 2013 American Mock Trial Association's case, *Allen v. Neptune Underwater Expeditions,* where a scuba diver died during a tour led by a professional scuba company.

Frankie Fernandez—plaintiff eyewitness to scuba diving accident	
Plaintiff facts	**Defense facts**
• Experienced diver (can explain how scuba diving works) • Fairly unbiased—no relationship to parties • Present during fatal dive • Saw defendant's scuba dive leader tell decedent to swim alone • Saw dangerous conditions (dark, strong current)	• Thought guides were excellent • Can support affirmative defense that decedent was negligent • Heard decedent ask beforehand if he could swim to lower part of shipwreck; heard guides say no • Saw decedent ask to swim ahead • Can identify flashlight found in lower part of shipwreck as belonging to decedent

2.3.2 Timeline

Make a chronological list of every date and time mentioned in the case. Include what is alleged to have happened at that point and who describes that as being the case. This timeline will help you sort out which "facts" are supported by multiple witnesses and which present clear contradictions.

When facts are duplicated, it might help you determine which witnesses are "optional" (in cases where you're choosing from a pool of witnesses rather than having them preassigned).

Some newcomers think such contradictions between witnesses or even in a single witness statement are "errors" in the case. They usually aren't. Case authors intentionally create contradictions to balance the case and provide fodder for cross-examination.

A timeline featuring the dates/times that are beneficial to your side can also be a worthwhile demonstrative exhibit at trial.

2.3.3 Exhibit Chart

It's helpful to track which witnesses are familiar with each exhibit. For one thing, an exhibit is only useful if it is admissible, and it is only admissible if it can be authenticated (established as genuine). So you will want to identify which witnesses can authenticate each exhibit. But even if an exhibit is easily admitted, it is most useful when it can be employed during the direct and cross-examinations of multiple witnesses.

Exhibit Number	Description	Notes	Jones	Smith	Lee	Rodriguez
1	Photo of victim		X	X		
2	Handwritten note	Admissible, per Stipulation #2	X			
3	Email dated 1/1/2014		X		X	X
4	Autopsy Report	Authentic, per Stipulation #1	X		X	

2.3.4 Case Updates

Be aware of how and when the governing body will release case updates. Case updates may be issued to correct typos and other errors that are discovered. They may address questions that teams have posed. If your competition allows you to submit questions, be aware of the deadline to do so.

Case updates may include substantive changes to try to make the case more balanced. Regardless of the reason, you need to have the most recent materials for trial and be prepared to use them. Just as the whole team needs to read the entire case packet initially, the whole team should read through and discuss any updates. Update your T-Charts and other materials as necessary.

Some organizations introduce new witnesses (or even a whole new case!) between the different levels of competition. The goals are to prevent the case from becoming stale and to provide new material to help differentiate between the top teams that have advanced to this point in the season. However, this process can be daunting for new teams. If such new material is expected, find out when the material will be released and build extra practice time into that portion of the season to address it.

2.4 Theory

A theory is a lawyer's explanation for why their client deserves to win. For example, a prosecutor's theory might be that the defendant murdered his business partner out of greed, to keep their profits all to himself. The defense attorney's theory, in response, might be that the defendant could not have committed the crime because he has an alibi. Your case will involve complicated facts, a timeline, multiple witnesses, and multiple exhibits. Your theory boils all of that down to something the jury can understand.

When you can choose between multiple criminal charges or multiple types of defenses, don't concern yourself solely with what would work in the real world. You have one and only one consideration: what theory will help you earn the most points during the round.

It cannot be emphasized enough that most of your scoring judges will not have read the case in advance. This is not appellate court[3], where the judges have read briefs in advance of oral argument and the result might hang on nuance. In Mock Trial, judges are learning the case start to finish in real time in less than three hours. When a judge is confused, lower scores result. Thus, one of the maxims for Mock Trial success is "Simple wins." If you have a case theory that can be spoon fed, the judges will understand it.

Choose a theory that you can present within your time limits. If you had a week to present evidence and the ability to call a dozen witnesses, you might choose a different theory. You don't. Most Mock Trial competitions give you less than an hour for all of your directs and crosses. Some give you less than half an hour. Choose a theory that you can execute

3. In the real world, an appellate court hears an appeal from a party that disagrees with a ruling made by the trial court. In Mock Trial, there are no appeals. However, in another competition called Moot Court, a trial is presumed to have already taken place and the teams are making arguments in front of a fictional appellate court. Moot Court sometimes also has a writing component.

clearly and thoroughly in the time you're given. This is the most common mistake made by coaches who are successful trial attorneys in real life. Rigidly using strategies from week-long real trials for three-hour Mock Trials will usually result in jury confusion and lower scores.

Come up with a theory that can be presented cleanly with minimal interruptions. Don't give the other team the chance to make worthwhile objections. Don't require your witnesses to make contentions that could be impeached. Remember the verdict is immaterial. *It's All About Points!*

Some competitions require the prosecution/plaintiff to try to prove all charges/claims. Others let you choose. The defense can normally pick whatever theory it likes. Check your competition's rules.

In competitions where you have a choice of which witnesses to call, choose a theory that allows you to select the witnesses that will earn the most points and that allows you to bring the most out of your witnesses. We are sometimes asked, "Do you choose the theory based on the witnesses you want to call, or do you choose the witnesses that support your preferred theory?" The answer is neither. A theory without great witnesses won't score enough points. Nor will great witnesses and incoherent theory. Select a strategy that produces strong witnesses that support a strong theory.

When you select your theory, make sure it's specific. "Means, motive, and opportunity" is not a theory. It's a cliché way of organizing evidence. "The defendant killed the victim" is not a theory. It's simply a statement of what the prosecution must prove in a murder case. Start with the key details. Consider the board game *Clue*, where players try to identify the murderer, the weapon, and the room in which the victim was killed. If you were to make an accusation, it might sound something like, "Professor Plum, with a candlestick, in the library." In non-*Clue* terms, this means "Professor Plum used a candlestick to kill Mr. Body in the library." We still need some additional information—motive, for one thing—but that's the beginning of a theory.

Of course, trials tend to be a lot more complicated than a *Clue* search for three facts. As an example, let's look at the fictional case of *State v. Perry*, the collegiate case from 2006: a child named Bailey Reynolds was kidnapped, and a family friend named Tyler Perry was arrested and tried for the crime. A viable theory for that case might sound like this:

> Tyler Perry kidnapped Bailey Reynolds because he needed money for his wife's operation. So, on October 22, he invited Bailey's parents to his house for dinner, snuck out under the pretense of buying a bottle of wine, and crept into the Reynolds

> home. He used a drug called chloroandromine to knock Bailey unconscious, dropped a ransom note in her room, and drove Bailey to a motel as he waited to collect his ransom money.

Notice how this theory answers the six classic "newspaper questions." Who did it? Tyler Perry. What did he do? He kidnapped Bailey Reynolds. When? On October 22, the night he invited the Reynolds to his house. Where? He took Bailey from her home and dropped her at a motel. Why? Because he needed the money for his wife's operation. How did he do it? With an incapacitating drug called chloroandromine.

Ideally, a theory describes the events and circumstances more concisely than the above example. The following is a tighter theory:

> Tyler Perry kidnapped Bailey Reynolds by using a dangerous, incapacitating drug. He needed money for his wife's operation, so he kidnapped his best friend's oldest daughter and held her for ransom.

The theory could be even more to the point:

> Tyler Perry needed money for his wife's operation, and he kidnapped a child to get it.

In a 2006 issue of *American Lawyer* magazine, an attorney discussed the importance of a simple, coherent theory. He tells the story of a Texas lawyer who was representing a plaintiff suing for breach of contract. The case was complex and its issues ranged from antitrust to patent infringement to accounting. But the famous advocate began his opening statement by distilling the complexity into something more approachable to a jury of lay people:

> These two men shook hands on a deal—and now one of them wants to take it back.

This is an excellent way to present the theory of the case because it cuts through the thorny issues of law, financing, and business, and presents something we can all understand. It is effective not only because of the theory itself, but also based on how it is presented.

2.5 Theme

Once you have your theory, you can decide on your theme. A theme is a word, phrase, image, or concept that encapsulates your theory. It's the lens through which you want the jury to view the evidence. The best themes are memorable, simple, easy to comprehend, and something you can repeat over and over. A good theme helps the jury understand your theory, which generally results in higher scores throughout the trial.

Let's Get Real: Professor Bernstein recalls a friend complaining about losing a real-life trial. "I can't believe we lost," the attorney said. "We had a smoking gun email where the other side admitted we were right. We had great admissions from all their witnesses. Their original set of lawyers missed the discovery deadlines, so they didn't get any information from our witnesses in advance. And three weeks before trial they brought in new lawyers who didn't know anything about the case. I honestly don't know how we lost the trial." Professor Bernstein asked his friend what their theme was. "Oh, we didn't have one," he said.

Most judges like and expect teams to have a theme. A few think they are corny or outdated. We strongly advocate the use of themes because experience has taught us that judges who like themes will usually score the opener and closer down if no theme is used. The judges who dislike themes may criticize them in giving oral feedback after a round, but they rarely will hand out lower scores based on using them. The reward outweighs the risk.

The best way to come up with a trial theme is to brainstorm early in the season after everyone has read the case. Start using it in scrimmages early. Your theme can evolve as the season goes on, but you want to start using a theme as soon as possible because using a theme correctly takes practice. Once you are proficient at working the theme into your arguments, it is relatively easy to plug in a newly improved theme. Also, guest judges can offer feedback on your theme and help improve it. You lose this benefit if you refrain from using a theme until you think you've "got it perfect."

Themes are hard. It's hard to take a complicated fact pattern, find a legally and factually persuasive theory, and reduce it to a single slogan. So if it takes your team a while to find the right theme, that's okay. But don't settle for something weak, generic, or confusing. Keep working to find a theme that will grab judges from the beginning.

As you work to find a strong theme, here are some common pitfalls to avoid:

Avoid generic themes. Plaintiff teams like to say, "This is a case about choices." Defenses like to say the case is about "reasonable doubt," "missing puzzle pieces," and "assumptions." None of these themes is specific enough. Every civil case is about someone's choices. What choices? What made those choices the wrong choices? Why did the defendant make those choices? Every criminal defense is based on reasonable doubt. Every civil defense is about pointing out the plaintiff's mistaken assumptions. This doesn't tell the judges what *your* defense is about.

WAR STORY

How generic is the "choices" theme? We once saw a trial where the plaintiff and the defense used that theme.

Avoid legalese. The best lawyers don't "sound like lawyers." They sound like real people. So avoid legal terminology as part of your theme. We've seen defense teams with themes such as, "Not negligent, not foreseeable." That's a succinct summary of a legal argument, but it's not a theme that will grab a jury's attention.

Avoid mere name calling. At least once a season, we see defense teams whose theme is, "The prosecution told you a story. We're going to tell you the facts." That's not a theme. That's an unsupported statement that the judges should blindly believe you and reject your opponent.

Avoid cuteness. California once had a high school case involving an employer's alleged exploitation of an immigrant employee. The employee was a chef, so many teams had cute themes involving cooking concepts such as "This was a recipe for disaster," and "The employee couldn't stand the heat." But the charge was human trafficking. That's a very serious crime. No real-life prosecutor would use a cooking pun as a theme when prosecuting human trafficking. If you're going to use puns or rhymes, make sure judges won't find the theme unrealistic, insensitive, or childish.

Avoid unnecessary length. Don't say, "This is a case about the defendant getting revenge because she was angry about being fired from her job." Instead, consider "First she got fired. Then she got revenge." Or "This is a case about revenge." Or even, "Revenge."

So what are some good themes? The following are themes used by Professor Bernstein's teams in some of their national championships.

At Tournament of Champions 2020, the plaintiffs sued the defendant grocery store for negligence when they served samples without allergy warnings. The plaintiff's son had a peanut allergy and got sick from trying one of the samples. As the plaintiff, we argued that the grocery store actively concealed the allergy information by instructing their employees to keep ingredient labels out of view and forbidding employees from proactively telling customers whether the sample contained a known allergen. The theme was, "The defendant hid the danger." Short, memorable, easily repeated, connected to the theory, and specific to that case. As the defense, we argued that the entire problem could have been avoided if the parents, aware of their child's allergy, had asked to see the packaging or asked if the sample contained peanuts. The theme was, "All they had to do was ask."

At Top Gun 2018, the plaintiff brewery sued the defendant brewery for misappropriation of trade secrets. The plaintiff's theory was that the plaintiff bought a local family's beer recipe and turned it into an award-winning beer. The defendant then paid one of the plaintiff's employees to steal a special beer recipe and give it to the defendant, who started selling it as their own. As the plaintiff, our theme was, "We paid for a recipe. They paid for a robbery." The sentences use parallel structure and alliteration. They involve two key words that are easy to remember: robbery and recipe. The theme is specific to that case. And it tells a story.

In the same case, as the defense, we argued that the story was more complicated. The beer recipe was developed by a man who passed it on to his two sons. One son sold his copy to the plaintiff, and the other sold it to the defendant. The defendant wasn't liable for misappropriation of trade secrets because when they bought the recipe, they had no idea that it had already been sold to the plaintiff by the other brother. Our theme was, "This case is about a family secret." The "family secret" language worked on two levels: The recipe itself was a family secret, and the fact that it was given to both brothers was also a family secret—our client didn't know that when it bought the recipe. Notice that this theme requires some explanation before judges will understand it. But that's okay—in fact, it can be a good thing. The theme—a family secret—grabbed the judges' attention at the beginning of the opening because it was a little mysterious. But once they heard the story and we repeated the theme, it all made sense.

At National Trial Competition 2021, the case involved a woman cut by broken glass when the bus she was riding in was hit by a car and flipped over. The woman sued the bus manufacturer for designing windows that were unusually likely to shatter in a crash because: (a) they were the largest in the industry, and larger glass panes break more easily; (b) the defendant used unglazed glass, which is flimsier than glazed glass; and (c) a safer alternative was available for less than 100 dollars per bus. Our plaintiff theme was, "Too big. Too weak. Too cheap." In the same case, our defense focused on the other driver, who caused the crash by driving into oncoming traffic. Our theme was, "Wrong direction, wrong defendant."

2.6 Witnesses

Many Mock Trial competitions have no witness selection. Each side must call designated witnesses. This is the rule in most high school and law school competitions.

In some competitions, including college competitions, you get to choose your witnesses. For example, the prosecution might get to choose three witnesses among five options. Or maybe there are eight witnesses, each side gets three, and they take turns selecting.

WAR STORY

When you run as many tournaments as we do, you think you've seen everything. Then something truly bizarre happens. In the last round of a college regional tournament, two brand new teams were facing each other. Midtrial, the captain of each team complained to tournament officials. "Their witness is changing his testimony! He is totally contradicting what he said the first time he testified," one complained. The "first time he testified"? The officials were perplexed. Witnesses only testify once in Mock Trial. Well, it turns out these brand new teams didn't understand witness selection. After the plaintiff team selected a witness, the defense decided they wanted that witness, too. So the teams decided that both teams would call the same witness, played by different people at different points of the trial. And they were shocked when the second person to take the stand in the role began his testimony by saying, "I'd like to correct some things I said earlier!"

If you get to choose your witnesses, whom should you select?

Choose witnesses who will collectively support a strong theory. Don't pick three witnesses who exclusively testify to motive but provide no forensic evidence or eyewitness testimony proving that the defendant committed the crime. Note that this is less of a concern for defense teams, who have no burden to prove anything. Defense witnesses need to be useful, of course, but they don't need to be as substantively useful.

Choose witnesses who present diverse personality types and testimony. A crying witness is great. But two witnesses who cry will feel redundant. Experts can be impressive and are often a great source of points. But calling multiple experts may leave judges tired and bored.

Choose witnesses based not only on maximizing the points you can score on direct, but also based on minimizing the number of points your opponent will score on cross. Remember that the object isn't just to score points; it's to score more points than the other side.

Above all, choose witnesses that fit your team's strengths. If you are deciding between a forensic pathologist and an eyewitness who works as a sports agent, ask yourself: Who on our team can play these roles? Which character best matches our roster? If the case includes the parent of the victim, but the witness has minimal useful testimony, don't immediately ignore this as a viable witness call. If you have a student who excels at portraying emotional witnesses, their ability to score big may be worth sacrificing the additional evidence you'd get from a different witness.

3

Performance

Mock Trial is not a legal competition with a public speaking component. It's a public speaking competition with a legal component. Successful Mock Trial starts with *performance.*

Why? Because attention must be earned. This isn't just true in Mock Trial. If a teacher isn't interesting, students tune out. If a TV show isn't interesting, we change channels. If a Facebook post isn't interesting, we keep scrolling. People have short attention spans, and Mock Trial judges are no different. No, they can't change the channel or get up and leave, but if they're not compelled to listen, they will tune out. It doesn't matter how brilliant your theory is or how clever your theme is if no one is listening.

The ability to present your ideas in a clear and compelling manner is by far the most important attribute of any successful attorney or witness. It is easy to get lost in the substance of what we are saying, easy to focus on the structure of a direct examination, and easy to focus on the illogical nature of our opponent's argument. But the minute we forget that our performance is only as effective as its delivery is the minute we lose—badly—to a team whose arguments and evidentiary knowledge are inferior to ours.

Thus, presentation is not something you should focus on *after* gaining a strong substantive foundation. Rather, it is what you should constantly hone *as* you gain that foundation. We often see teams that think about how an opening or cross should be delivered only on the eve of competition; before that, all focus was on writing content. This is a mistake. Performance skills need to be practiced and developed over time.

This chapter breaks down many of the skills that create a dynamic, effective performance. While there is more than one way to give a speech or answer a question on cross-examination, three traits are common to all effective deliveries.

First, delivery must be appropriate to the situation. You would not question a grieving widow in the same manner as you would a defendant accused of triple murder. This means every word and every facial expression must be consistent with the context.

Second, all aspects of your presentation should be consistent. Casual hand gestures look funny when one's voice is filled with fury. A gentle voice sounds odd when you're wagging your finger at the bad guy.

Third, delivery must be varied. Any volume, any tone of speech, any hand gesture—no matter how good—becomes monotonous after a while.

In sum: consider your context, vary your delivery and make sure all aspects of your presentation are consistent with the substance of what you trying to present. Ideally, your presentation should not only avoid detracting from your substance; it should also enhance it.

3.1 Speech

Our voice is our biggest weapon in the courtroom. It's our instrument of expression. It's the way we communicate feelings. There are six main attributes of how we use our voice in the courtroom: speed, volume, clarity, tone, emphasis, and pauses.

3.1.1 Speed

Speak slowly.

There are a lot of reasons to speak slowly. First, if you speak too fast, juries will not understand you. This means speaking more slowly than you would in everyday life. Why? Because in everyday life, you are usually speaking to people who already know what you're talking about. Suppose you tell your friend, "I heard that Donna and Josh were DMing, and Amy is super jealous." Your friend probably knows who these people are and what a DM is. Otherwise, you wouldn't use those names without context. But suppose you tell the same information to the jury in your Mock Trial round. Do you think they will be able to remember three names said quickly at the same time? A jury, especially at the beginning of trial, often knows nothing about the case. Many judges don't read the case packets ahead of time. You must speak slowly so they will be able to understand and absorb the information.

Second, speaking slowly shows confidence. It makes you look deliberate and unhurried. It makes you look comfortable in the courtroom. In contrast, speaking quickly is generally associated with being nervous. Confidence and a strong courtroom presence are some of the strongest signals to judges that you deserve a high score.

Third, speaking slowly when you know what you're going to say buys you time when you don't know what you're going to say. There will be times when you need to stop and think—objection responses, tough cross questions, an unexpected ruling from a judge. If you always speak slowly, then judges won't notice if you take your time searching for the right words.

The average newscaster speaks more than 150 words per minute. Many students, in conversation, will speak faster than 200 words per minute. You should generally be much slower. Professor Bernstein tells his students to stay between 100 and 110 words per minute in an opening statement. By closing argument, when the jury knows the case better, 120–130 words per minute is okay.

Be especially careful to talk slowly if you are reading anything. Because people read faster than they speak in conversation, words read aloud often come out way too quickly.

As we mentioned at the top of this chapter, you should vary your speed. Most of the time you'll speak slowly. Occasionally you should speed up for short periods—to create urgency, to tell the more chaotic part of a story, to add excitement. Occasionally you should get even slower—to create drama or suspense, to show grief (as a witness), or to explain something complicated. Changing speeds for emphasis is very effective and is one of the things even strong speakers sometimes forget to include in their repertoire.

3.1.2 Volume

Speak loudly.

First, you need to speak loudly enough to be heard. Many judges are older, and their hearing isn't excellent. Courtrooms are large, and some of them have bad acoustics. Many courtrooms have air conditioners that are loud and can drown you out, especially if the air conditioner is right next to where the judge or jury is seated. Your voice may be swallowed up. Before the trial, do a sound check where your teammates sit in the judges' seats and tell you if you're loud enough.

But it's not just about being heard. Speaking loudly is a way to show confidence. It says, "I'm not afraid." This isn't the same as yelling. You will want to practice speaking from your diaphragm so that your loud volume seems effortless. A big voice can take over the courtroom.

Once you've established a strong volume as your primary speaking voice, add variation. Get soft to introduce emotional testimony or to add drama. Don't be afraid to whisper. Get even louder—rarely, and only briefly—to show passion or significance. When you are getting loud, be especially careful about your positioning in the courtroom. Being loud when approaching judges or jurors can make it seem like you are yelling at them.

Notice the similarity between volume and speed. In both cases, there is a presentation style that should serve as your default: slow and loud. But in both cases, variety—occasionally getting quicker, occasionally getting quieter—will help convey the right emotions and retain the jury's interest.

3.1.3 Clarity

Speak clearly.

If judges are struggling to understand the words you're saying, their brains won't be able to focus on the significance of the words.

There are several things we can do to speak more clearly. Before each trial, make sure you open your mouth wide when doing your sound check. Tongue twisters before trial warm up our mouths. Drink lots of water before each trial. And of course, the first rule of public speaking—speak slowly—will usually force us to speak more clearly.

Professor Bernstein has his students do a pen exercise before each trial. It looks silly, but it works great. Before trials, the team leaves the courtroom and finds a quiet space away from the judges. Every team member puts a pen in their mouth and bites down. Then everyone starts reciting their lines as quickly as possible. The pen will make it hard to speak—and impossible to speak clearly. This forces us to open our mouths wider and make bigger tongue movements. After three minutes, take the pens out. Now say your lines. The words will flow more easily, and your voices will sound smoother. It's like running after taking a weight off your back.

3.1.4 Tone

Your tone must match your words. It can be appropriate to tell a victim, "I'm sorry for your loss." But how does that sound if you're shouting? Or sneering? Or mechanical? Or chuckling?

Always ask yourself, "Why am I asking this question? Why am I giving this answer? What do I want my audience to feel?" If you want the jury to think the witness is a liar, don't go for anger; go for incredulity or skepticism. If you want the jury to feel sympathy, your voice needs to carry pain and anguish. If you want the jury to feel suspense, your voice needs to convey peril, fright, and uncertainty.

Your tone needs to be varied—within each speech, within each paragraph, often within a particular sentence. This goes for witnesses, too.

Emotional witnesses can't maintain a judge's attention if they are sad the entire time. Funny witnesses can't be chipper on every question.

Your voice betrays how you're feeling, so make sure you aren't sending the wrong signals. Sarcasm, anger, and annoyance are rarely effective in trial, and, when they are, they need to be delivered in small, short doses. Condescension is almost never a good sound in your voice. Make sure that your voice generally sounds confident and energetic.

3.1.5 Emphasis

In writing, we can use **bold,** *italics,* and <u>underscore</u> to emphasize key words in a sentence. Orally we can do the same thing by stressing a key word in a sentence. This helps our jury understand our arguments.

Sometimes the emphasis completely changes the meaning of the sentence. A famous example is, "I didn't steal her money." It's a short sentence that seems straightforward. But consider how a different emphasis changes the meaning:

"***I*** didn't steal her money." This suggests someone else stole the money.

"I ***didn't*** steal her money." This sounds like a denial. This is probably the one you'd want your defendant to use.

"I didn't ***steal*** her money." This makes it sound like, yeah, you took the money, but you were just borrowing it. Or maybe she gave it to you. Yes, you were involved, but, no, it wasn't theft.

"I didn't steal ***her*** money." You took someone else's money!

"I didn't steal her ***money***." You stole something else that belonged to her!

Emphasizing the right words makes your meaning clearer and your argument more persuasive.

3.1.6 Pauses

Pauses are crucial. They make the last thing you said feel more significant. They give the jury a chance to digest your information. They show confidence.

Pause before you start your speech. Make eye contact with the jury and count to three in your head. This will show you are comfortable.

Pause after important moments. In your opening statement and closing argument, pause after the theme, after the introduction, and after each section. In your direct and cross-examinations, pause as you transition topics and to let big points sink in. Witnesses: pause before answering so it appears that you are thinking about the question. You can pause briefly mid-answer, or even mid-sentence, to build drama.

3.2 Nonverbal Performance

3.2.1 Facial Expressions

Your facial expressions should match the rest of your delivery. If your words and tone convey incredulity, you should look surprised. If you are expressing empathy—especially if you are expressing empathy for the other party—jurors should see that on your face.

Watch yourself in a mirror or, ideally, on video. Make sure your face expresses emotion. If your face is barely moving, it means you're holding back, and the jury won't trust you. Make sure your face expresses the emotion you mean to convey. If your face says one thing and your words say another, the jury will be confused. Keep in mind that the judge and jurors will be observing your facial expressions at all times—not just when you are the person performing.

Use your eyebrows. If they are furrowed, you look angry or concerned. You can use that sparingly on closing argument, or when directing a witness who says something concerning. On cross-examination especially, you can raise your eyebrows when confronting an evasive witness to show that you are reacting to the witness's comment with surprise, not hostility. It will show the jury that you remain in control and comfortable.

Another tip to being more expressive: ask yourself how you want the jury to feel after hearing a particular line. Adopt that emotion. Then deliver your line. Our facial expressions generally match how we're feeling.

3.2.2 Gestures

Let's start with hands. Many people get uncomfortable when speaking to an audience: "Where do I put my hands?" Some people cross their arms. This conveys irritation. Some put their hands behind their backs. This conveys secrecy; what is this person hiding? Some put their hands in their pockets. This is unprofessional in a courtroom. Many clasp their hands in front of them. This makes them look uncomfortable, unnatural, and nervous.

Instead, just do what you usually do with your hands when you are standing up and talking to someone: leave your hands at your sides. This might feel awkward, but it won't look awkward to others. Your default position should be standing with your hands at your sides.

Of course, you can't just leave them there the whole time. That will look stiff. Use your hands to bring your argument to life.

But don't confuse using your hands with simply waving your hands. If your hands are moving without purpose, that's not effective. Use your hands to enhance your message.

Pet Peeve: Many students think that using their hands means punctuating each syllable with a hand gesture. Moving your hand up and down at a speed that matches the cadence of your voice is not a gesture. It's just a distraction.

Your hands can represent objects: guns, phones, claws, spiders. Your hands can represent any number from zero to ten. Your hands can demonstrate size: the itty-bitty thing that fits between two fingertips, or the large heavy object that requires your wingspan. Your hands can demonstrate action: sewing, slicing, punching, blocking, waving, reaching, and so many more. Your hands can point to people or things for emphasis.

Pet Peeve: Don't hold a pen in your hand while speaking. It is incredibly distracting. The judges will be watching it and trying to predict if you will inadvertently or intentionally throw it like a dart.

Then incorporate your head. Nod to show agreement. Tilt your head to show disbelief. Tilt backward to show surprise. Shake your head when refuting.

Then incorporate your whole body. Don't just *say* the victim was on ground. Bend down a little and gesture to the ground. Don't just *say* the sun was in the eyewitness's eyes. Look up, block the imaginary sun with your hand, squint, and recoil slightly. Don't just *say* "maybe." Shrug. This is a performance. Don't hold back.

Attorneys, keep your feet about a pen's length apart. Not only does it signify strength, but it keeps you from moving or shuffling your feet unnecessarily. Also, always keep your feet firmly planted. The judges should never see the soles of your shoes.

WAR STORY

Professor Bernstein had a freshman who kept his feet so close together that they touched. Once, this student got animated during closing argument and leaned to his left. Because his feet were so close together, he lost balance and fell. He popped back up and said, "As I was saying . . ."

Finally, at the risk of sounding like your mother, stand up straight.

3.2.3 Movement

Changing locations draws attention. Moving in the courtroom is a crucial technique to maintain judge interest and enhance your message.

Mistakes here tend to fall into one of two categories. Some people never move. This makes them look stiff, and judges are more likely to grow bored. Other students pace back and forth. This doesn't enhance your message. It shows nervousness, and it will distract from your performance.

We want movement, but it must be purposeful. You can move to demonstrate transition. "Now let's talk about point number two: intent." You can move to recreate the scene. "The defendant crept down the hallway." You can move to show a timeline. "January. Sales are dropping. [step] February. Sales are dropping. [step] March. Sales are plummeting."

Don't move in the first sentence of your performance. It shows nervousness. Get set, and then begin. For the remainder of your presentation, consider whether each movement should be accompanied by speech or silence.

Most of the time, walk silently. If you are moving for emphasis—to show how far away something is, or how long ago something happened—walk silently. It will instantly command the room. If you move while questioning a witness—for example, when approaching a witness to hand them an exhibit, or returning to your original position after handing it to them—do not say a word while walking. A judge can focus on watching you walk, or hearing you talk, but not both. Plus, the silence will draw attention to the exhibit and make you look confident.

WAR STORY

In the 2010 college case, Professor Bernstein's UC Irvine team had a moment in opening statement where the attorney previewed the testimony of their expert. "Dr. Charney is a forensic entomologist. He examined the insects found on Mr. Bennett's body, and he will testify the victim didn't die on a Monday, like the prosecution says. He died two days later, on Wednesday. The reason that matters? You will learn that Ms. Owens [the defendant] left the state on Tuesday. Flew to England. At the end of this trial, we will ask the State, how could Ms. Owens commit a crime here in Midlands . . . [walks silently across entire width of the courtroom] . . . when she was all the way across the Atlantic." Consistently, that was the moment judges would remember and praise after trial: the long, silent walk that illustrated distance.

If you are moving as part of a transition, you should pause and then continue speaking as you take your steps. For a statement like, "Now let's talk about point number two," a long silent walk for a small transition will seem awkward or overdramatic.

Movements should generally be strong. Taking one step for a transition, for example, looks weak and scripted.

Movements can be creative. You can stroll. Or tiptoe. Or shuffle. Use whatever best tells your story and whatever best sells your message.

Sometimes judges will require attorneys to remain at the podium. This is a big disadvantage for teams that have incorporated great movement into their performance. If this happens, ask the judge if you can use the arm's length rule: you can move with anywhere within an arm's length of the podium. This allows you to demonstrate movement even as your opponent is stuck to the podium.

WAR STORY

In the 2018 Top Gun championship round, the judge told the attorneys—quite sternly—to stay within an arm's length of the podium. The plaintiff's attorney stood behind the podium. Professor Bernstein's student, Phil Pasquarello, took advantage of the arm's length rule and orbited the podium throughout the trial—moving from right to left, taking a step back, sometimes standing next to or even in front of the podium. The judge raised an eyebrow but never stopped him. Jurors praised Phil's use of the courtroom, and he won the national championship.

3.2.4 Props

Using props can increase the jury's attention. The most natural prop to use during a performance is an exhibit. Hold it up, point to something, put it down—the simple act of using an admitted exhibit will draw attention.

But there are other props you can use: your pen, pad, chair, counsel table . . . anything in the courtroom that you can pick up, move, or point to. If you can use your prop to enhance your message, it will also increase attention from your judges. It can also be impactful to hijack the other team's props and use them to enhance your own argument.

WAR STORY

In the 2012 American Mock Trial Association case, the defendant was charged with drunk driving and homicide. One prosecution eyewitness testified that she assumed the defendant was drinking a lot of alcohol because there were glasses in front of her. So anytime they were competing in a courtroom, Professor Bernstein's UC Irvine team checked to see if there were any cups or mugs in the courtroom. If so, they would incorporate that into their cross-examination. "You said Ms. Dawson had drinks in front of her?" "You assumed those were her drinks?" "There is a mug sitting right next to the judge?" "You can't tell us if that's his mug?" "You can't tell us if he drank from that mug?" The props helped illustrate the point, and the cross scored through the roof.

When you are not deliberately using something as a prop, keep your hands empty. Anything you hold will become the proverbial shiny object drawing their attention. If you are not using an item for a specific purpose, don't use it at all. If you are using it for a specific purpose, keep to that purpose. When taking notes at the counsel table, you need to have a pen in your hand. You do not need to click it. In fact, Judge Nelmark doesn't let his teams use click pens at all.

4

Opening Statement

"Openings are for winners. Closings are for heroes."

Closing arguments get the glory. They are your last chance to persuade the jury and the opportunity to drop the mic. How many people decided to become lawyers because they were inspired by Atticus Finch's closing argument in *To Kill a Mockingbird?*

But to win a Mock Trial—and probably a real trial—there is no element more important than the opening statement. That's what our research shows, and that's what our experience corroborates. Why?

The opening statement is the first impression. If the jury thinks your opening statement is better than the other team's, they will start to see you as the stronger team. That first impression is hard to shake—it creates "confirmation bias." Confirmation bias is the tendency to view new evidence as confirmation of the beliefs we already hold. If the judges think your team is stronger at the beginning of trial, they will subconsciously give you the benefit of the doubt during the rest of the trial.

Let's Get Real: Research has found that, about 80 percent of the time, a juror's ultimate opinion of the case matches their opinion after opening statement. First impressions matter in real life and in Mock Trial.

The opening statement is your first and best opportunity to make sure the judges understand your case. Most judges will not have read the case beforehand. They may know only the brief synopsis provided during judge instruction or nothing at all. They will rely on opening statements to understand what's happening. And if your opening statement is clearer than the other team's opening, the judges will naturally gravitate toward your version of the facts. The opening statement is your opportunity to tell your story uninterrupted, as most competitions don't allow objections during the opening.

The opening statement frames the issues for the rest of the trial. For example, if you plant the idea in the jury's mind that blood is important evidence for your prosecution theory, every time you mention blood during the rest of trial, the judges will think you're proving your case. If you plant the idea that the eyewitness has memory problems, the judges will later understand your point when you start asking the eyewitness about hitting his head.

So how do we build a stellar opening?

4.1 Goals

The most important goal of opening statement is for the judges to understand your case theory when you're done. More specifically, they understand why your party deserves to win, what you must prove or disprove to prevail, and which evidence and witnesses you think are most crucial. Opening statement is a roadmap for the rest of trial. If you tell the judges where they are going, they will be less likely to feel lost.

There are additional goals in opening statement. Some of them are substantive. You want the judges to understand how you will respond to the opponent's best evidence. Other goals are more emotional. As the prosecution, you want the jury feeling empathy for the victim and anger, frustration, or resentment toward the defendant. As the defense, you want the judges feeling empathy toward your client and skepticism or mistrust toward those accusing her (maybe the victim, maybe the police). And some of your goals are performance based. We want an opening statement that captures the judges' attention.

4.2 Persuade without Arguing

There is a reason it's called opening statement, not opening argument. You're not allowed to argue. In real life, if an attorney argues in her opening statement, the other side can object. In most Mock Trial competitions, objections are not allowed in opening statement. But if you argue, the judges will likely score you down.

What does it mean to "argue" in opening statement? It means that although you can state the evidence that will be presented, you may not state the conclusions you want the jury to draw from that evidence. For example, you may say, "Eyewitnesses will testify that they saw the defendant holding a gun when he went into the house. They heard a scream.

A gunshot. And then they saw the defendant run out of the house with a gun in his hand." Those are all facts that witnesses will testify to during trial. But you cannot add, "The only reasonable explanation for that series of events is that the defendant shot the victim." That's not a fact a witness will testify to. It's a conclusion—an inference—you hope the jury will eventually draw. Such a conclusion is proper for closing argument, but improper for opening statement.

A good rule of thumb: unless an exhibit states something or a witness will testify to it, then it doesn't belong in your opening statement.

So how do you persuade while not arguing?

First, use the facts to get the jury to reach your conclusion without you ever having to say the conclusion out loud. Consider the previous example. "Eyewitnesses will testify that they saw the defendant holding a gun when he went into the house. They heard a scream. A gunshot. And then they saw the defendant run out of the house with a gun in his hand." What is the jury going to think when they hear that series of events? Sure, there are innocent explanations. Maybe it was a different gun. Maybe someone else pulled the trigger. Maybe the defendant fired in self-defense. But when people hear that story, their natural inclination is to think, "The defendant is guilty"—especially if the lawyer tells the story in an incriminating tone. You don't need to add, "The defendant shot the victim" if the jury already thinks it. In fact, a lot of psychological research shows that people are more likely to believe a conclusion if they think they reached it themselves.

Here is another example, drawn from the 2015 Top Gun. Professor Bernstein's student, Rahul Hari, began his prosecution opening statement with this story en route to winning the national championship:

> It's September 2014. The defendant is holding a glossy color photograph. There are two people in the photo. One of them is James Moody, her husband. The other is her husband's 23-year-old graduate student. James is standing behind her, holding her tight. There are champagne glasses by their side. They're wearing bathrobes. They're smiling. They look like they're in love. And they're standing on the defendant's porch. At her home.
>
> The defendant puts down the photograph and picks up her phone. She calls the unlicensed private investigator who took the photos. She speaks to him for 32 minutes and, that afternoon, she wires him 10 thousand dollars. Four days later, the man she paid 10 thousand dollars walks into the Moody's home, finds James Moody in his study, and shoots him in the chest, dead.

Does it say that James Moody is having an affair? No. But everyone draws that conclusion from the bathrobes and champagne glasses. Does it say the defendant is angry? No. But everyone draws that conclusion because of course the wife would be displeased when looking at a photo like that. Does it say she hired the man to kill her husband? No. But that's the implication—and the conclusion jurors will draw—from the sequence of events. Fact: Wife discovers affair. Fact: Wife immediately pays man lots of money. Fact: Man then shoots husband. Conclusion: She hired him to kill.

When Professor Bernstein uses that example in his trial advocacy classes, he asks students what they remember from the opening statement, and they usually talk about those conclusions as if they were stated. They will refer to the affair, the anger, and the murder-for-hire—even though those words were never said. Some students are sure he explicitly talked about those things expressly! Our minds fill in the gaps. You can persuade without arguing by choosing the right facts and delivering them in the right order.

The second way to persuade without arguing is to introduce your conclusions with the magic words, "the evidence will show . . ." For example, it would be argumentative to say, "When Michael Ehrman walked into James Moody's study that night, James Moody didn't owe him money. They had never argued. They had never even met. Michael Ehrman was only there because he had been hired by the defendant." The first three sentences are perfectly appropriate in opening statement because they simply state facts that a witness will testify to. But the last sentence *feels* like argument, not fact. It's about why someone did something. It's a conclusion we ultimately want the jury to believe. We can introduce with reference to a witness to show it is a fact:

> When Michael Ehrman walked into James Moody's study that night, James Moody didn't owe him money. They had never argued. They had never even met. **Michael Ehrman will tell you himself:** he was only there because he had been hired by the defendant.

Or we can introduce with the magic words that tell the judge we are distinguishing between facts that will be presented (the first three sentences) and the inference we will ask the jury to draw (the last sentence):

> When Michael Ehrman walked into James Moody's study that night, James Moody didn't owe him money. They had never argued. They had never even met. **The evidence will show** he was only there because he had been hired by the defendant.

Even though the expression "the evidence will show" will usually keep your opening statement from being scored down as argumentative, don't overuse it. For one, it will make your opening boring and hard to listen to: "The evidence will show the defendant paid him 10 thousand dollars. The evidence will show they spoke on the phone. The evidence will show the defendant asked him to kill her husband."

Some conclusions are too argumentative even with the magic words. If you say, "The evidence will show the defendant is a cold-blooded murderer who is guilty as sin," judges will think that's argumentative because those proclamations don't even resemble facts. They're just accusation and rhetoric.

A third way to persuade without getting scored down for arguing is to sneak some argument into your theme. This is an unwritten rule. Judges expect you to have a theme, and they expect the theme to be argumentative. If you start and end your opening with the theme, you can get away with some argument. And that argument will help the jury understand the facts you're presenting in the middle. For example, in the murder-for-hire case, Rahul started his prosecution opening with the theme, "The defendant didn't pull the trigger. She pulled the strings." That's an argument. But judges didn't mind because it was part of the theme.

WAR STORY

In 2015, Professor Bernstein's student Rahul Hari was competing at Top Gun, which allows objections to opening statement. The opposing attorney repeatedly referred to Rahul's main witness as "Murderer Mike." Usually whether something is argumentative is a close call, but this was way over the line. Rahul stood up. "Objection, argumentative." The judge, with great Texas drawl, replied, "Overruled. That's why they call it 'opening argument.'" Of course, it's not called opening argument! It's opening statement, where argument is prohibited. But it's a good lesson that even when you do everything right, some judges still get it wrong. (It's also a good lesson not to be discouraged when you lose a big objection; Rahul still won the trial.)

4.3 Assume the Jury Knows Nothing

By the time you get to trial, you and your teammates will know the case backward and forward. The timeline will live inside your brain. You will know the exhibit numbers by heart. You will be able to quote key lines from the witness statements. But that preparation creates a challenge: while you will know every inch of the case, the judges may not know it at all. If you talk to the judges as if they already know the case, they will be confused. Here are some tips to help the judges understand your opening right away.

Don't use too many names at once. Suppose we're prosecuting Goldilocks for theft. The jury doesn't need to know the names of the three bears—at least not at the beginning of the story. By limiting the number of names, you can help the jury remember the names you give them.

Instead of names, use titles or descriptions that help the jury understand who you're talking about and how they fit into the story. In the murder-for-hire opening, Rahul didn't refer to the victim's mistress as Lila Green. He called her "James Moody's 23-year-old teaching assistant." He didn't say the shooter was Michael Ehrman. He called him "the unlicensed private investigator." This tells the jury the roles these people occupy in the story without immediately asking them to remember the names.

Avoid using too many dates or numbers. Juries forget them. Unless days or dates are relevant to something like an alibi, they are uninteresting. The drama is in the fact that someone got shot—not whether it occurred on the 22nd or the 23rd.

> On September 14, 2019, Michelle, Aaron, Allen, and Sammy attended the Santos Exhibition. At 8:15 p.m., Baker Hopkins asked everyone to come to the east room for the main event. But while Michelle and Allen and the other patrons entered the foyer, Aaron wasn't seen in the foyer until 8:40. The evidence will show that he was the one who stole the Shining Rose.

If you can stop, read, and re-read those four sentences, you might be able to get a general understanding of what happened. But your judges cannot hit pause. They hear the story once, while also trying to take notes and mentally evaluate what score they are going to give for the opening. If they hear that story, they will almost certainly be baffled. The first sentence introduces four people without telling us anything about them. The speech references the Santos Exhibit and the Shining Rose, without telling us what they are. It uses dates and times without identifying why they are important. What exactly was stolen? Why was it stolen?

> There's a crowd wearing their finest outfits. Tuxedos. Ball gowns. Diamonds. It's the annual art show here in San Diego. At exactly 8:15, the piano player stops playing and everyone begins to file into the east room for the auction. Everyone except the defendant, Aaron Charles. He heads to the south room. Where a million-dollar painting is about to go missing.

This version is the same length as the previous version, but this is much easier for judges to follow. They are given one piece of information at a time, so they know where to focus their attention. The only name they need to remember is the bad guy. They're not distracted by the name of the exhibition or the name of the painting. Instead, they're given the information they really need. You can fill in the rest later.

Although you generally want to avoid unnecessary details that don't enhance your story, theory, or theme, it is okay to have details. In the preceding example, "exactly 8:15" builds drama. The reference to an exact time suggests something important is about to happen. This perks up the jurors' ears, and they are rewarded with the key information of the defendant's name and the act that brought everyone to court.

WAR STORY

We once saw a prosecution opening statement in a high school round where the attorney made so many assumptions about what the judges already knew that he forgot to give them the necessary facts. After the attorney sat down, the defense attorney stood up and asked to begin. The judge said, "Just one second," and turned to the prosecution opener. "One question for you. What is the defendant charged with?" Make sure your opening hits the key details.

4.4 Formality

Historically, speeches to the court began by looking at the judge and saying, "May it please the Court." Some lawyers still use that expression. Others say simply, "May I proceed?" Others just begin speaking. Because the goal is to maximize scores, we recommend starting with one of those formalities. Judges who don't use those formalities in real life are unlikely to score you down for using one, but judges who think they're important may score you down for not using one.

Make sure to pause after you use the formality. The formality is not part of your presentation. It is how you seek permission to begin your presentation.[1] It's boring. Pausing afterwards shows poise and will increase the jury's attention for the good stuff that is about to follow.

1. Keep in mind that although it's not part of your presentation, opposing timekeepers may well start the clock as soon as the first word comes out of your mouth. Include this sentence, and the following pause, when determining how much content you can include. Squeezing in an extra 10 seconds of content is not worth having a debate about whether time has expired right before your big finish.

We strongly recommend making "appearances"—telling the judges who you are—during the pretrial conference. If you have done that, you don't need to waste time here re-introducing yourself. In the rare event that the judge did not allow appearances, don't waste valuable real estate at the beginning of your opening. You can introduce yourself later in the speech at the same time you introduce your client.

4.5 Structure

Like most aspects of Mock Trial, opening statements are part science, part art. We need to be creative—while still coloring inside the lines. Here is the structure we have seen generate the highest scores from judges: (1) introduction of the case, (2) introduction of your client, (3) the law, (4) roadmap, (5) preview of the evidence, and (6) finale.

4.5.1 Introduction of the Case

If opening statement is the single most important part of trial, then the beginning of the opening statement is the single most important moment of trial. Judges are paying maximum attention. They are excited to see each team perform. They want to know what the case is about.

We strongly recommend starting with a sandwich:

Theme

Story

Theme

The top slice of bread is the theme—the first words out of your mouth. Then comes the meat: your story. It grabs the audience and gives flavor to your speech. You finish with another slice of that theme—the last words of your introduction.

By saying the theme at the very start, and then a second time during the introduction, judges will know you have a theme and what it is. By crafting the introduction around a story, you can bring the case to life.

Notice that the theme does not have to make perfect sense on its own because it is followed by a story that helps explain it. Some themes make the theory clear without additional explanation. When the prosecution's theme is "He killed for money," you know the crime and the motive. When the defense's theme is, "No gun, no body, no witness," you know what shortcomings in the prosecution case the defense plans to attack. But some themes need explanation. For example, in the 2017 Tournament of Champions, Professor Bernstein's Drexel team used a prosecution theme of "Shut 'em up, shut 'em down." As the first words of the prosecution opening, these did not make the theory clear. But that was okay. The goal was to build suspense and draw in the audience—to make them wonder what those words meant. What followed was a gripping story about a sheriff who tried to thwart a government investigation into the fact that his deputies were brutally beating and abusing inmates in the jail. The sheriff tried to shut up the key informant—to keep him from talking—and he tried to stop the entire investigation. When the opener, Jessica Falkenstein, repeated the theme—"Shut 'em up, shut 'em down"—it all made sense. A good story makes the audience think, "Oh, I see why that theme makes sense. I buy that."

When we say "story," that doesn't mean a summary of the facts. For example, don't start your opening like this: "On September 14th, at approximately 7:02 p.m., Michael Ehrman shot and killed James Moody with a .357 magnum revolver. The evidence will show that Ellen Moody hired Michael Ehrman to kill James Moody because of his infidelity with Lila Green, a third-year teaching assistant at Baylor University." That's a summary. It starts with the conclusion. It takes an incredibly dramatic set of facts and strips all the drama.

A story brings the facts to life. Do you feel like you're "there" as you read that summary above? No, of course not. We don't know where this all took place or what it looked like.

A story has characters. Do we know anything about the four people mentioned in that summary? No. We don't know who they are, what they do for a living, or how they feel.

A story has action. That summary has a shooting, but it's so abrupt—it's the very first sentence—that we don't get to watch it happen. By the time we realize what's going on, the climax is already over. Then it goes back in time, from the shooting to the defendant hiring the shooter. That's not action. That's a rewind.

Here is that story sandwich from the Top Gun champion:

> The defendant, Ellen Moody, didn't pull the trigger. She pulled the strings.
>
> It's September 2014. The defendant is holding a glossy color photograph. There are two people in the photo. One of them is James Moody, her husband. The other is her husband's 23-year-old graduate student. James is standing behind her, holding her tight. There are champagne glasses by their side. They're wearing bathrobes. They're smiling. They look like they're in love. And they're standing on the defendant's porch. At her home.

> The defendant puts down the photograph and picks up her phone. She calls the unlicensed private investigator who took the photos. She speaks to him for 32 minutes and, that afternoon, she wires him 10 thousand dollars. Four days later, the man she paid 10 thousand dollars walks into the Moody's home, finds James Moody in his study, and shoots him in the chest, dead.
>
> The defendant didn't pull the trigger. But the evidence will show she pulled the strings.

This introduction drops the audience right into the action. It's present tense. A woman is holding a photo. The drama builds as the audience realizes what the photo is: her husband having an affair. Then she acts. She arranges for his murder. By the time the murder happens, we know who is responsible.

This introduction has characters. The defendant is the woman who wants revenge. James is the victim, the object of the defendant's rage. The shooter is her pawn—he doesn't get a name because he's not the one on trial, and we want the focus on the defendant.

This introduction has details. Instead of unimportant details (.357 magnum, 7:02 p.m., third-year teaching assistant) this introduction has details that tell the story we want. The bathrobes and champagne glasses tell the story of an affair. The porch tells the story of betrayal—*in her home*. The 32 minutes tell the story of two people planning.

Notice that the story does not try to tell every important detail. We don't learn how the defendant first became suspicious of her husband cheating or how she hired the private investigator. We don't learn that the shooter was promised another 10 thousand dollars after the shooting was done. We don't learn that on the morning of the murder the defendant disabled her home alarm, which allowed the killer to enter the house. We don't learn what happened in the study—whether James Moody fought back or even saw his killer.

That's a good thing. One of the biggest mistakes we see in most team's opening statements is that they try to tell the story of the entire case all at once. That's impossible to do well, and it forces teams into summarizing instead of storytelling. Relax. You can tell the jury about the rest of the case after you've told them what is most important. If you have their attention at the start, they will stay with you until the end.

What story should you tell? Tell the story that highlights your theme and theory. That isn't always the most action-packed moment. In the Moody prosecution, the most exciting single event is the shooting itself. But the defendant isn't in the room for that moment. Starting there would point the attention—and guilt—away from the defendant. It would emphasize the hitman's crime, rather than the defendant's crime. Instead, Rahul started with a story about the defendant: the story of when she decided to have her husband killed. The introduction describes the hitman not as "the killer" but as "the man she paid 10 thousand dollars." The introduction has more than 100 words describing the defendant deciding to have her husband killed, and fewer than 30 about the actual killing. Why? Because "she didn't pull the trigger; she pulled the strings."

A final word of advice: Although you're engaging in storytelling, don't call your side's version of events a "story." The other side has a story. Your side has the truth.

4.5.2 Introduction of Your Client

This is where you introduce the party you represent. There are four main scenarios. In the first scenario, you are the prosecution in a criminal case. All you need to say is, "As the State, we've charged the defendant with . . ." This assumes you've already identified the victim and their injury during your introduction. If not, make sure you do so here.

In the second scenario, you represent the plaintiff in a civil case. Your job here is to introduce them to the jury. "This is Natalie Garson." Then humanize them. "She is a doctor. A wife. A mother. During the day, she takes care of her patients. When she comes home, she takes care of her family." If you haven't already described their injuries, this is a good time to do it. "She loved to run. Last year she did her first half marathon. Now? She has trouble walking to get the mail."

In the third scenario, you represent an individual defendant: a person accused of a crime or a person being sued. You need to introduce them. If it works in your courtroom setup, touch them on the shoulder. If you like (and are not afraid of) your client, the jury will pick up on it. Humanizing your client is even more important on defense because presumably by the time you give your opening statement, the prosecution/plaintiff has already attacked your client. You need the jury to see the defendant in a new light. You can do this by refuting the prosecution's / plaintiff's introduction of your client. "The prosecution tried to paint Mr. Ryan as a bad driver. But what you're actually going to learn is that . . ." Or you can acknowledge weakness and pivot. "This is Darren Ryan. He will be the first to admit he could have been more careful that day. But what you'll learn . . ."

In the fourth scenario, you represent a company. Again, your job is to humanize your client. You don't want the jury to think of the defendant as a greedy, profit-seeking corporation. You want them to see the company as the men and women who work hard to provide important services that people need. If you have the owner or company representative at your counsel table, you can start with them. At Top Gun 2019, the defendant was a bicycle manufacturer. Kyle DeCamp, a law student at UCLA, personalized his corporate client:

> Today you'll meet Jamie Patterson. Jamie Patterson is the chief operating officer at Texera Cycling. She's going to tell you what kind of company Texera is. Twenty years ago, mountain biking was really only for rich folks. See, the outdoors might be free, the trails might be free, but 20 years ago mountain bikes sure weren't. If you walked into Bicycle World down on Mary Street and asked for a mountain bike, it was a thousand bucks. Usually more. Until this company changed that. They introduced a mountain bike for five hundred dollars. They didn't make as much profit per bike. But they were okay with that. Because they were able to sell a lot of bikes. They were able to bring bikes to everyday people.

This puts the defendant in a positive light even though they're a corporation. No matter who you represent—no matter who they are or what bad things they've done—they have some positive characteristics. Your job is to dig those out and then introduce the client in the most favorable way the evidence will support.

4.5.3 Law

Once you've introduced your theory, theme, and party, summarize the law for the jury. Specifically, your job is to present the burden of proof, identify the charges or civil claims, and summarize the key legal issues.

The burden of proof is the standard that the prosecution/plaintiff must meet in presenting their evidence. In a criminal case, the prosecution's burden is proof beyond a reasonable doubt. In most civil cases, the plaintiff's burden is proof by a preponderance of the evidence, which means proof that something is more likely true than not true.

If you represent the prosecution or plaintiff, your opening just needs to say that you have the burden of proof and what it is. "As the State, we have the burden of proof. We have to prove the defendant's guilt beyond a reasonable doubt."

If you represent the defense, you want to emphasize the burden of proof. There are several ways of doing this:

> As the defense, we have no burden of proof. That burden lies solely with the prosecution. They have to prove every element of their case beyond a reasonable doubt.

> As the defense, we have no burden of proof. We don't have to present any evidence. We don't have to call any witnesses. We don't have to ask any questions. That's because the prosecution has the burden.
>
> The prosecution has the burden of proof. The highest burden in our criminal justice system. Proof beyond a reasonable doubt.

Although openings should point out what the burden of proof is and who has it; don't go into great detail explaining it or use analogies to illustrate it. Some judges will consider this "arguing"—which is not permitted during opening—and score you down for it.

Your opening also needs to identify the charges or claims. "We have charged the defendant with kidnapping." "Mrs. Jones has sued the defendant for the wrongful death of her son."

Finally, the law section of your opening should identify the key elements or legal concepts. This does not mean putting the jury to sleep by sounding like a legal textbook. Don't do this:

> As the plaintiff, we have to prove defamation. Defamation has five elements. The first element is that the defendant made a statement. This requires a factual assertion, not merely an opinion. The second element is that the defendant published the statement. This means . . .

WAR STORY

We once saw an opening statement where the high school competitor began reading the statutes, word for word. "The defendant is charged with first degree burglary. California Penal Code section 459 states, 'Every person who enters any house, room, apartment, tenement, shop, warehouse, store, mill, barn, stable, outhouse, building, tent, vessel, floating home, railroad car, locked or sealed cargo container, inhabited camper, or mine or any underground portion thereof, with intent to commit grand or petit larceny or any felony is guilty of burglary.'" The judges visibly stopped listening somewhere around "barn." Summarize the law. Don't quote the entire statute.

Instead, ask yourself, what does the jury need to know? What is the least I can tell them about the law while still making sure they understand this case? Here are three examples:

> Ms. Jones is suing the defendant for defamation. As the plaintiff, we have the burden of proof. That means we have to prove—more likely than not—that the defendant made a false statement that damaged Mrs. Jones's reputation.

> As the prosecution, we have the burden. We have to prove our case beyond a reasonable doubt. Because the defendant has been charged with murder, we have to prove he killed Mr. Smith with premeditation. In other words, that he planned to kill Mr. Smith.

> As the defense, we have no burden. That burden lies entirely with the plaintiff. They have to prove every element of their case by a preponderance of the evidence. But there are two elements they won't be able to prove. They won't be able to prove Mrs. Garcia was negligent. And they won't be able to prove she caused Mr. Chang's injuries.

Notice how short these legal sections are. That's the goal. Tell the jury what they need to know, and then get to the evidence. This is necessary in Mock Trial, where there are tight time limits, but it holds true in the real world as well. If you get in the weeds on the law, you will lose the jury before you get to the evidence you need them to pay attention to. Additionally, the more you discuss the law, the more likely it is that a scoring judge will think you are "arguing."

The legal section can also be a place to tell the jury that some of the elements you have to prove are undisputed. This will help them focus on what's really important.

> As the prosecution, we have the burden. We have to prove—beyond a reasonable doubt—that the defendant intentionally killed Mr. Body. We expect that most of what we have to prove will be undisputed. It's undisputed that Mr. Body was killed. You'll see his autopsy. It's undisputed that this crime was intentional. There were six bullet holes in his chest. So this case will come down to one question: was the defendant the one who did it? Three facts will prove that he did . . .

4.5.4 Roadmap

One of the biggest shortcomings we see in opening statements, everywhere from high school openings to real trials, is the lack of a roadmap. The lawyer introduces the case, summarizes the law, and then . . . just starts talking. Sometimes the lawyer turns it into a witness book report. "First we will call Officer Perez. He will tell you ___. Then we will call Doctor Wu. She will tell you ___." This is an unexciting way to summarize your evidence. That's a witness list, not a roadmap. It is important to identify each witness you will call, by name and role, but you can do so in the process of telling a story.

Before you explain your evidence in more detail, give the jury a roadmap. Find two or three points that organize your case. Sometimes it's the three categories of evidence that prove the defendant's guilt. "Means, motive, opportunity." "The eyewitnesses, the forensic evidence, the defendant's own statements." Or the three points that summarize the defense. "No gun, no body, no witness."

Sometimes it's two or three facts that tell a story. "She wanted revenge. She got revenge." "The defendant wouldn't commit this crime. Couldn't commit this crime. Didn't commit this crime."

Sometimes it's as simple as framing the evidence around the elements you have to prove or dispute. "The defendant had a duty to his patient. He was negligent. His negligence caused Mr. Adams to die." "They won't be able to prove that Dr. Zahav was negligent. They won't be able to prove that he caused Mr. Adams's death."

4.5.5 Preview of Evidence

Now, follow your roadmap! For each one of the points on your roadmap, deliver one paragraph of information that previews the evidence in support of that point. For example:

> As the prosecution, we have the burden. We have to prove our case beyond a reasonable doubt. Because the defendant has been charged with murder, we have to prove he killed Mr. Smith with premeditation. In other words, that he planned to kill Mr. Smith. We will meet that burden with three key pieces of evidence. The threat. The ballistics. And the blood. Let's take those one at a time.
>
> The first piece of evidence that will prove the defendant's guilt is the threat. Nora Green will take the stand. She's the defendant's coworker, and she saw the defendant's reaction when he was fired. Rage. Ms. Green will testify to the defendant's exact words when Mr. Smith fired him. "You'll pay for this." Twenty-four hours later, Mr. Smith was dead.
>
> The second piece of evidence that will prove the defendant's guilt is the ballistics . . .

Notice how the witness—Nora Green—is part of the paragraph. That's the goal. Always mention all your witnesses in the opening statement. Just don't make them a list. Instead, weave the witnesses, exhibits, and other evidence into each paragraph.

4.5.6 Finale

The last paragraph of an opening should remind the jury of your theory and theme before previewing the verdict you will seek. This is also a good spot to address a weakness in your case. Here is how Professor Bernstein's Drexel team ended their opening statement at the 2017 Tournament of Champions when prosecuting the sheriff for obstruction of justice.

> Members of the jury, the defendant tried to be careful. You won't see many documents with his name on them. You won't hear many guards who got their orders directly from him. That's not how he worked. No, you'll learn that he gave his orders to the undersheriff, the undersheriff gave those orders to the sergeants, and the sergeants gave those orders to the guards. Chain of command. But the evidence will show that all of the obstruction, all of the corruption, started at the top. Started with the Sheriff. At the end of this trial, we will ask you to find the defendant guilty. Because he gave the order. Shut 'em up, shut 'em down.

First, this addresses a weakness: the lack of direct evidence that the sheriff obstructed justice. The defense is going to attack the prosecution for not having documents where the sheriff tried to obstruct justice or witnesses who saw the sheriff obstruct justice. But this conclusion tries to address that weakness and turn it into a strength by suggesting that the lack of direct evidence doesn't mean the defendant is innocent; it means he was careful.

Next, the final paragraph comes back to the prosecution's theory. The sheriff gave orders to obstruct through his underlings. It identifies the verdict the prosecution will seek. "At the end of this trial, we will ask you to find the defendant guilty." Then it ends with the theme. Sometimes it makes sense to end with the request for verdict and the theme. Sometimes it makes sense to end with the theme and then the request for verdict. But those should be the last two lines of your opening statement.

4.6 Prosecution/Plaintiff Opening

Going first is hard. You have to educate the jury about what happened *and* persuade them that your position is correct. But going first also has an advantage. The jury is a blank slate. You can shape the way they see the rest of trial.

Make sure to address any major weaknesses of your case. This is important for both parties, but especially the prosecution/plaintiff. If you don't mention a bad fact and then the defense brings it up in their opening statement, the fact will seem much worse. The jury will start to distrust you.

4.7 Defense Opening

Point out what the other side won't be able to prove or show. This is easier to do in Mock Trial than in real life because it's a closed fact pattern—a new piece of evidence won't suddenly show up during trial. "We'll want to see _____, but it isn't there." Or: "When __ takes the stand, see if he remembers ___."

But just because you are the defense doesn't mean you should be defensive. The opening shouldn't be entirely about what the other side can't prove. Make sure you have your own story to tell—a competing narrative. If your defense feels entirely about "reasonable doubt," it will feel technical and nonspecific. Even if your focus is the flaws in the prosecution's case, you still need to tell a story that suggests your client is innocent.

It can also be effective to respond briefly to the prosecution opening. This shouldn't be more than a sentence or two because you want to focus on your theory. But if you can respond to the prosecution's theory, it will help set you apart from your opponent.

Let's Get Real: In some jurisdictions, criminal defense attorneys may "reserve" their opening statements. This means they can wait until after the prosecution has rested its case. Reserving its opening allows the defense to see the prosecution's theory and evidence before presenting its own, but it also risks the jury forming conclusions before the defense has opened. In Mock Trial, teams may not reserve their openings.

4.8 The Opponent's Opening Statement

Listen carefully to the opposing team's opening statement. If you are an attorney, you need to understand their theory and theme so you can rebut it throughout trial. If you are a witness, the other side's opening will help you anticipate what they are likely to ask you on cross-examination.

The whole team should listen closely for promises the opponent makes in opening statement that they might not be able to keep. If they describe evidence that might be excluded or promise testimony that exaggerates what the witness will say, write that down. One team member should convert this into a combined list to use as a checklist during trial. Make sure your team's closing argument calls out the opponent for broken promises of anything discussed but not delivered.

4.9 Visual Aids

Using an enlargement or other visual aid can be helpful in holding the scorers' attention. It can also help the attorney remember key points without having to use notes. However, using enlargements takes practice.

Obtain permission from the judge to use a visual in opening statement. Do this before you start so it does not break up your flow.

Set up the enlargement beforehand. Ideally, place it on an easel but have it covered or reversed so the jury cannot see the visual before you reveal it. It looks great to have your co-counsel help set up the visual aid or shift from one to another if multiple visuals are being used. Judges love teamwork.

If you use a visual aid during opening statement, do not use it during your introduction. Some teams will show a photo of the victim at the start of their opening statement. But, as the attorney, you are the one receiving the score. You are the one who needs to develop a connection with the jury. Starting with a visual aid puts the jury's eyes and attention on something other than you. The other reason to use the visual aid later in the opening statement is that it will draw jury interest. You do not need the visual at the beginning—you already have jury engagement when you start—but you will benefit from the boost a few minutes later as their attention spans start to wane.

Beware of using visual aids with lots of text, even if enlarged. If you put text in front of a jury, they will start reading—and stop listening. The best visual aids for opening statement are photos and maps. Photos help a jury understand the key people or locations. Maps help the jury understand what happened.

4.10 Objections

Most competitions do not allow objections during opening statements and closing arguments. Do not try to take advantage of this by working in objectionable material. The judges will know what is and is not appropriate in real life and are likely to score you down for things the other side would likely have objected to if they were permitted to do so.

What should you do if the other side offers objectionable material? If the rules don't permit objections, you should generally do nothing. Some teams will, once the opening is finished, say, "Your Honor, objections to openings are not permitted in this jurisdiction, but if they were permitted, I would have objected to ________." We recommend against this as it rubs some judges the wrong way. The one exception is if a speech does something egregious such as commenting on the defendant failing to testify in a criminal case. In these instances, when the opening is over, just stand and say, "Your Honor, I'd just like to remind the Court that we are not allowed to object to openings in this jurisdiction." This helps the judge remember the rule and makes them less likely to score you down for failing to make an obvious objection.

4.11 Performance

Like every other part of trial, the opening statement should be performed with energy, drama, and precision. But there are a few differences in how the opening should be delivered, compared to other parts of trial, especially the closing.

Carefully memorize your opening statement. Other parts of trial require adaptation. Direct and cross may change based on objections. Closing must adapt to what's happened in trial. But the opening statement comes first, so practice it until your delivery is just right. You don't want to *sound* rehearsed—but you do want to *be* rehearsed.

The opening statement should be delivered extra slowly. The judges don't know the facts of the case yet, so you need to give them time to absorb the information. Aim for 100 words per minute. That may sound fast, but it's much slower than most of us speak normally.

The opening statement should avoid an argumentative tone. You need to be more restrained in opening than closing. This is partly because openings are not supposed to contain argument, and if you deliver a factual sentence too aggressively, judges will think it's argumentative. But the other reason to avoid being too aggressive in opening is that the judges don't know the case yet. If you deliver the opening with contempt, indignation, or fury, they likely won't yet share those feelings. In fact, it will probably make them resistant to your theory. Instead, ease them in and build the drama throughout the opening.

Opening statements should avoid sarcasm or humor. These might be appropriate for closing, but the judges don't know you yet. Once the judges trust you—later in trial—then you can show a greater range of emotion.

If you are wearing a jacket, button it. Set up any demonstrative aids before any words come out of your mouth. Apart from the time constraints, a measured beginning establishes your presence in the courtroom.

Finally, remember that it's not just the opener who has to think about performance. *When we are in court, we are always being scored.* During your own side's opening statement, everyone at the counsel table should be watching with rapt attention. Should a scorer glance at a teammate, their devoted gaze will promptly direct the scorer's attention back to the appropriate place. The opposite holds true during the other side's opening. Don't watch that person, but do take copious notes. And do not roll your eyes or make unprofessional remarks. A lack of professionalism will haunt you later when the judges score your performance.

5

Direct Examination

A direct examination is when a witness answers questions from the lawyer who called them to the stand. In real life, the lawyer and witness usually have a cooperative relationship on direct examination because they have the same goals. As a classic example, prosecutors often call police officers to testify; both want to convict the defendant. They have usually prepared together before trial.

In Mock Trial, the witness and lawyer have a cooperative relationship on direct examination because they are literally on the same team (the exception is "live witness" competitions discussed later in this chapter). They have worked together to carefully craft the attorney's questions and witness's answers.

Direct examination is a crucial part of Mock Trial success. This is where you present most of your evidence. Remember that *It's All About Points!* Direct examination usually has more points for your team than any other part of trial because your attorney and witness generally both receive scores.

Great direct examinations can be exciting: the witness captivates the jury, the attorney asks questions that highlight the witness's testimony, and the jury understands exactly how the testimony supports the team's theory of the case.

But, more than any other part of trial, direct examination also has the tendency to bore the jury. Because the attorney and witness are working together, there is less dramatic tension. Because no individual witness tells the whole story, direct examination can be difficult for scoring judges to follow. And perhaps the biggest reason direct examinations are often flat: most teams undervalue the importance of witnesses.

On some high school and college Mock Trial teams, the attorneys are the stars and the witnesses are the students who didn't qualify to be attorneys. Those teams lose. The best Mock Trial teams all realize that witnesses are just as—if not more—important as the lawyers.

> **Pet Peeve**: We hate when someone says, "I'm *just* a witness." That's like saying, "I'm *just* the starting pitcher."

Good witnesses score a ton of points. But they also impact the scores of the lawyers. A good witness will usually generate a strong score for her directing attorney (conversely, a strong attorney does not usually lift the score of a less skilled/experienced witness). A witness also impacts the score of the other team's cross-examiner.

There is a saying in the Mock Trial community: "Attorneys *lose* trials—witnesses *win* them." As a result, much of this chapter is devoted to witnesses.

5.1 Goals

A witness's goal on direct examination is to present their testimony in a clear and compelling way. This means creating a personality that will engage the jury from the start and developing answers that emphasize the key facts.

An attorney's goal on direct examination is to facilitate the witness's testimony by asking questions that highlight what's important, by asking questions that avoid objections (so the witness's presentation isn't interrupted), and by keeping the spotlight on the witness.

5.2 Witness Personality

We start with witness personality—before witness testimony—because it's vital and so often overlooked.

Think about your own experience in a classroom. If the teacher is dull—quiet, low energy, passionless, no fun—you are more likely to tune out during class. It doesn't matter what the subject is. If a person is unengaging, we all have trouble listening. That's the first half of being a great witness: you must be *engaging* so the jury will *listen* to your testimony.

Still, we can't go too far. If a witness is too loud, too angry, too sarcastic, too silly, or too theatrical, the jury won't believe them. That's the second half of being a great witness: you must be *credible* so the jury will *believe* your testimony.

So how do we do that? How do we make sure the jury listens to us and believes us? It starts with developing a strong personality. This includes the words we use on the stand, the way we say them, our posture, and (within the rules of the competition) our attire.

WAR STORY

The attire should make sense for the witness. In 2009, Professor Bernstein judged a trial between two inexperienced college teams. The defense expert was called to the stand. He wore a hat, scarf, gloves, and trench coat. When he reached the stand, the witness began to remove every accessory ***uncomfortably slowly***. We are talking "loosening one glove finger at a time" slowly. The witness would fold each article carefully and place it atop the witness stand. The entire presentation lasted more than a minute . . . and then no explanation was ever given! There was no witness personality, let alone a personality that could explain the disrobing. To this day, Professor Bernstein remains mystified.

Start by identifying who the witness is in the trial. A police officer is going to act and speak differently than a DNA expert. A rock star accused of a crime is going to act and speak differently than a librarian who witnessed a crime.

We divide witness personalities into four main categories:

- Law Enforcement
- Expert
- Eyewitness
- Party/Victim

Sometimes these categories overlap. For example, a crime scene investigator combines elements of law enforcement with scientific expertise. In those instances, you can decide whether you want to portray the character more as a cop, more as a scientist, or as a combination of both. You should make that decision by considering the person playing the role (does the person sound and look more like a cop or a scientist?), the nature of the testimony (is the direct more about their observations or analysis?), and whether you already have another witness who fits one of these categories (witnesses score best when their personalities are distinct from one another).

5.2.1 Law Enforcement

This category generally refers to police officers, but it can also include private investigators, military witnesses, and security guards. Law enforcement witnesses score best when they fit a stereotype: concise, confident, no-nonsense.

If you are playing a police officer, and if your competition permits, consider wearing a police officer uniform. If not, wear a dark suit (preferably blue) and white shirt. Men should wear a conservative tie (e.g., solid navy, solid dark red). Detectives should wear suits, not uniforms. The dress should remain conservative: dark suit and white shirt for all, conservative tie for men.

WAR STORY

A scoring judge, who happened to be a real judge, thought one of Judge Nelmark's teammates (who was in uniform, playing a witness that was a state trooper) was a real courthouse deputy. She asked him to close the door to the courtroom. He, of course, did so. The look on her face when that teammate was called to the witness stand was priceless.

Law enforcement witnesses should walk to the witness stand with a confident stride. Nod to the judge. Sit upright with your hands clasped in your lap. Don't fidget.

Speak loudly and confidently. Law enforcement witnesses testify regularly, so they should sound authoritative.

Change tones, but less dramatically than other witnesses. Establish a baseline speech pattern and alter it slightly depending on what you're saying. Avoid sounding emotional. For example, if you are describing the sight of a dead body, don't sound grossed out: you have probably seen dead bodies before. Instead, pause slightly before answering; hesitate just a little when answering. The small change will be noticeable to judges, and it will feel real.

Speak concisely. Eliminate unnecessary words. Consider this example:

Q. Please introduce yourself to the jury.

A. Hello. My name is Officer Sally Jones.

Q. What do you do for a living?

A. I'm a patrol officer. I work for the Los Angeles Police Department. It's my job to keep the streets safe. I handle routine traffic stops and I respond to reports from dispatch.

Q. How long have you worked in this role?

A. I have been a patrol officer for 13 years now. I love helping my community.

Q. Do you have any training that qualifies you to be a police officer?

A. I attended and graduated from the Los Angeles Police Academy. It's a six-month training that covers everything from traffic laws to evidence collection.

This is how the typical Mock Trial police officer answers questions. It's fine. It accurately states the content from the witness statement. But it doesn't *sound* like a police officer. This version will score better:

Q. Please introduce yourself to the jury.

A. Evening. My name is Officer Sally Jones.

Q. What do you do for a living?

A. I'm a patrol officer.

Q. Where?

A. LAPD. Los Angeles Police Department.

Q. What are your duties as a patrol officer?

A. I handle routine traffic stops and respond to reports from dispatch.

Q. How long have you worked in this role?

A. Thirteen years.

Q. Do you have any training that qualifies you to be a police officer?

A. Yes. Graduated from the academy in '08.

It's the same substantive information, but we've removed the commentary and the full sentences. You won't score well on your English papers writing like this, but you will score well portraying a police officer speaking like this.

Good law enforcement witnesses speak respectfully—on direct and cross-examination. This is as easy as adding "sir" or "ma'am" to yes/no answers and the occasional short answer. For example:

Q. Please introduce yourself to the jury.

A. Evening. My name is Officer Sally Jones.

Q. What do you do for a living?

A. I'm a patrol officer.

Q. Where?

A. LAPD, ***sir***. Los Angeles Police Department.

Q. What are your duties as a patrol officer?

A. I handle routine traffic stops and respond to reports from dispatch.

Q. How long have you worked in this role?

A. 13 years, ***sir***.

Q. Do you have any training that qualifies you to be a police officer?

A. Yes, ***sir***. Graduated from the academy in '08.

The officer on the 1950s/60s police show *Dragnet* isn't famous for saying, "I only want to gather objective information." The famous line was, "Just the facts, ma'am." Keep your answers short, to the point, and respectful.

Some teams have their police officers refer to attorneys as "counsel" or "counselor": "Yes, counsel." Don't do that. It will sound condescending to many, especially on cross-examination.

Make sure to use plenty of police lingo. Instead of saying, "I checked to see if the driver appeared drunk," say, "I performed a field sobriety test." You could say, "I received a report of a possible robbery." But it would be better to say, "Dispatch reported a possible 459. Burglary in progress." Instead of saying "four in the afternoon," say, "sixteen-hundred hours."

Police witnesses should also use appropriate detail. Law enforcement witnesses are excellent at noting details, such as time, location, direction, physical description, and vehicle information.

Decent Testimony	Better Testimony
The guy was on the highway.	The suspect was heading northbound on Interstate 5.
I found Mr. Harper's body in the alley.	In the alley, we found a white male, approximately 30 years old. Face down, no pulse. We later identified him as Bran Harper.
The person was driving a white car.	The suspect was driving a white Chevy Impala, license plate BRG142.

This will make some answers longer. But you will have saved plenty of time by shortening your other answers.

Present your law enforcement witness as genuine, experienced, assertive, and terse.

5.2.2 Expert

Most Mock Trial cases have expert witnesses. An expert is any witness whose specialized experience or education allows them to give testimony that a regular person could not. Common experts include a forensic scientist (DNA, fingerprints, blood spatter), pathologist (someone who determines cause of death), psychologist, or accident reconstructionist. But Mock Trial cases, like real cases, can have very specialized experts. For example, just in the last year we've seen Mock Trial cases with experts on handwriting, police conduct, product warning labels, bus design, food allergies, stunt work, fires, electrical wire installation, ethics, immunology, toxicology, and bed bugs.

All great experts should present themselves as part scientist, part teacher. The scientist part of their personality should show their precision, mastery of the subject, and credibility. The teacher part of their personality should make the complex information easy to understand with definitions, examples, analogies, and (if possible) charts or demonstrations.

An expert witness should dress professionally. Wear a suit. But you don't have to dress as conservatively as the law enforcement witness. You can wear a shirt that is not white, and if you're wearing a tie it doesn't have to be monochromatic. Bowties, though overdone, still score well. But don't be silly: doctors don't wear lab coats, scrubs, or stethoscopes to court. We've seen teams do this, and we advise against it.

An expert should walk to the stand confidently. Don't strut. Glide. Sit down and be comfortable. Maintain good posture but lean back a little in your chair. You've testified in court before. You're comfortable, and everyone should see that. But when you have something exciting to share, lean forward in your seat. Speak loudly and slowly. Use gestures to help make your point.

An expert's answers should be more articulate, formal, and grammatically correct than those of a law enforcement witness. Instead of saying, "I got my bachelors at Georgetown and my MD at Wisconsin," we recommend something like, "I earned my bachelor's degree in biology from Georgetown University and my medical doctorate from the University of Wisconsin."

An expert should use the vocabulary of their profession. This requires research outside the case materials. Don't make up information. Use authentic vocabulary when conveying the information in the case materials.

An expert should be specific. The brain of the victim didn't weigh "about 1300 grams"; it weighed 1,302 grams.

It would be easy to read everything we have said so far and think the expert's primary goal is to sound smart. But that's only half the battle. An expert must be a teacher, too. You don't want your expert to sound cold and distant. You want the jury to know you're there to help them understand the complexities.

Finally, and maybe most importantly, an expert must be passionate. The jury should see and feel how much you care about your subject. If you are passionate, the jury will be interested, too. It doesn't matter how boring the topic sounds to the average person—economics, mattress construction, the best way to brush your teeth—if an expert is passionate, the jury will listen.

Another reason to portray your expert with passion is that it conveys excellence. When someone tells us they are good at their job, we are skeptical. Of course, they *say* they are good at their job. But when someone is passionate about their job, we assume they are good at it. The most effective way to establish credibility as an expert witness is to be enthusiastic about your subject.

This does not mean you should be passionate for the entire direct. That will wear out the judges, and instead of viewing you as passionate about your subject, they will think you're just erratic or silly. Save your passion for moments when you are describing your subject of expertise. For example, you don't need to be passionate when asked, "Where did you go to school?" and "Did you have a sample of the defendant's fingerprints?" Save your passion for answering questions such as, "What are fingerprints?" and "How did you determine whether these prints came from the defendant?"

5.2.3 Eyewitness

An eyewitness is someone testifying based on firsthand knowledge, without a direct stake in the outcome of the case. For example, the 2012 AMTA case involved a woman who died in a single car collision. The driver was charged with driving under the influence and reckless homicide. The eyewitnesses included the bartender and server where the driver was drinking, the friend who was in the backseat during the crash, and a homeowner who saw the crash from her front porch. For the purposes of witness portrayals, we do not count the defendant as an eyewitness. Yes, the defendant was driving and has firsthand knowledge of what happened. But the defendant has a direct interest in the outcome of the case. We cover parties (plaintiff and defendants) and victims in the next section.

Eyewitnesses present an enormous point-scoring opportunity in Mock Trial. Because they don't have the professional obligations of a police officer or expert, and because they don't have a personal stake in the case like a victim or defendant, you can—and should—have more fun with these witnesses. Obviously, you don't want to go too far. It will be off-putting to many judges if a witness treats a trial where someone died like a standup comedy routine. But the best-scoring eyewitnesses will have distinct, engaging, fun personalities.

How do you decide on their personality? Let's start with the one thing that *shouldn't* dictate your character choice: the witness statement. Often case authors will create a witness personality on the page. They will write the character as dimwitted, or callous, or arrogant. Ignore that. As a witness, you must stick to the facts contained in your statement. You don't have to stick to the personality in your witness statement.

So how should you choose the witness personality? Consider the person playing the role. What is their natural personality? What do they look like? What roles would they play best? Can they do any accents (and does the competition permit accents)?

For example, in 2010, Professor Bernstein coached four UC Irvine teams that all called an eyewitness named Hunter Baxamusa. One student played the character as a nerdy high school student who was stargazing on his telescope when he witnessed a murder. Another portrayed the character as an Indian woman who was communing with nature. Another portrayed the character as a snooty rich guy who was out for an evening stroll. Another portrayed the character as a Russian graduate student doing research for an astronomy class. *They all won awards in that role.* They had the same witness statement, but they each played the character completely differently. Find the portrayal that works for you and your team.

Portraying a character with an accent or incorporating aspects of their background into the portrayal can create fun, lifelike characters. Be aware, however, that using a "Boston" or "Alabama" accent can be risky before a panel of judges who come from Boston or Alabama. The witness must also be understandable and able to maintain the accent during cross-examination. Finally, make sure you aren't perpetuating harmful stereotypes or doing something offensive.

The only frequently seen portrayal we recommend against is the shy/nervous/awkward witness. It tends to make judges uncomfortable, bored, or confused. It also runs the risk of judges not realizing it is a portrayal: they may think the student is truly nervous. That's a recipe for a low score.

Consider the witness's occupation. That can be a great source of inspiration for the witness's personality. For example, car salesmen, flight attendants, and movie producers are all naturally fun characters. If you get a witness like that, think about how you can bring that character to life. And you can also be creative. If a witness says, "I work in a bar," you can decide whether to portray them as the old, irritable waitress at a pub—or the sommelier at a fancy wine bar.

Consider the judges. They're adult professionals. They may not have the same sense of humor as high school or college students. *It's All About Points!* So, it's not about whether your teammates think a witness is funny. Evaluate whether the 55-year-old lawyer scoring your portrayal will find it funny.

WAR STORY

We once saw a trial where the witness chose an odd portrayal. Afterwards, one of the scoring judges said, "I found your character confusing." The student explained, "Oh, I was playing Squidward." The judge said, "I don't know what that is." The student explained further, "From SpongeBob." Pause. "I don't know what that is." You can guess how the witness scored on that judge's ballot. First moral of the story: know your audience. Second moral of the story: cartoon characters are rarely the best inspiration for witness portrayals.

Okay, so once you figure out the witness character, how do we bring them to life?

We have so many tools at our disposal! We can choose the attire. What would the witness wear to court? We can practice our body language. How would the witness walk to the stand? How would they sit on the stand? Where would their eye contact be? Most of all, we can design the witness's speech. How would they speak? What words would they use? What subjects would they discuss?

If the witness is a lady who lives alone with her seven cats, make sure to include a couple references to her cats. If the witness is nerdy, refer to her stamp collection or trusty TI-85 calculator—she never leaves home without it. If the witness is a grandma, make sure she calls the lawyer "sonny," "honey," or "young man." It only takes a few careful choices to convey the character's personality.

5.2.4 Party/Victim

This category includes people directly affected by the outcome of the case: the plaintiff or surviving family, a victim in a criminal case or their surviving family, or the defendant.

These witnesses all have an emotional stake. Victims want the jury to know they've been hurt. Defendants want the jury to know they are innocent (or, in a civil case, not liable).

Most teams forget to give party/victim witnesses a personality. For example, sometimes when we are consulting with teams and we ask these witnesses to describe their personality, they say, "Sad." That's a mood, not a personality. Or sometimes they will try to turn the witness into an angel. Every answer is delivered gently and sounds like Mother Teresa. When we meet these witnesses when consulting and we ask them to describe their personality, they say, "Nice." But "nice" isn't a character. Or at least it's not a very interesting or fully developed character. No one is simply "nice." We are all more multifaceted than that. Instead, ask yourself: Who is this person? What are they like apart from the events in this trial? You should be able to answer questions about the person even when the answers are not in the fact pattern. Learn how the person thinks. In short, present a real person.

At the same time, however, you don't want the witness to present a personality so "big" that it seems like they're not taking the case seriously. A defendant can't crack jokes or throw in asides the way some eyewitnesses can.

We have three pieces of advice for parties/victims. First, present a personality like you would with any other witness—but reduce the intensity by about half. Ideally, the jury will see that the witness is a real person and will also see that the witness is taking this trial seriously.

Second, find a character arc. If the witness is the victim to a crime, don't be sad the whole time. Even raw emotion, such as crying, becomes boring after a while. If the witness is the defendant, don't be indignant the whole time. It's not very likable. Find opportunities for the witness to show a range of emotions: sadness, anger, regret, empathy, kindness, contrition.

Finally, if your witness is a good actor/actress, keep the testimony understated. For example, imagine the witness is testifying that she found a dead body and realized it was her brother. Some teams might be tempted to have the witness say, "I rolled the body over. I couldn't believe it. It was my brother. My only brother. I was heartbroken." Remember, though, the mantra of "show, don't tell." If we can show the emotion through our facial expressions, tears, and voice, we don't need to *tell* the jury that we were devastated to find our brother dead. We can *show* them. In that case, all you need is, "I rolled the body over. It was my brother." The best emotional witnesses don't use a lot of words to convey how they are feeling.

5.3 Content

Once you have developed a witness character that the judges will listen to and believe, you can figure out what the witness is going to say.

5.3.1 Sources of Information

A witness knows everything in their witness statement. Comb it carefully for information that may help your case. This is the primary source of information for your direct examination. Also comb it for anything that hurts your case. You don't want to inadvertently set traps that will spring during cross.

Then study every document or exhibit with which the witness is familiar—every email, map, photo, and more. If a witness is familiar with the document, she can testify about its contents. For example, suppose a witness says, "Exhibit A is a photo of what the park looked like on the day of the murder." That means that in addition to everything written in the witness's statement, the witness can also testify about how the park looks, how it's laid out, etc.

5.3.2 Invention of Fact

There is a tendency to want to stretch the facts—to fill in the gaps in the witness's knowledge to help your case. This is called invention of fact. Don't do it. For one thing, it's against the rules, and judges are often instructed to score you down for doing so. Additionally, if you invent facts, your witness can be impeached on cross-examination. In some competitions, you can also draw objections to your direct examination. In other competitions, the teams can file a complaint against your team for inventing facts. This may result in sanctions, including a loss of points or even disqualification. Mock Trial is about using the facts you have, not inventing new ones.

Let's Get Real: The real-life consequences for inventing facts are severe. Attorneys can be fined, suspended, or disbarred. Then-attorney Nelmark once discovered that opposing counsel had altered the signature page on a set of discovery responses to make it appear they had been served earlier than they were. As a result, the Iowa Supreme Court suspended that attorney from the practice of law for six months.

But there is another reason not to invent facts: you don't need to. Judges are generally scoring based on the quality of your performance. They assess whether the witness is credible, whether the attorney is prepared, and whether the direct supports their theory of the case. They do not generally score a direct higher simply because it has some better facts presented.

Our rule of thumb is this: for every fact that comes out of a witness's mouth on direct examination, they should be able to point to a specific line in their affidavit that asserts that fact. If the opposing attorney tries to impeach you on cross-examination, you shouldn't be left saying things like, "I didn't know I needed to include that," "I didn't think it was relevant," "I wasn't asked that in my deposition," or "Well, I didn't say that, but . . . " Instead, you should be able to say, "It's right here on page . . . "

5.3.3 Keep It Simple

Your direct examination does not need to include every fact in your witness's statement. In fact, it *should not* include every fact in your witness's statement.

As we discussed in Chapter 2, "Building Your Case," simplicity wins. Instead of trying to cram every fact into your direct examination, choose the most important facts and emphasize them. If the crime scene investigator mentions five pieces of forensic evidence in her witness statement, maybe you only mention three of them during your direct. If the eyewitness sees two arguments between the defendant and the victim, maybe you only mention one of them during your direct.

5.3.4 Keep It Admissible

There are multiple reasons to choose admissible content for your direct examination. If the other team objects and the evidence is excluded, that evidence cannot help you prove your case. If an objection is sustained during your direct examination, it often lowers your attorney's score and increases your opponent's score. But even if the other side's objections are overruled, lengthy or repeated objections can still hurt your direct examination because they disrupt the flow between your attorney and witness. Those interruptions make it harder to maintain the jury's attention. Sometimes it makes sense to avoid great testimony that *might* be excluded, and instead focus on good testimony that cannot be properly excluded.

5.3.5 Support Your Theory and Theme

So far, we know that a direct examination should include *some* of the useful, admissible facts in our witness's statement. How do we decide which facts? Choose the facts that support your theory of the case.

Suppose defense witness Jimmy provides an alibi for the defendant and has evidence that implicates an alternate suspect. Maybe Jimmy's direct examination should include both topics. But it depends on your theory. If your defense is not alleging that the alternate suspect is the real killer, then do not raise that possibility on Jimmy's direct. Spend more time and attention on the alibi.

This leads to the question of whether the witness should say the exact theme. We think the answer is generally no. It usually sounds rehearsed and fake. It just reminds the jury that the witness and the lawyer are on the same team.

However, you can still support your theme. The theme does not have to be announced to be referenced. Similar words or concepts might be enough. It may be easier for the attorney to work the theme into a question than it is for the witness to work it into an answer.

5.4 Structure

The order in which we present witness testimony impacts how well judges understand and appreciate the testimony. It also affects admissibility. An eyewitness cannot testify to what the killer looks like until we *first* establish that she saw the killer.

Here are the structures we recommend for various types of witnesses.

5.4.1 Eyewitness Direct

This is the simplest direct examination structure:

1. **Introduction** (name, occupation, etc.). This is where you establish the witness's background and how they are involved in this case. This is also where you establish the witness's personality.
2. **Foundation** (how they know what they know). Before a witness testifies to anything, they must first testify to the foundation for their personal knowledge. For example, before Siegfried explains that he saw the tiger attack Roy, we must first learn that Siegfried was there when the attack occurred, that he was in a position to see what happened, and that he knows who Roy is. Laying a strong and thorough foundation is critical: it demonstrates the

attorney's proficiency at conducting a direct, supports the witness's testimony, and protects against objections from the other side.

3. **Observations** (what the witness saw, heard, did, or knows). In other words, the story. The story usually proceeds chronologically, ending with the last important event. Sometimes, however, the attorney may want to revisit an earlier point for emphasis.

5.4.2 Expert Direct

An expert direct examination requires the most careful, precise structure. That structure will help the jury understand complex information and it will ensure you lay the necessary foundation for the expert's conclusions.

1. **Introduction** (name, occupation). This includes a description of the occupation if it might be unknown to the jury. If the witness says, "I'm a heart surgeon," you probably don't need a follow-up question. If the witness says, "I'm a forensic entomologist," you definitely need a follow-up question. "What is forensic entomology?"
2. **Involvement** (how they are involved in this case). This is usually just one question. Typical answers here might be, "I was the doctor who performed the autopsy on Lacie Peterson's body," or "I was Martin Dutcher's treating physician during his stay," or "I was retained by the defense to evaluate the conclusions of the plaintiff expert."
3. **Credentials** (education, training, publications, honors, skills, experience). Balance including enough questions to make the witness seem impressive with keeping it short enough that the jurors pay attention.
4. **Foundation for expert conclusion** (the information the expert had and the methods the expert applied). For an expert conclusion to be admissible, the attorney must first establish that the witness had enough evidence to reach a conclusion and that the expert used reliable principles and methods when analyzing that evidence. The evidence is usually just the case materials: the other witness statements and the exhibits. Sometimes it also includes a site inspection (e.g., examining the crime scene). Showing that the witness used reliable principles and methods usually just requires asking whether the witness used methods that are standard in their field. Finally, confirm with the witness

that all their conclusions were drawn to a reasonable degree of scientific certainty.

5. **Conclusions** (what the expert determined on this basis of the information learned). The witness should summarize their conclusions in one sentence. "The victim died from eight stab wounds inflicted by a left-handed person." "Had he not been injured, I project that Mr. Kissner would have earned approximately four million dollars during an 18-year career." "I believe the car that left these skid marks struck the victim."
6. **Explanation** (the expert breaks down the conclusion to the jury). This is where the attorney asks questions so the witness can help the jury understand the conclusion. Suppose the witness concludes, "The victim died from eight stab wounds inflicted by a left-handed person." You might ask questions such as: How can you tell if a stab wound is inflicted by a right-handed person or a left-handed person? What tells you that these stab wounds came from someone left-handed? How many of these eight stab wounds came from a left-handed person?

Notice that the conclusion comes before the explanation. Don't think of an expert direct examination like an episode of TV where the killer is revealed in the last moment. You're not trying to surprise the jury. You are trying to persuade the jury. Give them the conclusion first, and then explain why it's correct.

5.4.3 Law Enforcement Direct

Most teams treat their police officer purely like an eyewitness. They ask a series of chronological questions: What did you do next? What did you do next? And then what did you do? It culminates with an arrest of the defendant.

That approach is a mistake. It treats the investigation as the main story of the direct examination. The main story should be the crime and how we know it was committed by the defendant. We recommend this approach, which is more like an expert direct examination:

1. **Introduction** (name, occupation).
2. **Credentials** (experience, specialty). Keep this section brief. For example, this section could be as short as: What do you do as a detective? How many years have you been a detective? If the witness has a specialty that's relevant to this case, you can establish it. How many kidnappings have you investigated?

3. **Summary of Investigation** (from how they got involved to who they arrested). Again, keep this section brief because you will get to the details later. For example, this section could be as short as: "How did you get involved with this case?" "Can you describe the scene when you arrived?" "After you found Mr. Garcia's body, what steps did you take in investigating his death?" "Detective, did you make an arrest?" "Whom did you arrest?"
4. **Evidence** (what evidence supports defendant's guilt). This question begins by segueing from the arrest of the defendant to the evidence on which that arrest was based: "What evidence led you to arrest the defendant?" The witness then summarizes the evidence. "The fingerprints at the scene, the murder weapon, and the defendant's statements during our interrogation." The attorney then says, "Let's take those one at a time." And the rest of the direct discusses those three pieces of evidence in order.

5.4.4 Victim Direct

1. **Introduction** (name, occupation, background). Use this section to make the jury like the victim . . .
2. **Summary of Injury** (short summary of what happened to victim) . . . so that when you turn to the injury, the jury feels bad for the victim. Don't go into detail here. One or two sentences is enough. "I was robbed. Someone broke into my house and robbed me at gunpoint."
3. **The Story** (a chronological telling of the key events). Start at the beginning. Establish the key people. Then tell the story of what happened to the witness. This is where you can go into more detail.

The most frequent mistake teams make with their victim direct is the lack of an emotional arc. If the witness is sad the entire time, it will be boring. Their emotions should rise and fall throughout the examination.

5.4.5 Defendant Direct

There are multiple effective ways to organize the direct examination of the defendant. We aren't fans of the most common: a chronological telling of the events with a denial on the last question. It's anticlimactic. The jury already knows what the witness is going to say. We recommend this approach:

1. **Introduction** (name, occupation, background). Use this section to make the jury like the defendant . . .

2. **Denial** (defendant says "I didn't do it") . . . so when you ask the defendant if they committed the crime, the jury is primed to believe them. You can do one question here (Did you kill Samantha Leung?) or multiple for effect (Did you enter Ms. Leung's house on March 24, 2019? Did you stab her with this knife? Did you kill Samantha Leung?). Usually the best answers are simply "no" or "absolutely not," rather than lengthier explanations. We want the denial to be dramatic.

There are two more things we need to accomplish with the defendant direct, and we can do them in any order. We need the defendant to tell their story of what happened. And we need to confront the defendant with the bad facts. Usually the story should come first, but you can play with the order to see what has the best impact for your case:

1. **The Story** (a chronological telling of the key events). Start at the beginning. Tell the story through the defendant's eyes. Find out why the defendant did what they did and what they knew.
2. **Confrontation** (the defendant explains why the prosecution's evidence is not incriminating). The best defendant directs don't hide from the bad facts. They confront the bad facts. "How do you explain your fingerprints being found on the gun?" "Is it true that you had an argument with the victim the day he died?" "Why were you talking with a known a heroin dealer if you weren't buying heroin?" Your witness and attorney appear more trustworthy because they addressed the bad facts. And, when the prosecution cross-examines the defendant on these topics, it won't hurt your case as badly because the jury just heard the defendant's explanation.

5.5 First 30 Seconds

The one element every direct examination has in common is the introduction. The most important part of any direct is the first 30 seconds. That is when judges form their impressions. Make sure that the first 30 seconds establish the witness's personality and credibility.

Pet Peeve: When beginning, the attorney should say, "Please introduce yourself." Don't say, "Can you introduce yourself?" If that witness "can't," everyone is in for a long trial.

For example, most teams have their expert say something impressive or scientific in the middle and end of the direct. That's okay. But if that's the first time the witness gives an impressive or scientific answer, it may be too late to get a perfect score. We like to ask something on the third or fourth question that lets the witness show off: "What is accident reconstruction?"

If you want the witness to be a cat lady, you need to mention cats in the first 30 seconds. If you want the witness to be a nerd, the jury needs to know that in the first 30 seconds. If the police officer is a gruff, confident sort who doesn't say a lot of words, the jury needs to see that in the first 30 seconds.

5.6 How to Phrase Questions

5.6.1 Open-Ended Questions

The rules of evidence impose one restriction on the way you may ask questions on direct examination. Attorneys may not ask leading questions on direct examination.

A leading question is one that suggests the answer, such as, "You saw the defendant holding the knife, right?" The phrasing of that question tells the witness what answer you want.

Questions can also be leading if they are so specific that they imply the answer. "When you arrested the defendant, did you find a loaded Winchester rifle in the trunk of his car?" It sounds like the lawyer is trying to get the witness to say yes.

Just because the question asks for a yes/no answer doesn't mean it's leading. For example, suppose the witness is a convenience store clerk and she has just testified that someone robbed her at gunpoint. The question, "Did you recognize the person?" is not leading. It does not imply an answer one way or the other.

However, many Mock Trial judges will mistakenly consider a question leading if it seeks a yes or no answer. To be safe, minimize the number of yes/no questions you ask on direct examination. Avoid questions that start with "do" or "did."

So far we've talked about the phrasing to avoid. So how *should* we phrase our questions on direct examination? On direct, you should use "open-ended questions."

An open-ended question is one that lets the witness tell their story. Think of the five Ws that journalists use: Who? What? Where? When? Why? Most direct examination questions should start with these words. Who did you see inside the car? What route did you take to get home?

Where did you find this knife? When did you last see Mr. Rodriguez alive? Why did you refuse to take a breathalyzer?

"How" is also a great word on direct examination. How did you find the knife? How many times did you see the defendant stab the victim? How sure are you that the defendant was the person you saw?

You can also use commands that require the witness to tell a story. "Describe the person you saw holding that knife." "Tell the jury what happened next." Phrasing like this grabs attention. Use it sparingly so it retains impact.

Although leading questions are objectionable, they can be used strategically to get a witness back on track if he gets lost.

Q. What color was the car?

A. Ummmm . . .

Q. Was the car green?

O. Objection, leading.

Q. I'll rephrase. What color was the car?

A. It was green.

Avoid verbal filler at the start of your questions. Beginning multiple questions with "Well," "So," or "And" starts to bore the jury and also wastes valuable time.

5.6.2 Looping

Looping is repeating part of the witness's answer in our next question.

Q. What happened next?

A. I stayed behind the counter. The defendant pulled out a gun and aimed it at my head.

Q. When the defendant aimed a gun at your head, what did you do?

This allows you to reinforce the key facts from the witness's answer. You don't want to do it on every question because that will annoy the judges and seem monotonous. It can also draw an objection that "counsel is testifying." But we want to loop at least a few times in every direct examination to emphasize the most important material.

5.6.3 Short Questions

On direct examination, shorter questions are generally better questions.

Question: "Now, Mrs. Jones, I want to ask you, where were you the day that my client, the defendant, Betty Smith, was arrested?" Better question: "Where were you the day Ms. Smith was arrested?"

Shorter questions are easier to understand. They show confidence. They take less time. They allow the witness to do most of the talking.

5.6.4 Signposting

On direct and cross-examination, attorneys are supposed to ask questions. They are not supposed to make statements. But judges will usually let you get away with a little bit of statement-making if it's short and designed to make things clearer.

We recommend a heavy dose of "signposting." Signposting is when an attorney tells the witness and jury how they plan to organize the examination. Consider two versions of the same excerpt of a direct:

Q. What were your conclusions?

A. The killer was right-handed and about six feet tall.

Q. How can you determine whether stab wounds come from a right-handed or left-handed person?

A. The angle of the wounds. If they go from the victim's left to right, that indicates the attacker was right-handed. If they go from the victim's right to left, that indicates the attacker was left-handed.

Q. How do you know the killer in this case was right-handed?

A. All eight wounds were from left to right. Definitely made by a right-handed attacker.

Q. How do you determine the height of an attacker?

This is a decent expert direct. But we can make it a lot clearer for the jury if we add signposts:

Q. What were your conclusions?

A. The killer was right-handed and about six feet tall.

Q. Let's break those down one at a time, starting with your conclusion that the killer was right-handed. How can you determine whether stab wounds come from a right-handed or left-handed person?

A. The angle of the wounds. If they go from the victim's left to right, that indicates the attacker was right-handed. If they go from the victim's right to left, that indicates the attacker was left-handed.

Q. How do you know the killer in this case was right-handed?

A. All eight wounds were from left to right. Definitely made by a right-handed attacker.

Q. Let's turn to your second conclusion, that the killer was six feet tall. How do you determine the height of an attacker?

By signposting throughout the direct examination, you will remind the jury what you have already proven and help them understand where you are going. Just like road signs help drivers know where they are headed—"30 miles to Las Vegas"—signposts make it easier for jurors to follow the direct examination.

5.6.5 Building Interest

Often an attorney should ask questions in the most straightforward way possible. But sometimes it's effective to build interest by setting the stage a bit more. Here is an actual transcript from a civil case where an inmate sued the government for an injury allegedly sustained during a transport from jail:

Q. Deputy Jones, what did you do following the accident?

A. I went around to open the back of the van and check on the inmates.

Q. Did the plaintiff say anything to you?

A. Yes.

Q. What did he say?

A. That he was paralyzed.

Q. Did you believe him?

A. No.

Q. Why not?

A. Because he was walking out of the van as he said it.

The answer is much more powerful because the attorney introduced the statements before the visual observation.

5.7 Conversation

The greatest advantage you have in a Mock Trial direct is also the greatest obstacle.

The greatest advantage is your ability to prepare the witness. In real life, attorneys can't develop "scripts" with their witnesses. It's unethical and can get the lawyers in serious trouble. In Mock Trial, it's allowed—and common—for teams to plan exactly what their lawyers will ask and exactly what their witnesses will say. This ability allows you to craft perfect questions and answers.

But it also creates a large obstacle: the risk of sounding rehearsed. If a direct feels rehearsed or unnatural, it will score lower. The ideal direct has the precision of a carefully practiced play but feels to the audience like a natural *conversation*.

So how do we make our directs sound like a conversation?

Keep the witness answers shorter. Imagine the witness has just said she found her father's dead body, and the direct continues from there:

Q. Tell us how you found the body.

A. I walked into the living room. I saw my father on the floor. There was blood everywhere. I walked over to his body. There was a hole in his head. He wasn't breathing. There was a gun about 15 feet from his body. I called the police.

Now consider a different way the direct could go:

Q. Where did you find your father's body?

A. In our house. In the living room.

Q. Describe what you saw.

A. My father was on the floor. There was a gun on the floor. There was blood everywhere.

Q. What did you do?

A. I walked over to his body.

Q. What did you see?

A. There was a hole in his head. He wasn't breathing.

Q. You said there was a gun. How far was the gun from your father's body?

A. About 15 feet.

The second example will almost always score better. It sounds more natural and more like a conversation. It also allows the attorney to show her skills by asking good follow-up questions.

One trap to avoid is having the witness "direct the direct." Sometimes we see witnesses conveniently add information at the end of their answer so the attorney can ask the next question.

Q. Do you know the defendant?

A. Yes, we were coworkers. We worked at the hardware store until 2020. He had a violent temper.

Q. How do you know the defendant had a violent temper?

The witness wasn't asked about the defendant's temper or even about the defendant's personality. The witness just volunteered that information, which just happened to allow the attorney to ask the next question about the defendant's temper. This feels forced and unnatural. The attorney should be the one introducing the new topic.

Q. Do you know the defendant?

A. Yes, we were coworkers. We worked at the hardware store until 2020.

Q. During the time you worked with the defendant, how well did you get to know him?

A. Very well.

Q. From what you saw, how did the defendant respond to stressful situations?

A. He had a violent temper.

5.8 Performance

Witnesses should perform with energy. Energy will demonstrate confidence and keep the judges engaged. Witnesses should speak slowly. The jury needs time to absorb the information. Witnesses should make eye contact with the jury on most answers. Doing so will help build credibility and connection.

Attorneys should also perform with energy and speak slowly. Attorneys should keep their eyes on the witness, except for occasional moments when they look at the jury to indicate something is especially important. Generally, an attorney's tone should match the witness's testimony. If the witness is introducing themselves, the attorney should be friendly. If the witness is discussing something emotional, the attorney should display empathy. If the witness is describing something exciting, the attorney should show great curiosity.

A lot of people say the attorney should blend into the background. That's true. The spotlight should be on the witness. But that doesn't mean the attorney should sound meek, bored, or flat. By performing with energy, the attorney will make the jury more interested in what the witness has to say.

The attorney should stand in a spot that helps the witness easily look at the jury. Standing at the podium makes it hard to establish rapport with the witness and jury, and it forces the witness to look away from the jury. We recommend standing here:

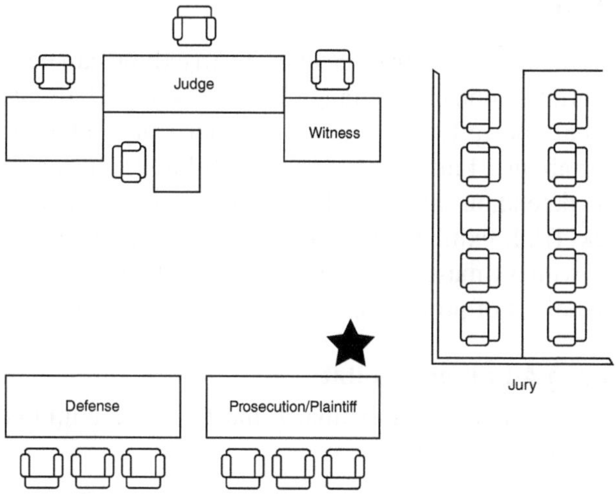

So far, we've discussed the witness and attorney separately. But they need to have a good rapport. That requires practice. Sometimes the attorney will forget a question, and the witness will need to add some information to remind the attorney. Sometimes the witness will forget part of an answer, or misspeak, and the attorney will need to ask a follow-up question. And sometimes the direct will need to be revised on the fly—either because time is running low or because the judge has sustained an objection—and the attorney and witness will need to improvise. All those situations will benefit from the attorney and witness practicing together frequently.

The other aspect of attorney-witness performance is timing. Both the witness and the attorney have a tendency to go too quickly. Because the witness will know what questions are coming, he could answer right away. Likewise, because the attorney will know what answers are coming, she could ask her next question right away. Avoid that temptation. For one thing, it will look unnatural. A witness who answers immediately does not appear to have thought about the question. The direct will appear rehearsed (which it is—but should not come across that way!). You also risk speaking over one another, a surefire way to reduce your score. The other reason to pause between question and answer is that it gives the jury time to digest the information—to understand the question being asked and to absorb the answer given.

5.9 Exhibits

An exhibit is an item you introduce at trial. An exhibit can be a document (email, blueprints, contact) or a tangible item (syringe, hair, baseball).

Exhibits are powerful ways of telling your story to the jury. It's one thing to hear about a knife. It's more powerful to see it. It's one thing to hear that the defendant said something. It's another to see it in writing.

In Mock Trial, exhibits are almost always introduced through witnesses. The witness must be familiar with the document, and we must follow a special set of procedures for introducing the exhibit.

5.9.1 How to Admit an Exhibit

Before the jury can view an exhibit, it must first be admitted into evidence. Here is how we do that:

1. **Set the stage.** The jury should understand why the exhibit is important before they see it. Usually this only requires mentioning the existence of the exhibit. For example, if you are about to introduce the murder weapon, you can simply ask, "Detective, did you find the gun you were looking for?" When the witness says yes and you begin to introduce the gun as an exhibit—or a photo of the gun as an exhibit—the jury will understand immediately why this matters.
2. **Mark the exhibit**. In trial, all exhibits have numbers. That is how we refer to them and keep track of which exhibit is which. In some courts, the prosecution/plaintiff uses numbers ("Prosecution Exhibit 1") and the defense uses letters ("Defense Exhibit A"). In Mock Trial, the exhibits are often pre-marked with numbers and letters. In that case, they keep those markings regardless of the order in which they are introduced. For example, if the first exhibit introduced is Exhibit 4, it doesn't switch to Exhibit 1. It remains Exhibit 4. But in the rare competition that doesn't pre-mark the exhibits, you will mark the exhibit before introducing it. Choose whatever number or letter is next in the sequence.
3. **Show opposing counsel.** Walk over to opposing counsel, hand them the exhibit, and announce what you're doing. "Your Honor, I am showing opposing counsel what has been pre-marked as Exhibit 4."
4. **Ask permission to approach the witness with the exhibit.** "May I approach the witness with the exhibit?"
5. **Hand the exhibit to the witness.** Ask the presiding judge if they would like a copy of the exhibit (or remind them that the

exhibit is in the bench notebook provided at the start of the trial). Walk to the witness stand. Hand the exhibit to the witness. Do not hover over the witness while asking questions. Walk back to where you were standing before.

6. **Establish that the exhibit is admissible**. First, have the witness identify the exhibit. Then ask whatever questions are necessary to establish the exhibit is admissible, including questions that show the exhibit is relevant and authentic. "Authentic" means genuine.

   Q. I just handed you what has been marked as Exhibit 4. Do you recognize it?

   A. Yes. This is my employment contract with the defendant.

   Q. Who signed this contract?

   A. I did. And the defendant did.

   Q. Is this a fair and accurate copy of your employment contract?

   A. Yes.

   That last question is standard when establishing that an exhibit is authentic. You can add questions such as, "Has it been altered in any way?" but that is not usually necessary and takes up valuable time.

   If you are introducing a photograph, don't ask if the copy is fair and accurate. Instead show that the thing depicted in the photo is actually the thing you're claiming it is.

   Q. I just handed you what has been marked as Exhibit 5. Do you recognize it?

   A. Yes, this is a photo of Main Street, at the corner of Pine Avenue.

   Q. Is this how Main Street looked at the time of the accident?

   A. Yes.

If you are introducing tangible evidence, authenticity may require establishing "chain of custody"—that the exhibit is the same one collected.

   Q. I just handed you what has been marked as Exhibit 6. Do you recognize it?

   A. Yes, this is the knife we seized from the defendant's glove compartment.

   Q. How do you know this is the same knife?

   A. It's in the same evidence bag as when I collected it. The seal has my initials and it's unbroken.

Q. Does the knife appear to be in the same condition as when you seized it?

A. Yes.

If the exhibit contains words, you should be ready to respond to a hearsay objection. Lay the foundation you will need before the other side objects.

Q. I just handed you what has been marked as Exhibit 7. Do you recognize it?

A. Yes. This is a receipt from my store. We gave it to the defendant when he came in and purchased a ski mask and baseball bat.

Q. Who generated this receipt?

A. I did.

Q. Was this receipt made in the regular course of your business?

A. Yes. We make receipts for every purchase.

Q. Is Exhibit 7 a fair and accurate copy of the receipt?

A. Yes.

If the defense objects to the receipt as hearsay, you will be able to say you've laid the proper foundation for the business records exception to the hearsay rule (which you will learn about later in the book).

7. **Offer the exhibit into evidence.** "Your Honor, the plaintiff offers Exhibit 12 into evidence."

   Some teams say, "Plaintiff *moves* Exhibit 12 into evidence." Some judges will bristle at this language because they think it's presumptuous. We have heard judges respond, "Counsel, the Court *moves* it into evidence." Other judges don't mind the expression. But remember our goal: *It's All About Points*! So we choose the path that offends no one, and say, "Plaintiff *offers*" the exhibit. Many people say, "The plaintiff would *like* to offer," or "The plaintiff *intends* to offer." Those are both wrong. They are statements of belief or intent. The statement that allows the court to enter the document into evidence is the affirmative action of *offering*.

WAR STORY

The American Mock Trial Association has sometimes allowed physical evidence (meaning something other than a sheet of paper) to be used in competition. This "real" evidence can add some entertainment value to the trial. In 2002, the evidence was an "access card" allegedly used by the defendant to enter an office building and commit murder. In 2011, the physical evidence was toy beads that (according to the fact pattern) were toxic and caused the death of a child. In each case, teams had to purchase the evidence from AMTA to ensure that all teams were on an equal playing field. The most notorious physical evidence was the 2000 case of *State v. Ellis.* The victim in that case was murdered with a shovel. Teams could procure their own shovel as long as it complied with certain size requirements. That wasn't the problem. The problem was teams attempting to get dozens of shovels through courthouse metal detectors.

8. **Respond to any objections.** Sometimes your opponent will not object and the exhibit will be admitted. But if the opponent objects, explain to the judge why the exhibit is admissible. If the judge overrules the objection, keep going to the next step.

   If the judge sustains the objection and you can resolve the judge's concerns with additional questions, ask those questions. For example, if the judge wants you to establish how the witness knows the email came from the defendant, ask, "How do you know this email came from the defendant?" The witness testifies, "We've emailed each other before. This is her email address." Then you offer the exhibit into evidence again.

   If the judge sustains the objection and you don't think you can solve the judge's concerns with additional questions, move on. Stay confident, and don't let anyone know you're disappointed. Reacting confidently during setbacks is an important trait for trial lawyers. Simply say: "Your Honor, may I approach and retrieve the exhibit?" This should happen rarely because we should adopt strategies of focusing on evidence and exhibits that are almost certain to be admitted.
9. **Publish the exhibit.** To this point, the jury has not been allowed to see the exhibit because it hasn't yet been admitted into evidence. Now you get to show it to them. That's called "publication."

   "Your Honor, may I publish Exhibit 3 to the jury?" Once the judge says yes, you can choose among several methods for publishing the exhibit. You may hand the jury a copy of the exhibit or multiple copies to pass around (if the exhibit is tangible and unique, you can hand them the exhibit rather than a copy). You may hold up the exhibit so they can see it. This obviously works better when the exhibit isn't text-based. Or you can display an enlargement on a poster board and easel.

Make sure to set up the easel and enlargement before you begin to talk about it. If a teammate can set it up for you, that's even better.

10. **Use the exhibit.** After going through all that effort to admit the exhibit, we need to show the jury why it matters. Ask the witness questions about the exhibit. It can be as simple as, "Detective, why was this knife important to your investigation?" or, "Mr. Jones, after you saw this photo, what did you do?"

5.9.2 Advice for Using Exhibits

In putting together the case, teams need to determine which evidence will come in through which witness. The primary consideration is which witness can best establish the foundation needed for the exhibit. This may be just one individual. However, if something can be authenticated and appropriately discussed by multiple witnesses, it should be entered through the examination that otherwise gives the attorney the least chance to shine, as using an exhibit is a good way to increase an attorney's score. The exception would be an exhibit (such as a map or contract) that you want to use with multiple witnesses. In that instance, enter it with the first witness who needs to refer to it during testimony.

Make sure to confirm that the exhibit is admitted. Sometimes after the parties have argued an objection, the judge will simply overrule the objection but forget to declare that the exhibit is admitted. If the judge forgets this last step, remind him or her by asking: "Your Honor, is the exhibit admitted?' Once admission of the document is confirmed, and you are finished using it, present it to the bench or publish it to the jury.

It is improper to write or otherwise mark on an exhibit after it's admitted. So, if you intend to do this, either write on the document first or use a copy of document—and state for the record that is what you are doing.

It is often hard for jurors to see exhibits, which are generally included in case materials as standard 8.5 x 11 pages. Using enlargements can be helpful. The best way to do this is to admit the exhibit, then seek permission to use or for the witness to use "an enlargement of admitted exhibit X for demonstrative purposes."

Pet Peeve: Many teams use the term "blow-up" for an enlarged exhibit. Don't. "Blow-ups" are pool toys. The professional term is "enlargement."

Whether in direct or cross-examination, when handling an exhibit, the attorney should have at least three copies of the exhibit at the ready: (1) the official copy to give to the witness and that will be given to the court after admission, (2) a copy for the attorney to keep for reference when asking questions, and (3) a courtesy copy for the presiding judge if all exhibits were not already provided in a pretrial notebook.

It is better to store your copies of exhibits (and witness statements) in folders rather than binders. The clicking sound of binders opening and closing can be distracting, and it takes time. Folders are smoother and safer (less likely to have everything fall on the floor). Just make sure your folders are properly labeled and easy to access.

5.9.3 Refreshing Recollection

Sometimes a witness forgets the answer to a question. As a lawyer, you can fix this by showing the witness their statement that contains the answer. This process is called refreshing the witness's recollection. It happens more in real life than in Mock Trial (because in Mock Trial, witnesses are trained to remember a specific set of facts). However, even in Mock Trial lawyers should know how to refresh a witness's recollection.

Refreshing recollection is different from impeachment. Impeachment is the process of discrediting a witness by showing that their testimony in court is contradicted by what they said before trial. Refreshing recollection is helping a witness remember a fact they once knew but have forgotten in court.

Like admitting an exhibit, refreshing recollection has a specific litany we follow—a list of questions that show we know proper courtroom procedure.

1. **Demonstrate the witness cannot remember information.**

   Q. You said you attended the UCLA-USC basketball game. Who won?

   A. I don't remember.

   OR

   Q. You said you attended the UCLA-USC basketball game. Who won?

   A. I'm not sure.

   Either of these answers indicates that the witness doesn't know. Sometimes, though, the witness will get a fact wrong, and you need to indicate that to the witness.

Q. You said you attended the UCLA-USC basketball game. Who won?

A. I think it was USC.

Q. Is your memory clear on that?

A. No.

Any time a directing attorney says, "Is your memory clear on that?" the witness should immediately know that's code for, "You said the wrong thing, and I am trying to fix it." The witness must say, "No." Otherwise the lawyer cannot refresh the witness's memory.

2. **Demonstrate the witness's memory might be refreshed by some exhibit or statement.**

Q. Is there anything that would help you remember?

A. Yes, I sent my friend an email after the game.

OR

Q. Would looking at your personal diary help refresh your recollection?

A. Yes. I always record basketball results in my diary.

3. **Mark-Show-Give.** This is the same process we followed when admitting an exhibit.

Q. Your Honor, I'm marking this as Exhibit 8. I'm showing it to opposing counsel. May I approach the witness with Exhibit 8?

J. Yes.

Q. I've just handed you Exhibit 8. Do you recognize it?

A. This is my diary.

4. **Refresh the witness's memory with the exhibit.**

Q. Please turn to page 20 and read the diary silently to yourself. When you're done, please look up at me.

(witness looks up)

Q. Has reading your diary refreshed your recollection about who won the UCLA-USC basketball game?

A. Yes.

5. **Retrieve the exhibit.** We do this so the witness is now testifying from memory, not simply reading the exhibit. Notice that we do not admit the exhibit into evidence. We just use it to jog the witness's memory.

   Q. Your Honor, may I approach the witness and retrieve Exhibit 8?

   J. Yes.

6. **Get your answer.**

   Q. Who won the basketball game between UCLA and USC?

   A. UCLA. It wasn't close!

5.10 Demonstrative Aids

Almost all Mock Trial competitions limit exhibits to those contained in the case packet. You can't create a new map and offer it into evidence. In many competitions, however, you can create new "demonstrative exhibits," also called "demonstrative aids." This might be an enlargement of an existing exhibit or it might be something new like a timeline. The information contained in a demonstrative aid must be based on information contained in the case. Demonstrative exhibits can be used by witnesses during examination or by attorneys during openings and closings. Although they can help explain or summarize exhibits or testimony in the case, demonstrative exhibits themselves do not become part of the trial record. Some demonstrative aids are created during trial. For example, a witness might draw a timeline of events on a whiteboard.

Q. If you had a whiteboard, would you be able to create a timeline of what you did on August 28, 2021?

A. Yes.

Q. Your Honor, may the witness step down and make use of a whiteboard?

J. Yes.

Q. Ms. Daniels, I just handed you a marker. Can you draw a timeline that starts with the first time you saw the victim on August 28, 2021?

When you are done, ask the judge, "May we mark this as Exhibit X and preserve it for use later in trial?" Choose the smallest number that won't be used in trial. For example, if the case packet has Exhibits 1 through 14, preserve the demonstrative aid as Exhibit 15. Preserving a demonstrative allows you to use it later with another witness or during closing. Note that you cannot offer the exhibit into evidence. If a judge invites you to do so, respond that: "Offering exhibits not included in the case packet is prohibited in this jurisdiction."

If you use a demonstrative aid with multiple witnesses, make sure the record is clear about who made which marks. For example, you can have each of them use different colors and state that you're doing that. You don't need to say, "The record should reflect that the witness is using a black marker." This creates a situation where the judge says, "The record will so reflect." This just wastes your precious time. If you simply say, "The witness is using a black marker," that statement automatically appears in the record (also known as the trial transcript). Although there is rarely a court reporter present in a Mock Trial, we act as if one is present and taking down everything that is said.

Some competitions allow pre-made demonstrative aids. These might include a timeline of events, a graph that illustrates data contained in the case, a flowchart an expert uses to explain their process, or anything else that helps *demonstrate* information to the jury.

5.11 Stepping Down

Try to find opportunities for the witness to step down from the witness stand during their direct examination. Doing so will increase the jury's attention. It changes what they're looking at, which always draws attention. It usually brings the witness closer to the jury, which will increase their interest in and connection to the witness. And it allows the witness to stand up, which gives them greater opportunity to gesture and draw attention.

A witness will typically step down for one of two reasons. The first, and most common, is so the witness can testify about an exhibit. Perhaps you have placed an enlarged version of the map on an easel, and the witness is going to point to where she found the body. Or the witness is going to highlight parts of an email and explain them. The second reason for the witness to step down is to perform a demonstration. Perhaps the police officer is going to show the jury how they performed the field sobriety test.

WAR STORY

While presiding over the 2021 AMTA One Last Time virtual championship round, Judge Nelmark asked a competitor if there was any re-direct examination for the witness. Counsel replied, "None. May the witness step down?" Judge Nelmark only heard the "step down" request and replied "Yes"—creating a very awkward pause as he then waited for the witness to use a demonstrative. The lesson for judges is to listen very carefully. The lesson for competitors is to, at the conclusion of testimony, just ask that the witness "be excused" to avoid any confusion.

For the witness to step down, the attorney must first seek permission from the court. Lay appropriate foundation and then ask for permission.

Q. Doctor, would it help the jury understand your testimony if you were able to use an enlargement of Exhibit X?

A. I believe it would.

Q. Your Honor, may the witness step down?

A. Yes.

You ask that opposing counsel be allowed to move if they need to *before* they ask permission for themselves. It sounds polite and avoids the possibility of them interrupting your flow with a "Can I move?"

Q. I'd ask that Ms. _______ be allowed to move if she needs to in order to see the enlargement.

If you haven't already established that the demonstrative aid is simply the larger version of the original exhibit, do so once the witness steps down.

Q. Is this an accurate copy of exhibit X?

A. It's exactly the same, only larger.

The witness should continue to be the star. The attorney's job is to make a record of what is happening such as, "I'm handing Mr. Johnson a red marker. Please draw on this map the path that the car was driving."

Other things the witness can do off the stand include acting out something that happened or indicating on their body where certain injuries were sustained. Again, describe what the witness is doing so their gestures or actions get into the record.

If the witness or attorney is going to write anything, make sure his handwriting is legible. Test your markers before every round. If you're using an enlargement laminated for re-use, make sure not to mix up permanent and dry-erase markers. Whatever kind of marker you are using, keep a backup handy.

5.12 Inoculation

The substantive goal of direct examination is to highlight your best facts. But it's vital to acknowledge your worst facts, too. If your witness has a perjury conviction—and the jury hears it for the first time on cross-examination—the witness will lose credibility. And you as the lawyer will lose even more credibility. It will look like you hid that fact from the jury. You need to bring out that bad fact on direct examination.

That process of addressing your weaknesses before your opponent can do it is called "inoculation." Informally, it's often called "pulling the sting" or "stealing the thunder."

In deciding whether to utilize inoculation be sure to consider whether the other side will (a) attempt to use the evidence and (b) be allowed to use it over any objections you plan to make. If you open the door to the issue on direct, you won't be able to keep it out on cross.

Put the inoculation in the middle of the direct. The jury will have had time to get to know and like your witness before you introduce the bad fact, and you will have time after to rehabilitate their credibility.

Inoculation will help your witness on cross-examination. The bad facts won't sting as much if the jury has already heard them.

Don't spend too much time on the bad facts because that can distract from your main point. Two or three questions is about right.

Let's Get Real: Although you don't want to spend much time on a bad issue, if you're going to bring it up, don't leave out the part that is actually the "sting." Then-lawyer Nelmark had a trial where the other side's witness mentioned Exhibit 67 (a crucial email exchange) in passing, saying it was no big deal. This led to following exchange on cross:

Nelmark: Mr. Witness, are you a *Seinfeld* fan?
Witness: I've seen a few episodes, why?
Nelmark: Because I think you just Yada-Yada'd Exhibit 67.
Jurors: [Laughter]
Opp. Counsel: Objection.
Judge: Sustained.
Nelmark: Let's see what Exhibit 67 actually says, shall we.

Although the objection was sustained without opposing counsel even needing to state the grounds for it, the point was made. The jurors were now awake and very interested to hear about the contents of Exhibit 67.

5.13 Objections

Making objections and responding to objections are both covered in a separate chapter. They are referenced here as a reminder that both present an opportunity to score points during direct examination.

On direct examination, limit opportunities for the opponent to object. Be ready to respond to objections. For every question you ask, be ready to defend against a foundation or relevance objection. For every question you ask that involves someone's words outside of court, be ready to respond to a hearsay objection. For every question that involves someone's actions apart from the events of your case, be ready to respond to a character objection.

On cross-examination, directing attorneys need to be ready to raise objections. In addition to the normal objections that will be discussed later in this book, direct attorneys should be prepared to protect their witness on cross-examination. If the cross-examiner is disrespectful or overly aggressive, stand up and object "badgering." If the cross-examiner is arguing with the witness instead of eliciting facts—for example, "Were you lying then or lying now?" or "Do you really expect the jury to believe that?"—then stand up and object "argumentative." If the cross-examiner interrupts your witness mid-answer, stand up and say, "Objection, badgering. I ask that my witness be allowed to complete his answer." Even if the judge overrules your objection, your witness will have a break from the cross and the judge will be more attuned to the cross-examiner crossing the line in the future.

5.14 Re-Direct Examination

After the witness is cross-examined, the directing attorney may—but is never required to—ask the witness some follow-up questions. That is called re-direct examination.

In most circumstances, you should do a re-direct. It can rehabilitate points raised by the opponent on cross-examination, clarify anything from cross that was confusing, and allow the witness to finish any answers where the witness had more to say.

When the cross-examination ends, stand up and say, "Your Honor, may I re-direct the witness?" Or if you feel comfortable being more colloquial, simply stand and say, "Re-direct, Your Honor?" A lot of lawyers, in real life and Mock Trial, say, "Brief re-direct, Your Honor?" Don't do that. It sounds apologetic, as if you have to promise to keep the re-direct short in order to get the judge's permission to do it in the first place. Besides, if the re-direct goes longer than you intend, you don't want to look like you broke your promise to keep it brief.

That said, re-directs *should* be short. They are counted against your time limit. But more importantly, re-directs score best when they are short and pointed. Almost never ask more than three questions. Try to ask only one.

Avoid objectionable questions on re-direct even more than on direct. If something goes wrong, it will be more glaring because the re-direct is so short. And it will be the last thing judges see before they finalize their score for your direct.

Re-direct is limited to issues covered during cross. If on re-direct an attorney strays into topics not covered by the cross, the cross-examiner may object to the re-direct as "outside the scope" of cross-examination. If the opponent raises this objection, you can say, "Opposing counsel opened the door to this line of questioning when they discussed _____."

When should you *not* perform the re-direct? Skip the re-direct when the cross went poorly for the other team and/or when the cross-examination ended on your objection being sustained. If you say, "No re-direct, Your Honor," it signals to the jury that you are confident that the cross went well for your witness. It also means the judges are likely to enter their scores at a moment when the other side doesn't look strong.

Judge Nelmark found success by usually having at least one attorney perform a re-direct and at least one attorney *not* perform a re-direct (assuming there was at least one cross that was not too damaging). The absence of a re-direct made the other re-directs more powerful and less like it was required.

5.15 "Live Witnesses"

Some competitions use "live witnesses," which refers to witnesses who are not part of your team. They can be members of other teams at the tournament (at some Empire competitions) or witnesses provided by the tournament host (at Gladiator, Trial by Combat, and the National Trial Competition). Live witnesses test an attorney's ability to react.

Let's Get Real: In actual trials, every witness is a "live witness" to some degree. Lawyers can prepare their witnesses, but they are not allowed to give the witness a script telling them what to say. And, no matter how much you prepare, witnesses are unpredictable.

Your strategy in preparing for the direct of a live witness depends heavily on the amount of time you have to prepare the witness. If you have hours or weeks, you can probably prepare the witness the same way you would if they were a teammate.

If you have only 15 minutes—which is the preparation time at Gladiator and Trial by Combat—then you need a different strategy. The witness cannot come close to memorizing an entire direct. Identify the main points of your examination, with no more than five things you want to emphasize. Practice some questions and answers so you and the witness are on the same page. If you are doing something unusual with the direct—either using an angle most teams aren't or ignoring facts that most other teams use—highlight that during your preparation.

What if you are playing the witness? If you only have 15 minutes to prepare with your directing attorney, make sure to accomplish two things. First, learn that team's theory so you can present your testimony in a helpful manner. Second, tell the directing attorney what introductory questions you need to establish your character. If you are getting scored, too, you need a strong introduction to make an impression with the jury.

5.16 Witness Order

On the prosecution/plaintiff side, the most important decision is which witness to call first. Your first witness should be someone who can tell your story broadly—someone who can introduce all the major events and people. But try to avoid calling an expert first. Even if they have a broad view of the case, juries may be bored if they hear from an expert witness first. Victims, eyewitnesses, and police officers often make good first witnesses.

Let's Get Real: Witness calls are quite different in real life. In criminal trials, the prosecution almost always calls more witnesses than the defense. In fact, a criminal defense lawyer sometimes will not call any witnesses. In Mock Trial, the defendant almost always testifies; in real criminal trials the defendant usually does not testify. In real-life civil cases, the plaintiff will often call the defendant as one of its witnesses (which almost never happens in Mock Trial).

On the defense, we recommend calling first the witness who most represents your theory of the case. If you are attacking the police investigation, call the witness who can criticize the investigation. If you are pointing the finger at an alternate suspect, call the witness who best implicates the alternate suspect. Try not to call the defendant first.

For both sides, try to call your lowest-scoring witnesses first and highest-scoring witnesses last. Research shows that judges give higher scores as the trial proceeds, but it also shows that judges tend to compare each witness with those who testified earlier. If you start with your best witness, judges are unlikely to give them the perfect scores they deserve—and then your later witnesses will receive lower scores in comparison to the first witness. Many coaches try to sandwich the witness they think will score lowest in the middle. This is dangerous. If the first witness is scored low because they're first, and the second witness is compared to the first witness, you are likely to get two low scores rather than one.

6

Cross-Examination: Attorneys

In many ways, cross-examination is the most exciting part of a trial, both for the audience and the participants. Cross-examination lies at the very heart of our adversarial system. We test witnesses' credibility by exposing them to cross-examination.

In many ways, cross-examination is also the hardest part of a trial for attorneys. You must make a witness agree to facts with which they probably do not want to agree. Witnesses want to advance the case of the party who called them. They want to protect themselves when you attack their credibility or conduct. In Mock Trial, opposing witnesses have practiced extensively on how to trip you up.

But attorneys have two significant advantages during cross-examination. The first is that they get to choose the questions. The witness can squirm all they like, but they must admit to facts that they've admitted before—either in a deposition, or to the police, or in a signed witness statement. If you develop your cross based solely around questions to which you already know the answers, it's hard for the witness to hurt you.

An attorney's second big advantage is the ability to perform. A witness is stuck in their seat. If they get too animated, they seem biased or less credible. But an attorney can move, gesture, change their volume, and change their tone in ways witnesses generally cannot. If you own the jury's attention, you own the cross.

6.1 Goals

The substantive goal of cross-examination varies by witness. Sometimes you want to show the witness is biased. Sometimes you want to show that the witness, even if honest, lacks critical information. Sometimes you need to establish some key facts for your case theory.

But the Mock Trial goal is always the same: *It's All About Points!* To score points on cross-examination, it's all about control. You need to show the judges that you are in control of the cross and that you are accomplishing what you intended.

Let's Get Real: Because real lawyers are focused on the evidence, not points, that means they will sometimes keep their cross-examinations extremely short—or choose not to ask any questions at all. This tactic is common with victims or witnesses whose testimony is so narrow that no cross is required. Professor Bernstein once gave a one-question cross: "The plaintiff is your son, right?"

6.2 Phrasing

On direct examination, attorneys should generally keep their questions open ended. But on cross-examination, the goals are very different. We want to restrict the witness from talking. So we use a very different questioning technique.

Cross questions should be leading. A leading question is one that implies an answer. We don't ask, "What did you buy at the store?" We don't say, "Did you buy milk?" We ask, "You bought milk, correct?" We aren't really asking questions, as if we are unsure. We are confidently making statements that the witness confirms as true.

Some competitors (and real lawyers) like to ask open-ended questions on cross-examination. They like forcing the witness to state the bad fact themselves. In Mock Trial, this is almost always a bad idea. Sure, it will work against less experienced opponents. But a really good witness will punish you for asking an open-ended question. Take the previous example: "What did you buy at the store?" The witness's affidavit says they bought milk. It seems harmless to ask the open-ended question. After all, the witness has to say milk, right? No. A smart witness might waste your limited time by saying, "I bought the one ingredient I was missing if I wanted to make an omelet. Milk. But not just any milk. I bought pasteurized, two percent milk. I don't remember which dairy farm it came from . . ." Some judges will punish the witness for giving such a long answer, but some will punish the lawyer for asking an open-ended question on cross. And the witness might also hurt you in another way. Question: "What did you buy at the store?" Answer: "I bought the ingredient your client told me to buy. Milk." The only way to *consistently* beat good witnesses on cross is with leading questions.

There are two other reasons to lead. First, judges expect it. Even if you "get away" with an open-ended question on cross, you may get scored down because judges remember the rule from when they learned trial advocacy: stick to leading questions on cross. Second, ask leading questions because it conditions the jury to ignore the witness. If you ask nonleading questions sometimes, they will look to the witness for the answer. *But if you are only asking leading questions, they won't need to listen to the witness because your question will tell them the answer.*

You should end your questions with "a leading phrase." Notice the "correct" in the previous example. "You bought milk, ***correct***?" That alerts both witnesses and the judge that you are asking a yes/no question. Make sure to vary your leading phrases so it doesn't feel monotonous. There are lots of leading phrases to choose from:

- You bought milk, correct?
- You bought milk, isn't that true?
- You bought milk, right?
- You bought milk, didn't you?

Once you're on a roll and the witness is answering yes-yes-yes to everything, you can drop the leading phrases. That will make your cross even smoother.

Q. You went to the store, right?

A. Yes.

Q. To buy milk, correct?

A. Yes.

Q. You planned to make an omelet, isn't that true?

A. Yes.

Q. You bought a gallon of milk?

A. Yes.

Q. Skim milk?

A. Yes.

Keep your cross questions short. This will make it easier for the jury to understand and harder for the witness to argue with you. Consider these questions:

Detective, you searched my client's house, right?

That search included the upstairs of the house?

It also included the downstairs of the house?

You also searched the garage?

You were looking for evidence connecting my client to the victim, correct?

You didn't find any of the victim's clothing?

You didn't find any of the victim's fingerprints?

You didn't find any of the victim's hair?

You didn't find any of the victim's blood?

You didn't find any of the victim's DNA?

When you searched my client's house, you didn't find any physical evidence connecting her to the victim in this case, did you?

We can make those questions a lot more powerful by eliminating unnecessary words:

Detective, you searched my client's house, right?

You searched upstairs?

Downstairs?

The garage?

You looked for evidence connecting my client to the victim, correct?

Didn't find the victim's clothing?

Fingerprints?

Hair?

Blood?

DNA?

In that search, you found no physical evidence tying my client to the victim, did you?

We made the same points with 49 words instead of 102 words. That saves time, sounds more confident, and establishes a rhythm that judges and juries love.

Avoid the taglines of "correct" or "right" when asking something in the negative. Saying, "You didn't see the car, correct?" may elicit a "No," meaning the question was incorrect, or a "No," meaning "No, I didn't see the car." Instead, look for something like, "You were looking away from the intersection, correct?"

Limit each question to one key fact. Don't ask, "You own a red Corvette convertible?" Instead ask, "You own one car, correct?" "A Corvette, right?" "It's red?" "It's a convertible?" You might not want to do this with every question because it could make your cross tedious. But every fact that matters should get its own question.

6.3 Structure

Your cross-examination should be a series of separate sets of questions, each of which supports a single conclusion. We call each set of questions a "pocket" or "chapter." For example, suppose Spider-Man were on trial for littering. You might structure your cross around the following three chapters:

- His web slinging creates a mess
- He has no right to make that mess
- He never cleans up his mess

You should organize the cross into smaller shots instead of one big cannon ball of an attack. We recommend three to five chapters per cross, each no longer than ten questions. This gives the jury bites it can digest instead of asking the jury to swallow a whole meal at once.

You don't even need to say the point you're trying to prove—as long as your questions make it clear:

On direct examination, you explained why you sling webs all over the city, correct?

You said it's to fight crime, right?

You're not a police officer, are you?

You're not an FBI agent?

The government has never hired you to fight crime?

The government has never asked you to fight crime?

The government has never given you permission to fight crime?

We never actually ask the question, "You have no right to make a mess, do you?" because that's a conclusion and the witness will argue with us. Instead, we stick to facts. One fact at a time. The jury will understand that's the point we are trying to make.

The jury is even more likely to understand our point if we signpost it:

Let's talk about whether you had a right to do what you did. On direct examination, you explained why you sling webs all over the city, correct?

You said it's to fight crime, right?

You're not a police officer, are you?

You're not an FBI agent?

The government has never hired you to fight crime?

The government has never asked you to fight crime?

The government never gave you permission to fight crime?

We never come back to that question: "You have no right to make a mess, do you?" We don't need to. By signposting the point of this chapter and then asking questions that illustrate our point, the jury understands our point.

Here is another example:

Let's talk about whether you were sober enough to drive. On October 1, 2021, you went to a bar, didn't you?

You drank beer, correct?

Six beers, right?

In less than three hours?

Then you got behind the wheel?

Notice the questions we didn't ask at the end: "You were drunk?" or "You shouldn't have been driving?" Questions like those are called "one question too many." Lawyers are often tempted to ask a question that sums up their entire cross-examination. "So you were lying?" "So your conclusions are incorrect?" "Do you still claim that you did a thorough investigation?" If these statements aren't in the witness's affidavit, a good witness will never say yes to them. *Don't ask one question too many* because it will turn an effective cross chapter into a fight you might not win.

There is another reason to avoid one question too many: You don't need it. After establishing that the witness drank six beers in the three hours . . . do we really need to ask whether the witness is drunk? The jury already assumes it. Do we really need to ask if someone who drank six beers in three hours shouldn't get behind the wheel of a car? The jury already believes that. If your cross chapter is effective, the jury will reach the conclusion you want without the witness admitting it.

Make sure to indicate the transition from one line of cross to another—and not just by changing the substance of your questions. After making each point, (1) pause, (2) move (whether it's a few feet or just a step), and (3) tell the jury you are switching topics.

Doctor, you're being paid, right?

Paid by the plaintiff?

The plaintiff is paying you 500 dollars an hour?

Now let's talk about the quality of your work. When serving as an expert witness, it's important to be thorough, correct?

Important to consider all relevant information?

By saying, "Now let's talk about the quality of your work," you are signposting to the jury that you have changed topics.

Put your best cross lines at the beginning and end of the cross. People remember best what they hear first and last, so sandwich your weaker points in the middle. This is the theory of primacy and recency.

Finally, never sit down following an objection sustained against you. It looks weak and undermines almost everything you accomplished during the cross. Therefore, end with a cross pocket that you know will not draw an objection. And, just to be safe, prepare a backup cross pocket in case an objection is sustained against your final point.

6.4 Content

There are three main categories of cross chapters. You can demonstrate a witness's lack of credibility. You can undermine their testimony from direct examination. You can offer facts that support your theory.

Suppose an eyewitness testifies for the plaintiff. On direct examination, he says your client, the defendant, punched the victim in the face. Your theory is that your client was attacking in self-defense. If you were going to attack the witness's credibility, you might point out that the witness is biased. He is friends with the plaintiff and has a longstanding feud with the defendant. Or maybe he lacks credibility because he was once convicted of fraud.

If you were going to attack the witness's direct examination testimony, that might mean pointing out that the witness didn't see what happened before the punch was thrown. Maybe you can establish that the witness was far away or had to view the events without much light.

If you were going to raise facts that support your theory, maybe you show that the plaintiff didn't just have blood on his face—he also had blood on his hands, indicating he threw a punch, too. Or maybe you establish that the plaintiff has a temper and had threatened your client in the past.

These aren't mutually exclusive. You can cover two of these three points, or—time permitting—all three.

As you can see, there are often multiple ways to approach a cross-examination. How do you decide which points to make?

6.4.1 Sources of Cross Content

Start by looking for "yes material": facts to which a witness must admit, "Yes, that's true." The first source is their witness statement. If the doctor said, "There are some flaws with my theory," they have to admit that "yes," there are flaws with their theory. If the police officer said, "I didn't search the alternate suspect's house," they must admit on cross, "Yes, that's true," they didn't search the alternate suspect's house.

The reason it's so important to find material the witness *must* admit is that on cross-examination we should never ask a question unless we already know the answer. This is one of the most fundamental rules of trial advocacy. Cross-examination isn't a time for surprises. It might go well in the movies, but in Mock Trial a good witness will punish attorneys who ask for facts outside the witness statement.

Look for necessary inferences from the witness's statement. By "necessary inference," we mean anything that must be true given the facts in the witness's statement—or which the witness would look silly denying. Suppose the police officer's witness statement says, "The victim was stabbed with a six-inch knife. Mr. Thames was an alternate suspect. But I never entered or searched Mr. Thames's house." You can cross-examine the officer by asking, "You have never been inside Mr. Thames's kitchen?" "You can't tell if Mr. Thames has six-inch knives in his kitchen?" "You can't tell us if there are knives in Mr. Thames's kitchen with blood on them?" The witness statement doesn't say that, but it must be true based on what *is* in the witness's statement.

Read the exhibits that the witness wrote or adopts. For example, a police officer can be questioned about what she wrote in a police report or citation. A witness can be questioned about what they wrote in an email. Even if those documents were not written under oath, the witness will look bad by denying statements they made in writing. You can also cross-examine witnesses with nontextual exhibits. Suppose an eyewitness's statement says, "Exhibit 2 is a map of my house." You can cross the witness based on the map: "Your house has three bedrooms?" "The victim was found in the guest bedroom?" "That's right next to your room?"

You can cross-examine a witness using common sense. You can ask a police officer, "It's important to collect evidence carefully? Important not to contaminate evidence?" even if those facts are not in the witness's statement. It's common sense. If the witness tries to get cute and say no, they look terrible.

Finally, you can cross-examine a witness on anything they say during direct examination. If you do, make sure to highlight that you are doing it. It will build interest from the jury and communicate to the jury that you are adapting to the direct examination. You can (and should) say, "You testified about X on direct examination, and I wanted to make sure I heard you correctly, so I wrote it down. You said ______________." This is incredibly effective, but you do need to make sure you wrote it down accurately.

6.4.2 Choosing the Right Content

So you've scrutinized the witness statement and the exhibits. You've thought carefully about all the things you can make the witness admit on cross. How do you decide what to cover? Are you going to attack the witness or use the witness against the other side?

The first thing you need to consider is whether you *need* to discredit the witness. Ask yourself this question: If the jury believes what this witness said on direct examination, does that mean we lose the case? If the answer is yes, you need to discredit the witness. Suppose you are the prosecution, charging the defendant with killing the victim on March 1, 2020. The defense calls an alibi witness who says, "I was with the defendant every minute of March 1, 2020, and we were a hundred miles from the scene of the murder." If the jury believes this witness, the defendant is not guilty. You *need* to discredit the witness.

Now consider another defense witness in the same case who testifies that the defendant is generally a kind person. That's relevant, potentially persuasive evidence for the defense. But if true, it doesn't cripple your prosecution case. A person can be kind in general, but still commit a terrible crime. You may want to discredit the witness. But you don't *need* to.

The second thing to consider when choosing your cross-examination content is your theory of the case. If you can use the opponent's witness to support your theory of the case, you should. This is generally the content that will score best because it will remind the judges of your theory and emphasize that your team has a cohesive strategy. In this scenario, it could be counterproductive to discredit the witness because you want the judges to believe them when their testimony supports your theory.

The third thing to consider when choosing your cross-examination content is your opponent's likely theories. It can be very powerful to undermine your opponent's theory on cross-examination.

Finally, consider the identity of the witness. Some witnesses are more vulnerable to aggressive crosses, where the content is designed to attack the witness. If you are a prosecutor or plaintiff's attorney cross-examining the defendant, the jury expects you to focus on facts that make the defendant look bad. If you are a defense attorney cross-examining a police officer, the jury expects you to criticize the investigator or investigation that led to your client's arrest. Likewise, if you are cross-examining an expert, the jury expects you to attack that expert's methods or conclusions. But some witnesses require more nuance. If you are cross-examining a victim or eyewitness with no stake in the outcome of the case, you may consider topics that are less aggressive.

6.5 Adaptation

Sometimes the witness will say something you didn't anticipate. Maybe they will add a fact on direct examination. Maybe they will say something interesting on cross-examination. The best cross-examinations seize on these opportunities and use them against the witness.

We are not referring to situations where you decide to demonstrate that the witness has just invented information. That process is called impeachment, and we discuss it later in this chapter. Rather, we are talking about instances when you decide to use the witness's own words against them.

Suppose you are a prosecutor set to cross-examine the defense expert. On direct examination, the defense criticizes your plaintiff's expert for not being thorough. You had not planned to attack the defense expert's thoroughness. But now it might make sense to do so:

> On direct examination, you criticized Dr. Jones for not being thorough, correct?
>
> Your exact words were, "A credible expert leaves no stone unturned," right?
>
> So let's talk about whether you left any stones unturned. Doctor, isn't it true that . . .

But what if you had already planned to cross-examination the defense expert about their lack of thoroughness? Add that same introduction! It will make your carefully practiced cross chapter appear to be responsive and spontaneous.

You can also show your adaptiveness by using the opponent's demonstrative aids against them. Be careful, however, about using the other team's equipment.

WAR STORY

Long ago, when Judge Nelmark was a Mock Trial competitor, his team had carefully created a demonstrative exhibit during the course of trial. It was a laminated piece of foam board and different witnesses wrote on it during the course of the trial. It then served as the centerpiece for the closing argument. "On one occasion, opposing counsel had a theme related to magic. He said that when you looked at the facts, our case 'disappeared.' With that, he grabbed an eraser off our counsel table and wiped the board. Unfortunately for him, nothing happened, even when he repeated the line and wiped harder. He eventually just took the demonstrative off the easel. That wonky eraser had been the bane of our team's existence all year, but it redeemed itself in that moment."

6.6 Performance

Sometimes attorneys with excellent speaking skills lose that great delivery on cross-examination. Why? Because they are embroiled in a game of chess with the witness. They are thinking exclusively about what they are going to say, not how they are going to say it. This is a terrible mistake. Cross, like every other part of trial, demands captivating presentation. Use your voice. Presentation remains just as important on cross-examination, if not more so—you are competing for center stage. Use a loud, slow, clear voice. It will show confidence to the jury, and it will intimidate the witness.

Vary your volume, inflection, and emphasis. Tell a story with your voice. Remember when we said, "Don't ask one question too many"? You don't need to ask that conclusion question if you've already implied it with your tone.

Pause. Pace yourself. It can be tempting to try to hurry and get done before the witness does something you don't want. Don't give in to the temptation. You need to give the jury time to digest your cross chapters.

Use your body. Keep your feet apart and remain balanced. Use hand gestures when appropriate. Move for emphasis. Pick up their demonstrative. Bend your knees. Hold up evidence. Point to the defendant. Get the attention on you.

The attorney should stand in a spot that makes it difficult for the witness to look at the jury and which puts the lawyer center stage. We recommend standing here:

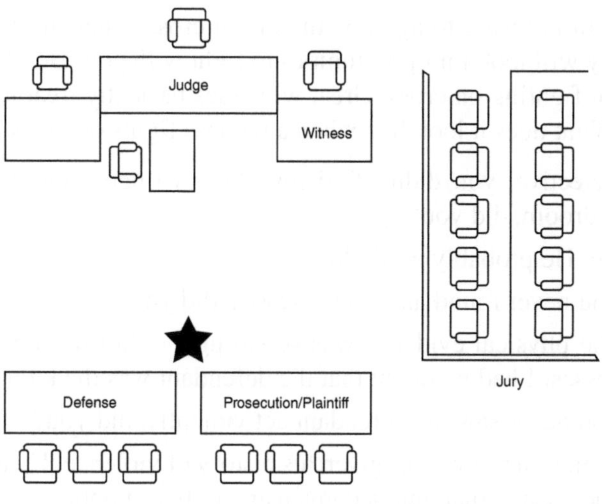

Keep your eyes on the witness much of the time, but occasionally (only a few times per cross) make eye contact with judges and jurors when delivering key questions. Doing so will engage the jury and tell them what's especially important.

Deliver thc questions not as questions but as facts. The witness is only there to affirm your story. Avoid ending questions with an upward inflection; it sounds weak and unsure.

Always use an appropriate demeanor. Most people think this means acting angry with the witness. Though there are times that it may be okay to act slightly angry with a witness, those times are rare. "Don't be cross on cross." Remain professional. With a sad witness, be a bit sympathetic. With a zany witness, rein them in. But if they lie, let them have it.

Don't interrupt the witness. Though they may be going off on a tangent and avoiding your question altogether, do not interrupt them. The judge will be upset any time two people are talking at once, and they will always blame the attorney—unless the witness interrupts a question. In that case, admonish the witness to wait until you have completed your questions.

Most importantly, always act like you're winning. If the witness destroys one of your answers, act like it's exactly what you wanted to hear. The jury may not understand or pay attention to your substance, but they'll always notice your demeanor. If you act like you are winning, you probably are.

6.7 Witness Control

Witnesses rarely want to agree with you on cross. They are your opponents. They will look for opportunities to fight with you. Good witnesses are good at fighting on cross. Great witnesses basically treat it like martial arts. What does it look like when a witness fights on cross?

Q. Detective, you didn't find my client's fingerprints in Bailey's bedroom, did you?

A. No. He probably used gloves.

Q. You never found any eyewitnesses, did you?

A. The physical evidence was so strong I didn't need any eyewitnesses. I had no doubt that the defendant was the kidnapper.

Q. You never saw the defendant act violently, did you?

A. Which surprised me, given his history of violence. I heard that he once beat a man into a coma using only a spoon.

In some of these instances, the witness is responding but adding damaging testimony after answering. In other instances, the witness is not directly answering at all. The witness is trying to tell their story and prevent you from telling yours.

Your job is to get the testimony you want and demonstrate control of the courtroom despite the witness fighting. This is called "witness control."

Let's Get Real: When it comes to witness control, Mock Trial is harder than real trial. In real life, most lay witnesses are intimidated and nervous about being in court, and they just answer the questions. The best Mock Trial witnesses are far more slippery.

Good witness control starts with preparation. Before trial begins, analyze and memorize the witness's statement thoroughly. You'll need to know every word of the document. That way, when the witness fights, you will know if their answers can be impeached. For every single question you plan to ask, you should know precisely where in that witness's statement to turn if you don't get the answer you want. Note, the answer must come from *that* witness's statement. You can't impeach one witness using any other witness's statement. You can, however, use another witness's statement to set up a question or to bait your witness into saying something that contradicts his or her own affidavit. This strategy works best when referencing the other witnesses on the sitting witness's side of the case.

Don't let the witness take control. If the witness responds to a question with, "You could say that," your immediate response is "*You* would say that, right?" The witness must agree because your question should use the exact same phrasing as the witness's own words in her witness statement.

You should exercise witness control the very first time a witness is clearly not responsive. This sets the tone and tells the witness that evasion will not be tolerated. It is difficult to control a witness in the middle of a cross if the witness has been fighting without resistance from you.

You need to have your pockets of questions memorized, but don't be afraid to change up the order of them. If a witness gives you an opening, say: "I'm glad you mentioned that," and proceed with the questions on that topic. Even if you were planning to ask the same questions anyway, the judges don't know that. You might earn bonus points for the perception that "you're thinking on your feet." Along these lines, be ready for the witness to "oversell" on direct examination. Example:

Q. Mr. Jones, you just testified in detail about the accident, correct?

A. Yes.

Q. Well, let's make one thing clear . . . you did not actually see the accident occur, right?

This works even if the witness does not cooperate with your initial question:

Q. Mr. Jones, you just testified in detail about the accident, correct?

A. Well, I would not say "in detail."

Q. Right, because it's tough to provide details when you did not actually see the accident, correct?

When crossing an expert witness, point out the limitations of her testimony.

"Just so I'm clear, that's all your opinion, right?"

"And there is a difference between opinion and fact?"

It's sometimes beneficial to comment on a witness's answer, if it can be done quickly. Don't lead into it with something like "Let me summarize." If you do, you'll draw an objection that the question is "asked and answered" or "counsel is testifying."

Don't let the witness take control by answering any questions the witness might throw out. Either ignore them, or, if necessary, ask a new question that indirectly responds to what the witness asked.

Q. Was the car blue?

A. The Corvette?

Q. Was the Corvette blue?

It would be faster to say yes to the question, but that puts the witness in charge. While you should not answer a witness's question, you should also not be snotty about it. Resist the temptation to say: "I'm the one who gets to ask the questions here."

Let's Get Real: Cross is much about "tone." Throughout the examination, you want to sound like you're in charge. This is also true in real trials, but not advisable in other real-life situations. The authors have been told by their families, more than once, not to use their "cross-examination voice" at home.

Similarly, maintain direct eye contact with the witness. If you look away or look down at notes, it's an invitation for the witness to try to get away with something. The exceptions are when you are making eye contact with the judges (which is advisable on occasion—generally during key questions) or intentionally looking away from the witness to convey that the answer is unimportant. The latter technique is used sparingly and done only when the witness is narrating and you're conveying an "are you done yet" vibe, prior to making a "witness control" comment as described below.

There is a series of responses you can use to control an evasive witness. It's important to escalate the level of control appropriately. Start gentle and increase the aggression if the witness persists in being evasive.

Gentle

1. "Is that a 'yes'?" This is usually your first attempt at witness control and is best used when a witness gives a long answer when they are really just saying "yes." It is short, to the point, and makes it harder for the witness to ramble. Beware: you can only use this if, in fact, the witness indicated agreement. You should also only use this when the answer you were looking for was "Yes." "Is that a 'no'?" gets confusing in a hurry.
2. "So that's a yes, that ____." This is similar to the previous control. This is preferable if you want to make sure the jury remembers your question.
3. "Bringing you back to my question, [repeat question]?" This is like the first two techniques, but it points out the witness was not responsive.

Stern

4. "That wasn't my question. [repeat question]?" Here we are expressly asserting that the witness was nonresponsive.
5. "My question was ___________? The answer to that question is yes, right?" This asserts that the witness was nonresponsive and tells the witness how to answer.
6. "I'll ask my question again. [repeat question]?" This is more sarcastic than the previous technique because it presumes that the witness was so nonresponsive you are entitled to ask the same question again.

Nuclear

7. "I didn't ask you [___]. I asked [____]. [repeat question]?" This is more aggressive because you are commenting on the witness's

answer. Done appropriately, it's also more effective because you are pointing out how nonresponsive the witness is.

8. "I asked you [____]. You told me about [____.] I'll ask my question again. [repeat question]?" Here we are characterizing the witness's testimony even more, which would normally be objectionable because it's argumentative. But judges will usually give attorneys leeway to push back when witnesses are extremely evasive. So when would we use this technique? Suppose we asked, "You entered the store at 11 a.m.?" The witness says, "I needed milk, eggs, and sugar." You can respond, "I asked what time you entered the store. You gave us a grocery list. I'll ask my question again. You entered the store at 11 a.m.?" This is aggressive, but powerful if the witness has persisted in being nonresponsive.

Judge Nelmark likes to use the "reversal" technique. If the witness is nonresponsive or refuses to confirm the truth of your question, you can ask if the witness is denying the fact.

Q. The car was blue, right?

A. Well, what I remember is that it was speeding. It came flying around the intersection.

Q. So . . . the car was *not* blue?

This reminds the jury of your original question and highlights the witness's evasiveness.

You also have nonverbal ways of controlling an evasive witness. When the witness is droning on and on, one effective technique is to walk away from the witness—either across the courtroom or to counsel's table. This can startle the witness and cause them to pause.

You can pick up an affidavit and stare at the judge. If the witness sees this, they may fear an impeachment. This may also cause them to pause and stop speaking. (You can only run this bluff so many times, and usually only against inexperienced witnesses.)

One tactic that often succeeds is raising your hand like a traffic cop. You will be amazed how often a witness will stop talking when you indicate "stop" with your hand. Use this sparingly, however, because it's likely to work only once with a witness.

Notice that we have not yet recommended objecting that the witness has been nonresponsive. You are allowed to say, "Objection, nonresponsive." But, for several reasons, we advise you to first try controlling the witness on your own. First, controlling the witness on your own is more impressive. If you have to go to the judge, it looks like you needed help.

Second, if the judge overrules your nonresponsive objection, you are in trouble. The witness will feel licensed to argue and evade even more. Third, if you try controlling the witness on your own first, then if you do need to object nonresponsive, the judge will be more likely to sustain your objection because it's clear you've exhausted your other remedies.

WAR STORY

Professor Bernstein's favorite moment as a competitor involved the judge's intervention on cross-examination. "I was a sophomore at Nationals, cross-examining Roger Holman, owner of a company that led expeditions on Mount Everest. One member of the expedition died during the climb, and his widow sued the company. I asked the final question of my cross: 'When you left Mr. Gilbertson on that mountain, he was still breathing?' The witness saw that time was running out, so he decided to evade the question with a lengthy answer until time was called. I asked the question again, the other team objected that time had expired, and I said the witness had not answered the question. The judge said I could ask again. Again, the witness refused to answer, giving a lengthy explanation. As I began to ask for a third time, with time still expired, opposing counsel stood up to object. The judge ignored us both and—though he had been quiet and reserved all trial—yelled at the witness. 'Answer the question. Was he still breathing?!' The witness was stunned. The whole courtroom was stunned. The witness looked at me, dumbfounded. After a pause, I said, 'Mr. Holman?' He responded, barely whispering, 'Yes.' To this day, the best cross question I ever asked was simply the witness's name."

How do you know whether to object that the witness is being nonresponsive? You have to consider multiple factors. Consider the judge. Do they look annoyed by the witness? Your objection is more likely to be sustained. That should make you more likely to object. Is the judge smiling at the witness's jokes? Probably don't object. Consider how many times the witness has been nonresponsive and whether you've already tried other methods of control. And consider where you are. Nonresponsive objections are more common and acceptable in some parts of the country than others. In our experience, judges in the South and Midwest rarely sustain nonresponsive objections. Judges in California will sustain them routinely. Do your homework when competing in a new locale.

When you do raise a nonresponsive objection, sometimes you will hear attorneys defend their overly explanative witnesses by saying, "The witness should be allowed to explain himself." They're wrong, and you shouldn't be afraid to say so. "Your Honor, I asked the witness if he sent the hair sample to the lab for DNA analysis. This clearly called for a yes or no answer. The kind of explanation opposing counsel is asking the court to allow is more appropriate on re-direct."

There are two things you should work hard to avoid when a witness is being nonresponsive. First, don't interrupt the witness. When a witness drones on and on, there is a temptation to interrupt. You want them to stop talking because you want control back in your hands. You want them to stop talking because they are eating up your cross-examination minutes. And you want them to stop talking because they might be saying something damaging to your case.

Avoid the temptation. Almost never interrupt a witness. It makes you look as bad as the witness, sometimes worse. You certainly don't want the jurors who were annoyed with the witness to turn their frustration to you. If you speak over a witness, you may draw an objection for badgering or an instruction from the judge that you must let the witness finish their answer. This makes you the bad guy when the witness was the one causing trouble. Instead, use the witness control techniques discussed earlier in this section.

Of course, if the witness keeps talking, you eventually need to stop them or you will have no time left. If you do *need* to interrupt, you have two options. One, you can go to the judge with an objection. Or, two, you can wait for a pause in the witness's answer (every witness needs air) and quickly snap their name: "Doctor" or "Mr. Jones." They'll stop talking and it won't seem nearly as harsh as if you simply spoke over him. Then pause and calmly repeat your question.

Lastly, there is one thing you should never ever do when a witness is being nonresponsive: lose your cool. Inside, you might be angry and frustrated. Externally, keep that poker face. If you act annoyed, that's when the witness wins, and you lose.

In fact, do the opposite. If the witness is obnoxious and you remain friendly, cheerful, and calm, you look fantastic—in stark contrast to the witness.

Maintaining composure requires practice. Practice having a witness argue with you, not give you an answer, talk nonstop, and do all the things that evasive witnesses do. Practice controlling the witness. Develop your own style. Try different techniques and phrasing. That way when you face a difficult witness in trial, you won't be flustered. You will be ready.

6.8 Impeachment

Impeachment is the process of showing the jury that the witness's testimony in court is contradicted by something the witness said in the past—or that the witness just invented facts that they have never said before. The former is called impeachment by contradiction. The latter is impeachment by omission.

In law, "impeachment" can also have a broader meaning: any attempt to undermine a witness's credibility is impeachment. For example, if you show that the witness once committed perjury, we call that impeachment by evidence of criminal conviction. But for the purposes of this book, we are defining impeachment to mean the process of showing the jury that the witness just lied on the witness stand.

Impeachment is attempted far more times than it is successfully executed. However, when done right, it can be one of the most successful weapons in Mock Trial. It can increase the attorney's score because it shows the attorney's comfort with procedure. It can decrease the witness's score because it devastates their credibility.

6.8.1 Impeachment by Contradiction

Impeachment by contradiction, also known as impeachment by prior inconsistent statement, means the witness testified during the trial to something contradicted by a statement the witness made in the past. The dishonest statement in trial can be something they said on direct examination or something they said on cross-examination.

How will you impeach them? Usually you impeach a witness with their witness statement—their affidavit, deposition transcript, etc. For example, if the witness testifies on direct examination that the traffic light was red when the defendant drove through the intersection, but in their affidavit the witness said the light was green, you can use the affidavit to impeach them.

But you can also impeach a witness with any document they have written or adopted a belief in. For example, suppose the witness testifies on direct examination that the traffic light was red when the defendant drove through the intersection. In their affidavit the witness says that Exhibit A is a photo they took of the intersection when the defendant drove through it. In Exhibit A, the light is green. You can use Exhibit A to impeach them.

As another example: The witness testifies on direct examination that the traffic light was red when the defendant drove through the intersection. But in Exhibit B, an email to their friend dated the next day, the witness says the light was green. You can impeach them with Exhibit B.

Note, however, that you cannot impeach a witness with someone else's affidavit. That's the rule—and common sense. Just because someone else has a different opinion or recollection doesn't mean this witness is lying or wrong. Indeed, if you show them a contradictory statement from someone else, the witness may say the other person is lying.

Don't try to impeach a witness unless the impeachment is important. If the fact seems trivial, the jury may be annoyed that you are wasting time. For example, whether two people met in second grade or third grade isn't important. What's important is that they've known each other for a long time. It's not worth impeaching on the difference between knowing someone since second grade and knowing them since third grade.

Don't try to impeach a witness unless the impeachment is clear. If the jury thinks, "I'm not sure if that's a contradiction," the witness wins and the attorney loses.

These are some of the reasons that most impeachments fail: the attorney impeaches over something unimportant or the jury is unsure if there is actually a contradiction.

If you decide to impeach the witness based on something they said on direct examination, we recommend you do so at the start of your cross. It tells the jury, "Everything the witness just said is untrustworthy." If you decide to impeach the witness based on something they say on cross-examination, do it as soon as they make the dishonest statement.

Okay, so you've decided to impeach the witness. How do you do it? Judges will expect you to follow a customary method for impeaching by contradiction. There are three main steps: commit, credit, confront.

First, we **commit** the witness to their lie. Make sure they can't backtrack and wiggle out of the impeachment later.

Q. On direct examination, you told this jury that when you saw the accident you were sober, right?

A. Yes.

Q. You claimed that when you saw the accident you had not had any alcohol, correct?

A. Yes.

We like asking essentially the same question twice to lock in the witness and make sure the jury understands the fact we are about to impeach.

Second, **credit** the prior statement. Your exact questions will differ depending on the type of statement—deposition, affidavit, police report, etc. But the goal is always the same: make the prior statement seem as reliable as possible.

Q. You wrote an affidavit in this case?

Q. When you wrote that affidavit, you promised to tell the truth?

Q. You signed that affidavit under penalty of perjury?

OR

Q. This isn't the first time you've testified in this case?

Q. Your deposition was taken on May 14, 2017?

Q. At that deposition, you understood you had to be truthful?

Q. An oath to tell the whole truth and nothing but the truth?

Q. The very same oath you took today?

OR

Q. Officer, you wrote a police report?

Q. When you write a police report, it's important to be accurate?

Q. Important to be truthful?

Q. When you wrote your report in this case, you were accurate?

Q. You were truthful?

Finally, **confront** the witness with her lie.

Q. Your Honor, I am showing opposing counsel a copy of this witness's affidavit. May I approach with the witness?

J. Yes.

Q. Would Your Honor like a courtesy copy?

J. No, thank you.

Q. The document I just handed you is your affidavit, correct?

A. Yes.

Q. It's a fair and accurate copy of your affidavit?

A. Yes.

Q. Please turn to page three, line 16, and look up when you're there.

Q. I would like you to read silently to yourself as I read aloud to the court. "I had six shots of tequila an hour before I saw the car accident. By the time of the accident, I was drunk as a skunk. That is to say: extremely drunk. Definitely not sober." Did I read that correctly?

A. Yes.

Q. Your Honor, may I approach and retrieve the affidavit?

Once you hand the affidavit to the witness, don't stand over them while impeaching. Return to wherever you were standing. That prevents you from looking like a bully and allows you to present more easily to the jury because you aren't tethered to the witness.

Have three copies of any document you might use for impeachment: one for the witness, one for you, and one for the presiding judge if they want one. You don't need to give opposing counsel a copy—they should already have a copy—and you are not allowed to give a copy of an affidavit to the jury.

Don't offer the exhibit into evidence. You are only using it for impeachment.

Above all, do not ask one question too many. Do not ask, "So you had been drinking?" Do not ask, "Do you still claim you were perfectly sober at the time of the accident?" Do not ask, "So you lied?" Do not ask, "Were you lying then or lying now?"

Asking these questions gives the witness an invitation to explain or argue. You don't need to ask these questions. If the impeachment was clear, the jury got it.

6.8.2 Impeachment by Omission

Sometimes the witness will invent important information that is not contained in their witness statement. They are trying to create facts that aren't there. Doing so is cheating, and it's impeachable.

Just as we discussed with impeachments by contradiction, do not attempt an impeachment by omission unless the invented information is important. If an eyewitness creates a back story about once performing in the circus, that's probably not important to the case. If the doctor says she went to medical school because she likes helping people, that's probably not important to the case.

If you impeach by omission, you do the same three steps—commit, credit, confront—but the questions are slightly different.

First, **commit** the witness to their lie.

Q. On direct examination, you said you saw a car hit a boy, and then drive away?

A. Yes.

Q. You said the license plate was STR 442?

A. Yes.

Q. I want to be clear. It's your testimony that on January 1, 2017, you saw the license plate of the car that hit the boy?

A. Yes.

Q. In fact, it's your testimony that you saw all six digits of that license plate?

A. I sure did.

Next, **credit** the prior statement. Notice that with impeachment by contradiction, our primary focus is honesty. Here, it's about completeness.

Q. On January 3, 2017, you gave a statement to the police?

Q. A written statement?

Q. This was just two days after the accident?

Q. In your written statement, you described what you remembered from the accident?

Q. When you gave that statement, you knew a boy had been hurt?

Q. You knew the police were involved?

Q. You knew the police were looking for the driver who hit the boy?

Q. You knew it was important to tell the police everything you knew?

Finally, **confront** the witness with their lie.

Q. Your Honor, I am showing opposing counsel a copy of this witness's affidavit. May I approach the witness?

J. Yes.

Q. Would Your Honor like a courtesy copy?

J. No, thank you.

Q. The document I just handed you is your statement to the police, correct?

A. Yes.

Q. It's a fair and accurate copy of your statement?

A. Yes.

Q. Please turn to page three, line 16, and look up when you're there.

Q. In this paragraph, you describe the car that hit the boy?

A. Yes.

Q. You describe the color of the car?

A. Yes.

Q. The make?

A. Yes.

Q. The model?

A. Yes.

Q. But nowhere in this paragraph do you mention the license plate?

A. No.

Q. Nowhere in this entire written statement did you mention the license plate?

A. I didn't include that, no.

Q. Your Honor, may I approach and retrieve the document?

Notice how the context helps emphasize the invention. It's bad enough that the witness didn't include the license plate. But the fact that the witness included so many details other than the license plate makes it seem like they would have included the license plate if they knew it. It makes their invention in trial even more implausible.

6.8.3 Re-Cross-Examination

In some competitions, you are permitted to cross-examine a witness after a re-direct examination. This is called re-cross.

Re-cross is rarely a good idea. If you already did well, you may have little to gain. If you already scored well and the witness scored low, you may have nothing to gain. But because a re-cross is the last thing the judges see, you may have a lot to lose.

Only re-cross if you are sure it will score you points and/or cost the other team points. Impeachment is a good reason to re-cross.

Re-crosses are limited to the scope of testimony from re-direct. If you forgot to ask something on cross, you can't just re-cross to slip it in.

If you do a re-cross, make sure it's short. If it's not an impeachment, keep your re-cross to one or two questions.

7

Cross-Examination: Witnesses

Most witnesses prepare carefully for direct examination. The best witnesses also prepare carefully for cross-examination. A strong witness performance on cross is worth double because you can earn a good score for your team and damage the opponent's cross-examination score.

7.1 Goals

Too often witnesses think their primary goal on cross-examination is to help their team prove its case. No. Your goal is the same as always: *It's All About Points!* Arguing your case is not the best way to score more points. If you argue for your case, you will usually seem biased.

The goals on cross-examination are to remain credible, remain in character, and minimize the impact of the unfavorable facts.

7.2 Special Powers

Each witness type has what we call special powers: weapons they alone can deploy on cross-examination.

7.2.1 Law Enforcement

Police officers have the ability to score well without saying much. If any other witness simply says "yes" to more than half the questions, they will lose control of the cross and probably get outscored by the attorney. But police officers can score great merely by keeping their answers short, responsive, respectful, and confident.

Q. You searched my client's house, right, detective?

A. Yes, ma'am. Three days after the victim was reported missing.

Q. You were looking for physical evidence?

A. Yes, ma'am.

Q. You didn't find any blood in my client's house, did you?

A. No, ma'am. We didn't find any forensic evidence in the house.

Q. No gunpowder?

A. That's correct.

Q. None of the victim's DNA?

A. No, ma'am.

The witness admitted to all these unfavorable facts—but will still score great if they deliver these answers confidently.

Why? Remember the quintessential attribute judges want from law enforcement witnesses: credibility. "Just the facts." You want to seem unbiased. *Here is what I found. I will admit what I didn't find. I'm just here to tell you the facts.* Most police officer witnesses will try to explain why they didn't find blood in the defendant's home: "Oh, well, I wouldn't expect to find blood three days after the crime. The defendant could have cleaned it up." That might beat weaker opponents. Against strong attorneys, that will result in witness control that leaves the witness looking biased. Stick to the facts.

The key is the delivery. "Yes, ma'am" (or "Yes, sir") scores poorly if the witness sounds defeated. "Yes, ma'am" scores poorly if the witness looks hesitant—because it looks like the witness wanted to argue but couldn't find a way. "Yes, ma'am" scores poorly if it is delivered the same way every time. Instead, deliver the "yes" confidently. You know the facts aren't damaging. Otherwise, you wouldn't have arrested the defendant. So convey that confidence in your voice.

Vary the way you say "yes." Most of the time it will just be a strong "yes." Occasionally throw in a hint of confusion, as if to say, "Yes, that's true, but it's so irrelevant that I'm unsure why you're asking." Occasionally sound extra confident, as if to say, "Yes, absolutely, that fact helps me, not you."

Also make sure to remain respectful. Good law enforcement witnesses are very professional in court. Adding "sir" or "ma'am" after most yes/no answers will make the witness likable and credible all at once.

7.2.2 Expert

An expert witness has two special powers. The first is the power to explain. You can't launch into a monologue (unless opposing counsel is foolish enough to ask an open-ended question). But you can usually add a sentence to explain the area within your expertise. Most witnesses will look like they're being nonresponsive if they explain. If the answers are brief, an expert who explains will look helpful.

An expert's second special power is the ability to parse—to be nitpicky with words and phrases. If most witnesses do that, they will look biased and difficult. But an expert who parses the attorney's questions will look detailed, professional, and reliable.

Consider this exchange on the cross-examination of a crime scene investigator:

Q. You searched the crime scene, right, doctor?
A. The interior and exterior of the residence, yes.
Q. You were looking for physical evidence?
A. Forensic evidence.
Q. You didn't find any blood in my client's house, did you?
A. Correct. We used a Luminol spray. There was no blood.
Q. No gunpowder?
A. We test for gunpowder *residue*, not gunpowder itself. Gunpowder residue refers to the metal particles dispelled from a firearm when it's discharged.
Q. You found no gunpowder residue?
A. Correct. GSR only remains on a surface for seven hours.

For the most part, the witness is agreeing. But in each instance, the expert is phrasing their answer in a way that scores points.

Q. You searched the crime scene, right, doctor?
A. The interior and exterior of the residence, yes.

The witness is being specific. The attorney said, "crime scene," and the expert parses the question and identifies more precisely what area was searched.

Q. You were looking for physical evidence?
A. Forensic evidence.

This is nitpicky, but the witness is being specific about the professional terminology. For example, a knife would be physical evidence, but it probably would not be forensic evidence (an expert would probably say that the materials found on the knife—blood, skin, DNA—are forensic evidence). If the attorney had asked "You were looking for forensic evidence?" our expert might have said, "Trace evidence." Find ways to show off that you're the expert; the lawyer is just a lawyer.

Notice that that witness doesn't say, "No, forensic evidence" because we don't want to give off the impression that we are looking to argue. We just want to use the right phrase.

Q. You didn't find any blood in my client's house, did you?

A. Correct. We used a Luminol spray. There was no blood.

The witness isn't arguing with the lawyer. In fact, the witness is agreeing. This is one of the tricks for successful expert answers on cross: You can talk more when you agree. When you disagree and explain, it looks biased. If you agree and explain, it sounds credible and helpful. And then how can the lawyer control you?

Q. You didn't find any blood in my client's house, did you?

A. Correct. We used a Luminol spray. There was no blood.

Q. So you didn't find any blood?

A. Correct.

The lawyer loses patience and tries to control the witness. But the jury is thinking, "Why are you arguing with the witness? They just agreed with you."

Q. No gunpowder?

A. We test for gunpowder *residue*, not gunpowder itself. Gunpowder residue refers to the metal particles dispelled from a firearm when it's discharged.

Here the witness is flexing their scientific muscles. The attorney used the wrong term, and the witness corrects them.

Q. You found no gunpowder residue?

A. Correct. GSR only remains on a surface for seven hours.

This is an excellent answer, and not just because the witness sounds like a scientist. The witness agrees but undermines the value of the fact elicited. The jury doubts whether the lack of gunpowder residue means anything because maybe the search was conducted more than seven hours after the crime. This works so well because the witness doesn't say "but." If the witness had said, "Correct. ***But*** GSR only remains on a surface for about seven hours," then it looks like the witness has an agenda. They want to make a point. Instead, we just say, "Correct. GSR only remains on a surface for about seven hours." Here the witness is a helpful scientist offering a relevant fact. This answer also works because it's so short. It's hard for the attorney to object "nonresponsive" when the answer is so brief.

Experts should avoid fighting on cross. But they should find ways to explain.

WAR STORY

Professor Bernstein's favorite answer on cross came from an expert witness: "I had the pleasure of coaching a lot of All-American witnesses, but Ryan Cardenas was the best. He was a physics major who was so earnest, even when ripping the cross-examiner apart. At Nationals in 2011, he was portraying a toxicologist who had treated the child who had died after swallowing a children's toy coated in a poisonous chemical. On cross-examination, the attorney tried to make Ryan look biased. You have a daughter? 'Yes.' You were angry that the defendant put this chemical on children's toys? 'I was.' You want the defendant to go out of business? 'I want them to stop putting children in my emergency room.' The answer was sincere, real, and devastating."

7.2.3 Party/Victim

The party/victim's special power is emotion.

You have a stake in the outcome of the case. You have an inherent bias. After all, you are either the victim of something terrible or accused of something terrible. How could you not have an emotional investment in the outcome of the case? But since those downsides are unavoidable, you might as well harness them.

That means when you are cross-examined about the day you were injured, you can be emotional. You can tear up, or pause, or struggle to speak. You can have moments of anger. You can stare off while describing the events, as if you are reliving them. All these emotional moments will bring attention to you and take attention away from the lawyer. They also make you more believable. Truthful people show emotion when talking about emotional things.

Similarly, if you are the defendant, you can show emotion when attacked on cross-examination. You can be indignant when accused. You can be sad when asked about the person who was injured or killed. You can plead to the jury—"No, I wouldn't do that"—when confronted. The jury knows you are on trial, which means you don't need to worry as much as other witnesses about looking biased. Of course you are biased. But if you react the way an innocent person does when accused of something bad, you will seem more believable.

7.2.4 Eyewitness

The eyewitness's special power is personality.

You can use your character traits to distract attention from the cross-examination. Usually this requires some humor. If your character still lives in his mom's basement, find a way to mention that on cross-examination. If your character is pretentious and loves to name-drop celebrities that they know, make sure to name drop a celebrity on cross, too. Whatever shtick you used on direct needs to be used a couple times on cross, as well.

It's easy to go too far, which can cost you credibility. How do you make sure you stay on the right side of that line?

First, a little goes a long one way. Some high school crosses are less than two minutes. You only need one joke. Even a normal-length college cross—five minutes—only needs a couple humorous moments.

Second, you can be funny—but don't act like you're trying to be funny. The guy who lives in his mother's basement at age 35 probably is not proud of it. The pretentious name-dropper thinks they are being cool, not lame, when they reference people they know. These witnesses think they are being serious, which is what makes them funny to the jury. If you smile at your own jokes, it will usually look fake.

7.3 Techniques for All Witnesses on Cross

7.3.1 Listen to the Questions

Attorneys will often ask something similar to the facts in your affidavit. That is not good enough. As a witness, you only have to concede facts that are stated in your affidavit.

Suppose you are portraying the detective. Your affidavit says no forensic evidence was recovered during a search of the crime scene. On cross-examination, you are asked these questions:

Q. When you searched the crime scene, you found none of my client's blood?

Q. None of her hair?

Q. None of her fingerprints?

Q. None of her DNA?

Q. You found no evidence placing my client at the crime scene?

You have to say yes to the first four questions. But the last question is too much. "No forensic evidence" does not mean "no evidence." Did an eyewitness tell you they saw the defendant at the scene? Did an eyewitness see the defendant's car near the scene? Does the defendant have a parking ticket placing her near the scene?

It's easy to hear those first four questions and reflexively say yes to the fifth. It's easy to think, "I know the attorney *means* forensic evidence." But that wasn't the question. Listen carefully to each question and pounce when the attorney makes a mistake.

7.3.2 Answer the Questions

The best witnesses answer the questions.

Sure, you can defeat an inexperienced attorney by not really answering the questions.

Q. Doctor, it's important to be thorough, right?

A. I was thorough.

Q. You didn't interview any witnesses?

A. That wasn't necessary.

Q. You didn't visit the scene of the crime?

A. Well, I wasn't hired until a month after the crime.

Here, the attorney isn't controlling the witness. The jury might think the attorney is weak and the witness is winning the cross. (They might think the attorney is weak—but also think the witness is evasive and not credible.) But we don't want strategies that only work against inexperienced opponents. The strategy above falls flat against good witness control:

Q. Doctor, it's important to be thorough, right?

A. I was thorough.

Q. You didn't interview any witnesses?

A. That wasn't necessary.

Q. We will let the jury decide if it was necessary. For now, I'm just asking if you did it. And you didn't interview any witnesses?

A. No.

Q. You didn't visit the scene of the crime?

A. Well, I wasn't hired until a month after the crime.

Q. Again, that wasn't the question. You never visited the crime scene?

A. No.

Now the witness looks evasive *and* defeated. Not a good combination.

Answer the questions. But do so in a way that sounds confident.

7.3.3 The Power of Yes

The most counterintuitive trick on cross-examination is that we score the most points by simply admitting the worst facts.

Here's why. When we try to deny the bad facts, or argue about the bad facts, or squirm around the bad facts, all we do is invite the attorney to re-ask the question. Let's revisit our combative witness:

Q. Doctor, it's important to be thorough, right?

A. I was thorough.

Q. You didn't interview any witnesses?

A. That wasn't necessary.

Q. We will let the jury decide if it was necessary. For now, I'm just asking if you did it. And you didn't interview any witnesses?

A. No.

Q. You didn't visit the scene of the crime?

A. Well, I wasn't hired until a month after the crime.

Q. Again, that wasn't the question. You never visited the crime scene?

A. No.

Because the witness fought, the attorney was able to establish twice that the expert interviewed no one and establish twice that the witness never visited the crime scene. It's not like you can make the bad facts disappear by arguing. You are either going to eventually admit the bad facts or get impeached. If you fight the bad facts against a good opponent, the jury is going to hear the bad facts *double*.

But it's worse than that. By arguing about the facts, the witness increases the jury's attention. If you are walking down the street and see people talking, you don't pay attention. But when you see two people arguing, you suddenly wonder, "What's all this about?" It's the same with cross-examination. The jury has a limited attention span. They cannot absorb every detail. But you can be sure the jury is listening the moment you fight.

So say yes. Admit the bad facts easily.

Q. Doctor, it's important to be thorough, right?

A. Absolutely.

Q. You didn't interview any witnesses?

A. That's correct.

Q. You didn't visit the scene of the crime?

A. That's correct.

If you are confident when saying "that's correct," the jury may not even realize the significance of the fact you just admitted! "It must not be important," their brain tells them, "because this witness admitted the fact so freely."

7.3.4 Get Ahead of the Attorney

In fact, if you know a series of bad facts is coming, try to get ahead of the lawyer.

Q. When you searched the crime scene, you found none of my client's blood?

A. No, ma'am. We found no forensic evidence of any kind.

Q. None of her hair?

A. No, ma'am.

Q. None of her fingerprints?

A. No, ma'am. No forensic evidence of any kind.

Q. None of her DNA?

A. No, ma'am.

If you have studied the case packet and paid attention to the trial so far, you have a good idea of what cross-examination questions are coming. The witness here realizes that the blood question is just the first in a series of questions about what wasn't found. The witness could sit there and get hammered, one question after another, about all the things they did not find. This lets the attorney look in control and get points. But instead the witness volunteers the bad fact: no forensic evidence was found.

This reduces the sting of the ensuing questions. The jury knows the answer. Some jurors might even be annoyed about hearing this list of things that were not found when the witness already said it. Some judges would sustain a cumulative objection to the last question because the witness has twice said that there was no forensic evidence. Scorers may even assume the attorney does not understand what forensic evidence is.

Notice that the witness does not repeat that fact every time. It would look like the witness is biased or annoyed:

Q. When you searched the crime scene, you found none of my client's blood?

A. No, ma'am. We found no forensic evidence of any kind.

Q. None of her hair?

A. No, ma'am. We found no forensic evidence of any kind.

Q. None of her fingerprints?

A. No, ma'am. No forensic evidence of any kind.

Instead, the witness does it the first and third times only.

Q. When you searched the crime scene, you found none of my client's blood?

A. No, ma'am. We found no forensic evidence of any kind.

Q. None of her hair?

A. No, ma'am.

Q. None of her fingerprints?

A. No, ma'am. . . . No forensic evidence of any kind.

The witness tried to be helpful and upfront, which could save everyone some time: *No need to ask again because I'm telling you now, no forensic evidence was found.* The attorney asked the second time, and the witness was patient. But the third time, the witness pauses and acts—just slightly—confused, as if to say, *I thought I told you already.*

If the attorney has a grocery list, don't let them go ingredient by ingredient. Give them all the information at once to reduce the impact of the cross.

7.3.5 Phrasing to Avoid

There are certain phrases that witnesses like, but many judges will not. Avoid them.

"Yes, but." This is the hallmark of a witness who is biased, fighting, and evasive. *You hated the victim?* "Yes, but I wouldn't kill her." That sounds defensive. *You were paid in this case?* "Yes, but that did not affect my testimony." Again, defensive. *You didn't interview any witnesses before reaching your conclusions?* "No, but I read their witness statements." Defensive.

You can often make the same point without sounding defensive merely by dropping the "but." *You didn't interview any witnesses before reaching your conclusions?* "No. I read their witness statements." This sounds so much less defensive. The second sentence implicitly says, "No, *because* I read their witness statements." By avoiding "but" we make it sound like we are explaining rather than arguing.

"It wasn't necessary." Experts like to explain that certain procedures weren't necessary. You didn't visit the scene of the accident? "That wasn't necessary." You didn't interview any witnesses? "I didn't need to." This language sounds defensive. A more confident answer is, "That's correct."

"Counsel." Some witnesses like to refer to the attorney as "counsel." This is especially tempting when the witness is an expert. *You didn't actually see the accident itself, did you doctor?* "No, counsel." It sounds snarky. Don't do it.

"As I already said . . ." Witnesses sometimes get snippy when asked about the same fact multiple times. An attorney is entitled to cross-examine about a topic you've already discussed on direct examination. They are entitled to ask multiple questions about the same topic on cross-examination. If you act annoyed or impatient, the jury may not like that.

You might be thinking, what if the attorney genuinely *is* annoying everyone, including the jury, by beating a dead horse? Is it okay to show annoyance then?

Still no. If the jury is annoyed by the attorney, you don't need to do anything. Stay upbeat and polite, and the jury will reward you for your patience and punish the attorney for wasting their time. If the jury is not annoyed by the attorney, acting impatient will only reflect poorly on you. In sum, there is no upside to acting impatient with your cross-examiner.

"Would you like me to explain?" Some experts love this response on cross-examination. They figure it is lose-lose for the lawyer. If the lawyer says yes, the witness crushes them with a lengthy explanation. If the lawyer says no, the lawyer looks like they are afraid of the explanation. But an experienced lawyer has easy retorts. "No, you've answered the question." "You can explain on re-direct examination. For now, you can just answer the questions." Or they can just ignore you and ask their next question. The problem with "Would you like me to explain?" is that it looks like you are trying to pick a fight or lay a trap. If you need to explain, then do it. But don't ask permission against a prepared, experienced opponent.

However, if the lawyer isn't getting what you're saying or is asking a bad question, you can point it out. An expert can say: "That is a common misconception," or "That was not my answer." The attorney may be tricked into asking you to explain without you having to offer to do so. If the attorney asks you to explain, it's game on. But, even if the crossing attorney does not take the bait, the issue has been flagged for the jury and for your attorney to come back on re-direct examination.

7.3.6 Don't Throw the Attorney a Life Preserver

Every now and then, an attorney will make a big mistake on cross-examination by getting their facts wrong. Or they will overreach with one of their facts. Let's return to the example from earlier in the chapter. Suppose a detective found no forensic evidence during a search, and she is asked these questions on cross:

Q. When you searched the crime scene, you found none of my client's blood?

Q. None of her hair?

Q. None of her fingerprints?

Q. None of her DNA?

Q. You found no evidence placing my client at the crime scene?

You are the witness. You admit the first four facts. But you recognize the last question goes too far. You say, "No, an eyewitness saw her there 15 minutes before the crime." Success, right?

Wrong. That is a wasted opportunity.

If you give that answer, yes, you score points. You look good. The attorney looks bad. But then they fix their question. "Detective, you found no forensic evidence placing my client at the crime scene?" Now their cross is back on track, with a one-question detour.

A much more devastating response is a strong denial—without explanation.

Q. You found no evidence placing my client at the crime scene?

A. No, ma'am. That is incorrect.

What does the attorney do? They probably cannot just fix the question and limit it to forensic evidence *because you haven't clued them in to what's wrong with their question.* They can't just move on to the next chapter because it will look like they were defeated. They are stuck. Some attorneys will stand there, dumbfounded. Some will just repeat their question angrily. "So you found evidence that places my client at the crime scene?!?" "Yes, ma'am. I found significant evidence placing the defendant at the crime scene." Some will try to impeach you, and that will end in disaster for the lawyer when you point to the line in your affidavit about the eyewitness. Some will crumble and ask the open-ended question: "Okay, what evidence did you find connecting my client to the crime scene?" Then you drop the hammer.

By saying "no" without explanation, you just increase the jury's interest in what is happening. It makes your ultimate victory on this point seem more dramatic and compelling. It puts your opponent on edge. It makes them more likely to make a bigger mistake. And you will eventually get to give your explanation anyway. Either the cross-examiner will soon give you a chance to say it on cross, or your attorney can ask you on re-direct.

7.4 Impeachment

7.4.1 Avoiding Impeachment

Do not get impeached. You are not being scored on which side is right. You are being scored on your credibility, likability, and speaking ability. If you get impeached on an important fact, your score will suffer.

You should be able to avoid getting impeached. The first step is the most important. Know your facts. Know your facts inside out. Have your teammates quiz you on the facts before competition. If you know the facts better than your opponent, you should never be impeached.

The second step: when in doubt, say yes. If the attorney asks you a question and you're not sure if the fact is in your witness statement, say yes. Suppose the lawyer says, "Doctor, you think it's probable that the killer was right-handed." You can't remember if your witness statement says "probable" or "possible." Say yes! For one thing, the lawyer likely is not bluffing. If they are using the word "probable," there is a good chance they chose that word because it's in your affidavit. (When in doubt, adopt strategies that assume your opponent is good. If they are not good, you will beat them anyway.) And, moreover, it does not really matter. The jury likely does not care about the difference between "probable" and "possible"—certainly not enough to risk an impeachment.

7.4.2 Handling Impeachment

Suppose the opposing attorney tries to impeach you. Let's consider multiple scenarios.

Impeachment by contradiction when you have contradicted yourself. On direct examination, you said the light was red and your affidavit says the light was green. This is not going to end well for you. Admit the mistake as soon as possible—ideally at the beginning of the impeachment before you are holding the affidavit. "I'm sorry, I meant the light was green. I misspoke."

Impeachment by contradiction when you have not contradicted yourself. On direct examination, you said the light was red and your affidavit says the light was red. This is going to end great for you. Answer all the attorney's setup questions with confidence. Don't argue. Don't tell them it's in your affidavit. We want this impeachment to last a while. It will make the ending—where the jury sees you were right all along—look that much better for you and that much worse for the lawyer.

Impeachment by omission when you have omitted a material fact. On direct examination, you said the light was red and your affidavit says nothing about the color of the light. This is not going to end well for you. But don't make the situation worse by fighting. When the lawyer says, "That's not in your deposition, is it?" don't say, "I didn't think it was relevant." Don't point to something else in the affidavit that has nothing to do with the question. Just confidently say, "No, I didn't say that." There is a chance the jury mistakes your confidence for correctness. Even if not, at least you're not making the problem worse.

Impeachment by omission when you included the material fact. On direct examination, you said the light was red and your affidavit says the same. The lawyer somehow does not know this and begins to impeach by omission. Again, this is going to end great for us. Answer all the attorney's setup question with confidence. When the lawyer asks you, "Nowhere in this affidavit do you say the light was red?" don't just say, "It's right here on page 16, line 22." The attorney will look bad. But you can have a lot more fun than that. "Sure I do. Page 16, line 22. 'I saw the car speed through the intersection. The light was red.' See, right there I say the light was red."

7.5 Performance

The most overlooked part of scoring well as a witness on cross is the performance component—the acting.

Remain in character. So often witnesses have a fun character on direct, and then they are humorless on cross. This change makes the personality seem fake. Or the witness will be sad on direct, but fine on cross. This makes the emotion seem fake. Or the witness will seem professional on direct—a great cop or expert—but then biased on cross. This makes their credibility disappear. Or the witness has an accent on direct that fades in and out on cross. This makes the witness seem like a role instead of a real person. You want to come across as the same person on cross that you were on direct.

Remain energetic. The attorney gets to move around, gesture, change volumes, and do all sorts of things to keep the jury's attention. Compete for that attention. Maintain your volume, confidence, and energy from direct examination.

Speak slowly. When we get nervous, we tend to speed up. Doing so will sound scared and defensive, and it also eats up less of the other team's cross-examination time. No matter what happens on cross, we have to seem in control.

Remain unfazed. If the lawyer introduces your perjury conviction, look momentarily—and appropriately—regretful. Then return to your confident self. If the lawyer introduces other bad facts, act like they did not hurt you. If the lawyer impeaches you, act like it did not happen. The jury will not grasp every fact in trial. But they rarely miss the signs in our voice and body language. If we act like we are winning, we probably are. If we act like we are losing, we almost certainly are. So act like you're winning.

8

Closing Argument

In movies, the closing argument is the biggest moment of trial. It's the moment when the hero stands before the jury, searches for inspiration, and speaks from the heart without preparation or a script. It is the moment when the trial is won.

The movies are not reality. A closing is rarely the product of a charismatic and quick-witted attorney who "wings it" through pure ability. Instead, it is a carefully crafted synthesis of law and fact, performed with well-chosen rhetoric and the same excellent delivery demanded throughout the trial.

However, a closing argument is not just a recitation of a well-written speech. A good closer must improvise when things go wrong, incorporate helpful facts from trial, and respond to opposing counsel's theme, theory, and evidence. Use the framework of your script as a launching pad but respond specifically and powerfully.

Because closing argument is the speech at the end of trial, it is your last chance to win the trial. Hopefully, by the time you get to closing argument, you have already separated from your opponent with outstanding witnesses, examinations, and objections. Hopefully, the closing will only add to your lead. But some rounds are close. Closing argument can make all the difference.

We have also found that closing argument is the most objectively scored part of trial. Judges tend to agree least about which team won opening. They agree more about which team won each witness examination. They agree *most* about which team won closing argument. By closing argument, the judges have already been educated about the facts of the case and can focus on each closer's performance. When it comes to critiquing that performance, there is little variation in judge preference.

This chapter covers what judges want from closing argument.

8.1 Goals

The substantive goal of closing argument is to persuade the jury that your client deserves to win the verdict. If you are the prosecution or plaintiff, this means persuading the jury that you met your burden of proof. If you are the defense, this means persuading the jury that your opponent did not meet its burden of proof—or, even if they did meet their burden, you still win because of an affirmative defense.

The chief performance goal of closing argument is to engage the jury's attention and direct the jury's emotion. We want the jury to hang on our every word. We want the jury to relive specific moments from trial. We want the jury to feel the emotions that support our case: anger toward a callous defendant, empathy for our client, etc. The challenge is that closing arguments are often significantly longer than opening statements. In some high school competitions, each closing argument is five minutes; in other high school competitions, closing can be as long as ten minutes. In college competitions, closings are usually eight or nine minutes. In law school competitions, closings are often 15 minutes (and sometimes longer).

Let's Get Real: In the famous murder trial *People v. Orenthal James Simpson*, closing arguments lasted four days.

Of course—and by this point in the book we hope you know what we are about to say next—*It's All About Points!* In closing argument, we want to maximize our points and, if possible, knock points off our opponent's score.

8.2 Argue

It's not closing statement. It's closing *argument*. One of the most common mistakes that people make is flipping the purposes of their two speeches. They want to argue in opening and tell a story in closing. No. It's the other way around. We tell a story in opening. We argue in closing.

What is the difference? A story involves facts—people, places, events. An argument tells the jury what they should *conclude* from those facts.

Let's use the Top Gun 2015 case. The defendant, Ellen Moody, is on trial for murder-for-hire. She allegedly hired a hitman to kill her cheating husband. One of the prosecution's best facts is that the defendant left her home alarm disabled, which allowed the hitman to sneak in undetected. This fact helps prove she and the hitman were in cahoots.

This is how a closing argument might sound if the prosecutor were telling a story or merely summarizing facts.

> Michael Ehrman testified that the defendant left the home alarm disabled. He testified that this allowed him to sneak into the house without the victim realizing and without the police being notified. Exhibit 17 is the record of the home alarm system. It shows that the home alarm system was activated on other days, but it was not activated the day Mr. Moody was murdered. This proves the defendant was responsible.

This version includes the key facts, and it has the conclusion, but it does not connect the dots for the jury. It summarizes. However, the following version *argues*:

> That brings us to the third reason we know the defendant was involved. The alarm.
>
> When the hitman crept into the house, the alarm didn't sound. The police weren't called. Why? Because the defendant decided not to turn on the alarm.
>
> The defendant called that a mistake. "I was in a rush." But this was no mistake. Look at this security log, Exhibit 17. Every weekday the defendant is in town, she sets the alarm before she leaves the house. Every day. Monday. Tuesday. Wednesday. Thursday. Friday. The first day—*the only day*—the defendant didn't set the alarm was the day a man snuck into her house to kill her husband. That's not a mistake. That's murder.

This version addresses the defendant's argument head on. It gets into the details of the exhibit. It uses rhetoric to make the point more compelling. And it tells the jury what inferences to draw from the facts: The defendant's decision to disable the alarm proves her complicity.

Argument often takes longer than summary. That means we have to be more judicious about which points we argue. It is better to use fewer facts but use them convincingly. It is better to make fewer arguments but make them compelling. This is why attorneys must focus their preparation on what the best pieces of evidence are to prove specific points. Sometimes it's a quote. Sometimes it's an exhibit. Sometimes it's a demonstrative exhibit created to make that very point.

We can also be efficient. Some points can be addressed quickly:

> The defense expert said the fingerprints might not be a match. But that expert has never tested the fingerprints. Never even seen the fingerprints. The only expert who actually did the tests told you the defendant's prints are a match.

8.3 Structure

If the most common mistake we see in closing argument is summarizing instead of arguing, the second most common mistake we see is a lack of organization in the closing. The attorney stands up and just starts arguing. Even if all the arguments are good, the jury will often still be confused. The closing needs a clear structure: a beginning, a middle, and an end. It needs a roadmap: a set of directions to the jury about where you are now and where you are going.

The best structure for a closing argument is (1) introduction, (2) the law, (3) roadmap, (4) argument, and (5) finale.

8.3.1 Introduction

Just as you did with your opening statement, the closing argument begins with a formality. You can say "May I proceed?" or "May it please the Court?" We recommend using the same phrase used by your teammate who performed the opening statement. Pause before—and after—delivering the formality. That shows your poise, builds anticipation for your closing, and lets everyone know that the formality isn't the real start of the show.

The beginning of a closing argument needs to accomplish two things. One, you need to grab the jury's attention. Two, you need to repeat your theme. Those two things must connect: *You have to grab the jury's attention in a way that relates to your theme.*

There are a lot of ways to grab the jury's attention at the start of a closing argument. For this section, we will use several high-scoring examples from the 2013 college Mock Trial case, *Allen v. Neptune*. Lee Allen paid Neptune Underwater Expeditions to take him scuba diving. When he died during the deepest dive—to 170 feet—his wife sued the company for recklessly causing his death.

The simplest effective way to start a closing is with a few sentences that build to your theme. Here is a plaintiff example using the theme, "The defendant saw the signs—and looked the other way."

> The defendant saw the signs. At 70 feet, they saw Lee Allen struggle. At 80 feet, they saw him fall behind the group. At 100 feet, they saw him signal that he couldn't breathe. They saw all the signs that Lee Allen wasn't ready for 170 feet. But they let

> him dive because they didn't want to refund his money. Members of the jury, Lee Allen is dead because the defendant saw the signs—and looked the other way.

This introduction reminds the jury of the warnings the defendant saw—Lee struggling at shallower depths—that should have alerted them to the fact that Lee was not ready for greater depths. Then it attacks the defendant for allowing him to dive anyway. This comparison is simply an illustration of the theme: "The defendant saw the signs—and looked the other way." Instead of using *facts* from trial to build to your theme, you can use *analogies* to build to your theme. Here is an introduction using the theme, "They crossed the line."

> The defendant crossed the line. Members of the jury, there's a reason we have limits. You can't drive a car if your blood alcohol concentration is above a 0.08. You can't gamble in a casino until you're 21. If you want to ride the roller coaster, you have to be this tall. These limits, these lines, they exist for our safety. But today you heard about a company that ignored the limits. They knew the limit for recreational divers was 130 feet. They knew Lee Allen shouldn't be going deeper. Lee Allen lost his life . . . because the defendant crossed the line.

None of the facts that start the closing argument here are facts from trial. They are commonly known facts about the world: lines that get drawn about who can drive a car, who can gamble, who can ride the ride. Instead of proving that the defendant crossed the line, this rhetoric emphasizes why we have lines. In this example, the plaintiff was confident it could prove the defendant crossed the line—the industry standard that requires amateur divers not to dive deeper than 130 feet. So the plaintiff focused its introduction on explaining why that line is important.

Let's look at one more introduction that builds to the theme; in this case, "Profits over people."

> Why?
>
> Why did the defendant allow a man who had struggled at 100 feet . . . to dive to 170? Why did the defendant allow a man who struggled at amateur depths . . . to go where only certified professionals should go? It wasn't safety. It was money. If the defendant had stopped Lee Allen from diving, if they said, "I'm sorry, you're just not ready," they would have had to return his 10 thousand dollars. That's why we are here. Because the defendant put profits over people.

This introduction starts with the rhetorical questions. The single-word first question—"Why?"—grabs attention. The jurors do not know exactly what you are asking, which makes them curious. The next question clarifies what you are asking: "Why did the defendant allow a man who had struggled at 100 feet . . . to dive to 170?" Questions force the jury to think, to try to answer the question. If you phrase the question right, it will often lead the jury to the answer you want before you say it. And if the jury thinks your answer is *their* answer, it will be very persuasive.

Here, the ultimate answer to this series of questions is the theme. This example is similar to the first two, where we used facts to build the theme, except here we use rhetorical questions to build to the theme.

Notice how you can place the theme in different spots. In one example, the theme acted as a bookend. The introduction starts and ends with "they crossed the line." In the first example, the theme is cut in half. The first sentence is the first half of the theme: "The defendant saw the signs." The last sentence repeats that first half and then completes the theme: "The defendant saw the signs—and looked the other way." And in the other example, the theme was not introduced until the last line of the introduction: "They put profits over people." Any of these approaches can work well. It just depends on what you want to emphasize and how many times you want to say the theme.

Other creative ways can be used to start your closing argument. You can start with a word that grabs attention (such as, "Why?" in the example above). Here is another introduction that uses a single word to build to the theme, "They were supposed to be the professionals."

> Seven.
>
> Seven times the defendant's CEO used the expression "personal responsibility." As if it were Lee Allen's fault for going to a depth he wasn't ready to face. Funny. Because that phrase—"personal responsibility"—was nowhere to be found in their brochure. There the defendant said things like, "*We* are professionals." "*We* will keep you safe." "*We* will make sure you are ready before you get in the water." The defendant was the one that was supposed to be responsible. Because they were supposed to be the professionals.

The numerical reference to "seven times" was adjusted, depending on how often the CEO used the phrase. And obviously this approach only works if you know what your opponent will say—or if you are willing to improvise the introduction to your closing.

You can start your closing with a moment from trial. The next example builds to the theme, "The defendant gambled with a man's life."

Think back to our cross-examination of the defendant's CEO. My colleague, Laureen Bousmail, asked him, "You let a man who had struggled at shallower depths dive to professional depths?" The defendant's answer? "I figured he was probably ready." Probably ready. We are talking a man's safety. We are talking about a man's life. "Probably" isn't good enough. That's why we are here. That's why Andy Allen no longer has a husband. The defendant gambled with a man's life.

Starting with a specific moment from trial can be a very powerful introduction. It grabs attention because it is dramatic and specific. When done well, it resonates with the jury because they saw this moment happen right in front of them. Hopefully they felt the same emotion you did. In this instance, if the jury found that "probably" answer troubling, then they will feel a connection with you and your argument.

Can you script this introduction ahead of time? It depends. If the word "probably" is used in the witness's statement, then yes. You can always get that answer. If not, then this would be an introduction you improvise.

This chapter has illustrated a half dozen different ways to start your closing, but there are many more. Be creative. Closing argument, and especially the introduction, gives you lots of room to be creative in selecting the most powerful way of grabbing the jury's attention. There are only two unbreakable rules for the introduction. It has to grab attention. It has to use your theme.

Here are some things to avoid during your introduction.

Do not retell the same story that began your opening statement. The jury has heard it before. They will be bored hearing the same story again.

Do not summarize all your best facts. This is rarely exciting. And even if you manage to make it exciting, you have stolen your own thunder: when you repeat those facts later in closing, the jury will be bored.

Do not start with a philosophical quotation from history. *Winston Churchill once said* . . . Real life juries find that boring, and Mock Trial juries do, too.

Do not start with a personal anecdote. This case is about your client, not you.

WAR STORY

We once saw a competitor start his closing argument with a two-minute story about his friend's recent romantic breakup. The three scoring judges gave the closing a 10 . . . combined.

One final note: When should your introduction simply be your theme and nothing else? In other words, when would it be wise to say your theme and then move immediately to the next section of your closing argument?

There are two circumstances when that approach makes sense. First, in some high school competitions you have very little time for closing argument. For example, in the High School Mock Trial National Championship Tournament, each side has only five minutes for closing argument. That is not enough time to thoroughly argue what are often complex cases. This means we must look for shortcuts. Starting with your theme and then segueing immediately to the law is a great time saver.

> May it please the Court?
>
> Lee Allen is dead because the defendant put profits over people.
>
> As the plaintiff, we had the burden of proof . . .

The second instance is when your legal paragraph is complicated and long. In that instance, you may want to repeat your theme and turn immediately to the legal discussion. This tactic works particularly well when the theme relates directly to the legal discussion. For example, in the Neptune scuba diving case, Professor Bernstein's UC Irvine team used the defense theory of contributory recklessness, arguing that the plaintiff died because he recklessly chose to ignore instructions and dive deeper than the rest of the group. The theme was, "If you are reckless, you cannot recover," which means if a plaintiff himself is reckless he cannot recover monetary damages (i.e., win) in a lawsuit. The team began its defense closing like this:

> May I proceed?
>
> If you are reckless, you cannot recover.
>
> At the beginning of this trial, we told you that if the plaintiff was contributorily reckless, the law requires a verdict in favor of the defense. But what does that mean, contributory recklessness?
>
> . . .

Because the legal discussion was lengthy and related to the theme, it made sense to the start the closing with a one-sentence introduction.

In all other situations, we recommend an introduction that includes more than just the theme itself. This is an opportunity to persuade and engage. Exciting, creative rhetoric can capture the jury's attention. If you still have the jury's attention after the introduction, you may be able to maintain it the entire time.

8.3.2 Law

Next, summarize the law. This includes (1) the burden; (2) the charge, claim, or defense; and usually (3) a summary of the elements of the charge, claim, or defense.

For example, the plaintiff's law paragraph could look like this:

> As the plaintiff, we had the burden of proof. We had to prove our claim of recklessness by a preponderance of the evidence. Which means we had to prove four elements were more likely true than not. First, the defendant owed Lee Allen a duty of care. Second, they breached that duty by acting recklessly. Third, Lee Allen suffered injury. Fourth, the defendant's recklessness caused Lee Allen's death.

Sometimes it can be useful to identify the elements no longer at issue. The plaintiff's law paragraph could look like this:

> As the plaintiff, we had the burden of proof. We had to prove our claim of recklessness by a preponderance of the evidence. Which means we had to prove four elements were more likely true than not. One of those elements is undisputed. We know Lee Allen suffered injury because he died. That means we have three elements left to prove. First, the defendant owed Lee Allen a duty of care. Second, they breached that duty by acting recklessly. Third, the defendant's recklessness caused Lee Allen's death.

Here is how that might look for the defense in the same case:

> As the defense, we had no burden of proof. The plaintiff did. They had to prove every element of their claim was more likely true than not. But there were two elements the plaintiff could not prove. Recklessness and causation.

Notice how different the defense legal section is. The plaintiff legal section mentioned the burden of proof. The defense legal section emphasized it. The plaintiff legal section gave the technical term—"preponderance of the evidence"—and then defined it. The defense legal section only gives the colloquial expression, "more likely than not," because the plaintiff has already done the technical work. The plaintiff legal section lists every element. The defense only states the elements it intends to challenge.

In a criminal case, the defense will often want to explain that the prosecution has a heavy burden of proof. There are many ways to do that, but here are three examples:

> As the defense, we had no burden of proof. The prosecution did. They had to meet the highest burden in our justice system. Proof beyond a reasonable doubt.

> The prosecution had the burden of proof. They had to meet the highest burden in our criminal justice system. Proof beyond a reasonable doubt. What does that mean? If you think it's possible that the defendant hired a hitman to kill her husband, you must find her not guilty. If you think it's likely that the defendant hired a hitman to kill her husband—if you think, "yeah, she probably did it"—you must find her not guilty. The prosecution has to convince you beyond all reasonable doubt.

> The prosecution had the burden. They had to meet the highest burden in our criminal justice system. If someone gets sued in civil, sued for every dollar they own, the other side must prove its case more likely true than not. When the State wants to take a child away from his mother, it must prove its case by clear and convincing evidence. The burden in this case is even higher. The prosecution must prove its case beyond a reasonable doubt.

Be careful to avoid misstating the law. You cannot assign a percentage to "beyond a reasonable doubt." You cannot say "95 percent" or cite some other number. In real court, that is objectionable and might turn your trial into a "mistrial" (meaning the trial is ended and you have to start over from scratch with a new jury).

Similarly, do not take on a greater burden than necessary. As the prosecution, you do not need to prove the defendant is guilty "beyond all doubt." So don't claim that you did. As the defense, you do not need to prove that your criminal defendant is "innocent." You just need to show there is reasonable doubt in the State's case. Some judges will score you lower when it sounds like you raised your own burden.

Notice that in the examples above, we identify the elements of the claim. But we do not, as many teams do, define each of the elements in the legal section. Offering one legal definition after another will bore and likely confuse the jury. The concepts will feel abstract and will quickly be forgotten. Instead, save your definition of each element until the point in your closing when you tell the jury how you proved (or challenged) that element.

8.3.3 Roadmap

This is the most forgotten ingredient in closing arguments. Tell the jury what structure you used to prove your case. It does not need to be more than a few sentences. It should be the same structure you used in your opening statement.

> As we told you in our opening statement, we proved the defendant's recklessness with three facts. First, they knew Lee Allen was struggling at shallower depths. Second, they knew this dive was far more dangerous. And third, they let him dive anyway. Let's discuss those facts one at a time.

Often your subpoints will simply be the elements you have to prove. If so, that makes the roadmap easy. If we continue the legal section discussed earlier in this chapter, it might look like this:

> As the plaintiff, we had the burden of proof. We had to prove our claim of recklessness by a preponderance of the evidence. Which means we had to prove four elements were more likely true than not. One of those elements is undisputed. We know Lee Allen suffered injury because he died. That means we have three elements left to prove. First, the defendant owed Lee Allen a duty of care. Second, they breached that duty by acting recklessly. Third, the defendant's recklessness caused Lee Allen's death. [roadmap] Let's discuss those elements one at a time.

8.3.4 Argument

Your argument section should follow the points in your roadmap. Each individual point should be self-contained. Don't talk about point number two until you have completed point number one. Use transitions between each point: "Now let's talk about our second fact, ____".

Beyond that, there aren't many rules for the argument. This is where you can be creative. What is the best way to argue each point? How can you keep the jury engaged? Here are some tips.

Don't overstate the evidence. Judges will score you down if they think you are exaggerating.

Use your theme. Teams often say their theme only twice in the closing argument—once at the beginning and then once at the end. In a five-minute closing argument, that can be okay. But in a longer closing argument, we recommend using it at least once in the argument section.

Use gems from the trial. If judges hear specific quotes from trial, they will know you are incorporating and improvising. This does not require rewriting entire sections of your closing. It can be as simple as swapping or adding a few words to the points you already planned to make.

Explain the law. In the "Law" section of this chapter, we recommended *not* going into the details of the elements. But later in the closing, when you begin to prove a particular element, explain how that element works.

> That brings me to point number two. The defendant was negligent. As the judge will explain, negligence is a failure to act with ordinary care. A failure to do what a reasonably careful person would do in similar circumstances.

> Connect the law to your facts.

> That brings me to point number two. The defendant was negligent. As the judge will explain, negligence is a failure to act with ordinary care. A failure to do what a reasonably careful person would do in similar circumstances. Here, the circumstances involved a car approaching a red light with a pedestrian in the crosswalk. A reasonably careful person would see the red light and slow down. A reasonably careful person would see the red light and stop. A reasonably careful person would not hit a pedestrian in the crosswalk.

As the plaintiff or prosecution, remind the jury when you have proven your elements. It will make the jury feel like you are marching toward meeting your burden of proof.

> That brings me to point number two. The defendant was negligent. As the judge will explain, negligence is a failure to act with ordinary care. A failure to do what a reasonably careful person would do in similar circumstances. Here, the circumstances involved a car approaching a red light with a pedestrian in the crosswalk. A reasonably careful person would see the red light and slow down. A reasonably careful person would see the red light and stop. A reasonably careful person would not hit a pedestrian in the crosswalk. **We've proven the second element of our claim, that the defendant was negligent.**

As the Defense, remind the jury when you have demonstrated that the prosecution failed to meet its burden—and remind them of the consequences.

> That brings me to the second element the prosecution failed to prove. That Ms. Williams was the one who caused Mr. Johnson's death. The law says that when you have more than one explanation

> for the facts, one pointing to guilt and one pointing to innocence, you must choose the one pointing to innocence. In their closing argument, the prosecution said, "Ms. Williams must have been the shooter. She was at the office. She disliked Mr. Johnson. Her prints were on the gun." But on cross-examination, we learned every one of those facts was also true of Doug Fiero, the suspect the police chose not to arrest. He was there that day. He hated Mr. Johnson. Two of his fingerprints were on that gun. The prosecution failed to prove that Ms. Williams was the killer because they failed to prove that Mr. Fiero *wasn't* the killer. That's reasonable doubt. For that reason alone, the law requires a verdict of not guilty.

Use visual aids. Hold up exhibits. Walk over to the demonstrative aid on your easel. Pick up your legal pad to reference a quote from trial. The jury will be more engaged if it has different things to look at.

Humanize your client/victim. Many teams that remember to do this in opening statement forget to do it in closing argument. Make sure there is at least a moment where you create empathy for your client or victim. It can be verbal, reminding the jury of facts that make them sympathetic. It can be nonverbal, as you walk to your client and place a hand on their shoulder.

Attack witness credibility. If your opponent is relying on evidence from their own witnesses, find ways to undermine their credibility. You can attack using facts elicited during cross (bias, inability to see the events, bad investigation, etc.) or the witness's performance on cross-examination ("The witness wouldn't give us a straight answer").

Don't give "book reports." We often see attorneys summarize the witnesses and their testimony:

> First, the prosecution called Jim Smith. But he admitted he wasn't wearing his glasses. Then they called Officer Guerillo. But she admitted she hates my client. Finally, they called Dr. Park. This is the same doctor who was once suspended for mishandling evidence.

This is lazy argumentation. It's just a list of witnesses and their flaws. There is no real analysis or explanation of how these items fit into your overall argument. Instead, place those witness attacks in the portions of the closing where you are trying to attack certain evidence presented by those witnesses.

This is especially true for attacking witness credibility. Don't just say, without context, that a witness is biased or that a witness could not see clearly. Explain what testimony you are challenging and *then* argue the witness's lack credibility. For example:

> The photos tell us the defendant caused this accident. Our eyewitness told you the defendant caused this accident. The only person who *doesn't* say the defendant caused this accident is Jim Smith. A man who wasn't wearing his glasses.

Prove all your elements. If you are the prosecution or plaintiff, make sure to demonstrate that you have met your burden on each element. That includes proving that the events of the case occurred within the jurisdiction, if it has not been stipulated. If the case is not bifurcated, it includes damages. You will want to ask for a specific monetary sum of damages.

In real life, jury instructions are read by the judge to the jury either at the close of evidence and before closing argument, or after closing argument immediately before deliberation. The instructions will directly address the elements of the claims or charges. Whether to reference jury instructions depends on how much time you are allotted for closing. If you have time, it can add a bit of realism and enhance your score. But, if you are pressed for time, it's not a requirement. If you do plan to address the jury instructions, you may wish to ask the presiding judge in pretrial if you may assume the instructions have been constructively read to the jury before closing arguments.

Some case packets include written jury instructions. If your packet does, you can quote them in closing. If the practice in the local jurisdiction is that instructions are read after closings, you can say the judge *will* instruct you. . . . If the local practice is that instructions are read before closings, prior to starting your speech you should ask the judge if you may presume that instructions have already been read.

Finally, use rhetorical devices. The closing argument should be fun and exciting for the jury, and that starts with good writing. Consider all the things your English teacher is always talking about: repetition, alliteration, parallel structure, action verbs, vivid language, and short sentences. And then forget the formal things your English teacher is always telling you: write in complete sentences; never end a sentence with a preposition. Instead, write like you speak. Good speaking starts with good writing.

8.3.5 Finale

Once you have proven your case, it's time to land the plane. A good finale includes one argument, the theme, and a "prayer." The prayer is the legal phrase for the result you are seeking (e.g., a verdict of not guilty).

The argument should be short, ideally no more than a few sentences. It should summarize your case and connect to your theme. Beyond that, be creative. You can attack the argument the jury is about to hear from the other side after you conclude. You can remind the jury of the injury or loss suffered by the victim. You can acknowledge a weakness in your case and then spin it in your favor. Look for rhetoric that will motivate the juror. Avoid repeating arguments already made earlier in your closing.

Here are two plaintiff finales that scored well in the *Neptune* scuba case. In each example, the theme is highlighted. Notice that you can place the theme right before or right after the prayer.

> We ask you to put this company on notice. Tell them they cannot write the rules, and then break them. Tell them they cannot promise to keep people safe and abandon them 170 feet underwater. Tell them that they cannot put money before safety. Tell them, they're liable. *Because they knew the risks. They just didn't care.*

> Members of the Jury, the Allens were not experts. That's why they hired the defendant in the first place. They trusted the defendant to ensure their safety. But the defendant betrayed that trust. They saw Lee fall behind. They saw Lee clutch his chest. They saw Lee using too much oxygen. *They saw all the warning signs. And they did nothing.* We ask you to find the defendant liable for Lee Allen's death.

When you are requesting the verdict, use the right terminology. As the prosecution, you are asking the jury to find the defendant guilty. As the plaintiff, you are asking the jury to find the defendant liable. As the defense in a criminal case, you are asking the jury to find the defendant not guilty. Do not ask for a verdict of innocence. That is not the standard and not something you need to prove. As the defense in a civil case, you are asking the jury to find the defendant not liable.

8.4 Addressing Bad Facts

Do not run from unfavorable facts. There is a tendency to think that if we ignore the facts that appear to hurt our position, the jury might forget them. No. This just gives your opponent the chance to slam you for not addressing the bad facts and gives the jury the impression that we have no response.

You have several ways to deal with unfavorable facts, and you should choose the approach that works best under the circumstances. You might be able to dispute whether the facts are actually true. You can argue that the fact is not actually bad for your position. You can acknowledge the bad fact, but find a way to justify it, minimize it, or contextualize it. You can acknowledge the bad fact, and then explain why other facts are more important.

WAR STORY

Professor Bernstein says the best job of addressing bad facts he has ever seen came in 2005 from Lawrence Hilton, a student at Furman University. "We represented the prosecution and challenged the defense to explain one of the key facts making the defendant look guilty. Lawrence Hilton closed for the defense. He finished his closing with about 90 seconds to spare and began to walk back to his counsel table. Then he stopped, paused, spun, and said, 'I almost forgot! The prosecution challenged me to answer a question. Challenged me to explain the evidence. Maybe they forgot. They have the burden. Not us. We didn't have to call any witnesses. Or present any evidence. I don't have to answer their question . . . [long pause] . . . . But I will.' And he did. It was devastating and brilliant."

8.5 Responding

The best closing arguments are responsive to the trial. They incorporate witness testimony and the opponent's arguments. They address the opponent's theme. And they do so in a manner that makes it obvious to judges that you are adapting to what happened in this particular trial.

That last sentiment is key. If you reference your own witness's testimony, or facts you established on cross-examination, that does not feel especially responsive. Everyone knows you planned to elicit that testimony. Judges want to see adaptation, and they will usually reward it in their scores. So that requires using the opponent's material against them: things they said in opening statement or closing argument, unusual answers their witnesses gave on cross-examination, or arguments they presented during their directs or crosses. We recommend quoting the exact language, at least occasionally, to make it obvious to the judges that you are responding to what happened in trial rather than merely reciting your prewritten closing.

If your opponent objected to evidence and the objection was overruled, you can point out that they tried to keep the jury from learning that information. If your opponent objected to evidence you planned to present, and it is sustained, remove it from your physical outline or mental checklist so you don't get caught overstating the evidence.

You should always address the opponent's theme in your closing argument. You can explain why the concept is wrong, why they failed to prove it, why it is irrelevant, etc. You can use their theme against them: "The prosecution said this was a case about revenge. But let's talk about another person who had a motive for revenge. . . ." You can twist their theme to your advantage: "The defense has focused all trial on the missing body. They said it over and over. No body, no proof. But who was the one person capable of getting rid of the body? Who was the one person with no alibi right after Susan went missing?"

Sometimes the prosecution/plaintiff will wait until rebuttal to attack the defense's theme and theory. We recommend addressing it in your main closing argument. If you do it well, it will hurt the defense closing by making it sound less persuasive. And if you do it right before the other side gives their argument, it can be particularly devastating.

8.6 Things You May Not Say in Closing Argument

Don't ask the jury to "put yourselves in the victim's shoes" or imagine "how you would feel in that situation." This is called the Golden Rule. The reason we are not allowed to ask jurors to put themselves in the shoes of the parties or victims is that it is *too* persuasive. The law fears that jurors will not be rational. How can a person rationally evaluate whether a driver was negligent if the juror imagines it was *her* daughter who was run over? For the same reason we would never let the victim's mother on the jury, we cannot ask jurors to imagine how that person feels. In competitions where objections are allowed in closing argument, the opponent would be able to interrupt your closing and likely sustain an objection. In the competitions where objections are not permitted during closing argument (which is most competitions), the judges will often give you a lower score for violating the Golden Rule.

Don't ever—EVER—quote something a witness said during trial unless you're positive it came out the way you are quoting it. Sometimes attorneys forget to ask questions. Sometimes witnesses deviate from their witness statements and get away with it. Sometimes judges make bad rulings and keep out key testimony. What you expected to happen during trial is not necessarily what happened. Teams need to have a checklist of all evidence that their closer intends to offer during closing. The attorney doing the closing must be the best listener during the trial. Their teammates need to help them by checking to see if all the expected evidence is admitted. If your opponent refers to evidence that was never admitted, call them out during your closing or rebuttal.

In a criminal case, don't "shift the burden." As the prosecution, you always have the burden of proof. The defense does not have to "disprove" any elements. In real life, saying or implying that a criminal defendant has a burden will result in a mistrial (automatic dismissal of the case). In Mock Trial, any judge who notices will score you down.

This does not leave prosecutors unable to attack preposterous defense theories or testimony. Just be careful about how you phrase it. Make it clear you are not shifting the burden.

> The defense told you the defendant couldn't have committed the murder because he was with his mother that night. Now, of course, we have the burden of proof. But when the defense tells you something, you get to evaluate whether it's true, just like any other piece of evidence. And there is absolutely no support for the defendant's alibi. Even his mother doesn't remember seeing him that night.

Similarly, in a criminal case, do not criticize or even comment on the defendant not testifying. The Fifth Amendment allows criminal defendants not to testify. Prosecutors may not argue that the defendant must be guilty because she didn't testify or make any similar arguments.

8.7 Rebuttal

In almost every competition, the prosecution or plaintiff is given a chance to respond to the defense's closing argument. This speech is called "rebuttal."

Rebuttal must be short. Do not address every argument made by opposing counsel. That would be exhausting for the jury, and it would make it seem like every argument was equally important. Choose one or two of the opponent's strongest arguments and attack them. It is better to rebut one point effectively than cram in multiple issues and race through them. We generally recommend rebuttals be 60 seconds or less.

A note about timing: In some competitions, rebuttals have a specific amount of time reserved. For example, you might automatically have one minute. In other competitions, your rebuttal time is whatever remains after your first closing argument is done. For example, if you have nine minutes for closing and you use eight, you will have one minute for rebuttal. Check your competition's rules—some competitions require rebuttal to be reserved before beginning closing argument or even during the pretrial conference.

Make sure you save enough time for rebuttal. Even if you lose some great content from the main close, it's worth it. Many judges will score you down for not giving a rebuttal, no matter how excellent the closing.

Rebuttal should be responsive. This is not a time to give a canned speech that merely recites your theory and theme. Many judges will recognize that you are not actually rebutting the defense closing and score you down accordingly. Listen to the opponent's closing argument. Find one or two arguments that you want to attack. Then focus on those arguments. Ideally, you can use the defense's exact words so the jury knows you are responding—and so they know your rebuttal was not prewritten.

Rebuttal should focus only on the most important issues. In the heat of the moment, it is easy to get caught up on something that feels important to *you*—opposing counsel misstating a witness's testimony, opposing counsel omitting a portion of the law. In some trials, those issues might be the most important issues. But ask yourself: What are my opponent's main arguments? What are their biggest strengths? What are the judges thinking right now? Then hit those issues.

Notwithstanding the advice to not be scripted, do have your last line of rebuttal planned out. This is the last thing said during trial. Use your responsive points to lead into it, but have it ready. And be careful to not run out of time before you say it.

8.8 Performance

Opening statement requires restraint. You are not allowed to argue, and the jury does not know you yet. Direct examination requires deference. You do not want to steal attention from your witness. Cross-examination requires force. If you do not grab control, the witness will.

Closing argument, on the other hand, allows you the full spectrum of performance. You can tell a soaring story as you would in opening statement. You can perform with force as you would on cross-examination. You can dial it back for quieter moments as you would on direct examination. You can show empathy, indignation, sorrow, confusion, sarcasm, and conviction. It is your chance to shine. Seize the opportunity!

The most important thing to remember about delivery during a closing argument is that you must *vary* your delivery. No matter how powerful, loud, and impassioned you are, it will become monotonous after a while. No matter how slow, calm, and dramatic your delivery, it will become monotonous after a while. Get loud, get soft, get slow, get fast, use silence for emphasis—vary your delivery.

Because closing arguments are often longer than opening statements, you especially need to incorporate movement. If you stand in one place the entire time, the jury may grow bored. Find opportunities to move. Move for transitions. Move toward the witness stand when recounting testimony. Move for emphasis. Move toward your counsel table when explaining your burden of proof. As much as the presiding judge will allow, use the whole courtroom. But don't move so much that it is distracting. Be still for some portions of the closing to let the words sink in.

9

Before the Judges Arrive

As soon as you are within earshot or the line of sight of the judges, you are on stage. Accordingly, there is a lot you will want to accomplish before the judges walk in the room. You will want to set up your materials, including your easel and enlargements, determine the spacing to perform in this particular room, and confer with opposing counsel to get the details you need for trial.

Sometimes you have almost no time in the courtroom before the judges arrive. This happens when the room is unlocked for everyone at the same time and the judges enter when you do. Sometimes you have way too much time before the judges arrive.

No matter how much time you have, these guidelines will help you use that time wisely. If you're in a hurry, the list will help you prioritize. If you've got lots of time, it can help you fill it so you get less anxious waiting for the judges to arrive.

9.1 Have a Plan

Know what you are going to do before you arrive in the courtroom. Know who will confer with opposing counsel. This should usually be one of your attorneys. Know who oversees setting up the counsel table and easel. This should usually be a timekeeper or witness because, as discussed later in the chapter, your lawyers will probably have other responsibilities here.

Your case materials should be stored in an exhibit box, separated by labeled folders. This way you can quickly remove the exact items you want. Do not use a binder. It takes too long to open and shut the rings every time you want a document.

9.2 Arrive Early

Arrive early. You don't want to be rushed. If it can be avoided, you don't want the judges to walk in while you are setting up. We recommend getting to your courtroom at least 30 minutes, and ideally 45 minutes, before the trial is supposed to start.

If you arrive before the other team, you might get to claim the better counsel table. However, determine whether the local jurisdiction has a protocol for seating arrangements. For example, in some locales the party with the burden of proof sits closest to the jury box. If there is such a local protocol, follow it. But not all Mock Trial courtrooms are set up the same way. If there is no jury box, or if the room has an unusual configuration, you may have a choice of counsel tables by arriving first.

9.3 Room Setup

Start by setting up your counsel table.

Make sure there are enough chairs for the attorneys and any person who is seated at your counsel table as a party representative. In a civil case, the plaintiff sits at the counsel table. In any kind of case, the defendant sits at the counsel table.

Each attorney should have a pad, a pen, and water. The pads should match. The water bottles should match. It subconsciously tells the judges, "We are a team."

There are different ways to arrange the various documents you will need during trial: affidavits, stipulations, and exhibits. Some successful teams like to place a copy of every document neatly across their counsel table. The advantage is that every document is always within arm's reach. The disadvantage is that the counsel table can look cluttered, which is not a great look in front of the judges.

Other successful teams like to place on the counsel table only the documents they expect to use during the trial. They might swap documents at the end of the prosecution case-in-chief, replacing the affidavits of prosecution witnesses (who have already testified) with affidavits of defense witnesses (who are about to testify). The advantage is that the counsel table looks cleaner. The disadvantage is that you might have to find a document during trial by reaching for the exhibit box at your feet or behind you. We tend to prefer this approach because the counsel table looks more professional, but there is no right or wrong answer here. Be prepared to alter your plan if you get a small or oddly shaped counsel table.

Set up your easel. Make sure the legs are locked. We cannot tell you how many times we have seen easels collapse midtrial because they were not set up properly. If you plan to use the easel in the well of the courtroom, set it up off to the side of the courtroom, but as close as possible. If you plan to use the easel in a less obtrusive place—say, right next to the witness stand—then you can probably just place it there before trial.

WAR STORY

We once watched an attorney admit an exhibit and then ask to publish it to the jury. But he then set up the enlargement so that the ***back*** was facing the jury. All they could see was blank cardboard. The jury and judge looked at each other in confusion. Why would he do that? When the attorney was done setting it up, he asked the judge, "Your Honor, would you ask the jury if they can see the enlargement?" The judge, holding back laughter, asked the jury. "We can see the back of it," said a juror.

Do not place your enlargements on the easel before trial. The judges should not be able to see them until the proper foundation is laid, and you don't want them getting knocked over. Place them nearby, with the backs turned around so no one can see the content until you reveal it.

9.4 Sound Check

Every courtroom has different acoustics. You need to test your volume at various spots in the courtroom to make sure judges will hear you properly. We call this a sound check.

Most teams don't do a sound check, and most teams who do a sound check do it wrong. They have teammates or coaches, who are standing about the room, say, "Yeah, that sounds good" or "Maybe a little louder." But it doesn't matter if people in the gallery can hear you. *You need to have people sitting where the judges are going to sit.* It will often sound different in those spaces, depending on the acoustics, the distance from where people are speaking, and whether there are air conditioners nearby.

Put one person in the presiding judge's seat and at least one in the jury box. Each witness needs to take the stand. Each attorney needs to stand wherever they intend to stand and perform during trial. The team members on the bench and in the jury box can tell them whether they are loud enough.

Don't just tell your teammates to be louder or softer. Make them actually continue speaking until they get a thumbs up. This will help them remember how it felt to do it correctly.

WAR STORY

In one Memphis courthouse, the courtrooms have the state seal on the floor. The local custom is not to stand on the seal. In fact, if someone speaks while standing on the seal, the courtroom acoustics make it almost impossible to hear them. We have seen teams that forget to do a sound check suddenly go mute during a trial.

9.5 Practice Choreography

Courtrooms come in many layouts and sizes. This will affect where attorneys stand for direct and cross-examination and where you place your demonstrative aids and easel. When you get to your courtroom, figure out the best placements. Make these decisions as a team because uniformity is important. All attorneys should conduct direct examination from the same spot. All attorneys should conduct cross-examination from the same spot.

The choreography you practiced for your opening or closing may also require adjustment when you see the courtroom for your trial. If the space is very large, your movements will need to be bigger. If the space is very small, your movements will need to be smaller. If the space has an unusual design, you will need to figure out where to stand for various portions of your speech. Many attorneys will feel more comfortable if they walk through the physical steps in their speech before trial. Do it silently because you never know when the other team will enter the courtroom.

9.6 Confer with Opponent

Always greet your opponent before trial. Shake hands. Smile. Wish them luck. It's professional and appropriate.

You may have procedural or substantive issues to discuss with them as well. What are the genders of your witnesses? Where should the timekeepers sit? Do we want to agree that certain exhibits are admissible?

If enlargements are not approved during a separate captains meeting, address those. The goal is to get anything you can out of the way so disputes do not break up your flow—or count against your time limits—when trial starts.

Be friendly. Some teams think the best way to gain an edge is to be mean, rude, or standoffish with the opponent. They think it's intimidating. Not only is it unprofessional, but in our experience it's also ineffective. Friendliness shows confidence and comfort. Nothing is more intimidating than an opponent who seems confident and comfortable.

WAR STORY

In Professor Bernstein's first year competing in Mock Trial, his UC Berkeley team was facing College of the Holy Cross in the third round of Nationals. The captains of both teams were chatting, and the Holy Cross captains were especially loose and friendly. When it came time to do the coin flip for sides, the Holy Cross captain said, "Oh, no need for a flip. You can just pick your side." Professor Bernstein recalls his reaction even 20 years later: "They let us choose our side?!? Now, *that* was intimidating!"

9.7 Huddle

After you have completed everything on your checklist, the team should step outside the courtroom and huddle. Remind everyone of the goals. Make sure everyone is energized and feeling good.

Pet Peeve: It has become trendy for teams to do a yell or cheer or chant during the huddle. While this looks fun, we advise against it. Anything loud disrupts other trials that may have already started. Also, judges could be walking around the corner at any time. A key to maximizing scores is looking like real lawyers. Legal teams do huddle up before a trial. They do not scream.

WAR STORY

Professor Bernstein's college teams were some of the worst offenders of Judge Nelmark's pet peeve against chanting during preround huddles.

9.8 Game On

Walk back into the courtroom and take your seats.

One of the more nerve-racking aspects of Mock Trial is getting to your courtroom and then having to just sit and wait for your judges to arrive. People deal with this tension in different ways—looking over an outline, doodling, singing a song in one's head. Anything silent will work. What you don't want to do is goof around or start a conversation you have to end abruptly when the judges walk in. Plus, judges are known to peer in the windows to make sure they are in the right place before they open the door and announce themselves.

10

Pretrial Matters

This chapter focuses on how to score points from the moment the judges enter the room. Opening statement is the first time we get to tell the jury about our case, but it is not the first time we are being evaluated.

As soon as the judges enter the room, they begin forming impressions about the teams. *Who seems more prepared? Who seems more organized? Who seems more confident?* Even though the events before opening statement generally aren't scored, they create the judges' first impressions—which means they affect all the scores in the trial. Teams should practice their pretrial presentation.

WAR STORY

When Professor Bernstein coached UC Irvine, he sometimes had four or five teams competing at once. Sometimes he would watch pretrial and decide to switch courtrooms to watch a more competitive trial. Even though pretrial isn't scored, you can often tell who is going to win just by seeing how teams introduce themselves. Practice your pretrial!

10.1 Stand

This part is easy. When the judges enter the room, stand up. This includes every team member, coach, and spectator. This is how we show respect for judges in American courts. Some judges don't care about this, but some judges really care. Don't take any chances. The judge will tell you when you can be seated.

Each time you speak to the presiding judge throughout trial, you should stand. This is true even when your statements are brief—even if you are just saying, "No objection, Your Honor." This is true even when the judge gives you permission to sit. When given a choice, stand. It helps your performance. The only time to remain seated when speaking is when the tournament rules prohibit standing or the presiding judge tells you to sit (as opposed to giving you the option to sit). In real life, some jurisdictions do prohibit standing during witness examination, so in some tournaments judges may insist on sitting while conducting directs and crosses.

10.2 Appearances

"Appearances" is the legal term for introducing yourself to the judge. Before you do anything else, all your attorneys should introduce themselves.

When the judge asks if there are pretrial matters, try to be the first one to respond. "Yes, Your Honor. May we make appearances?" It lets you take charge and set the tone. Don't, however, jump out of your chair so quickly that you look foolish. Just be ready to stand (or remain standing if the judge has not yet told you to sit down) and speak as soon as the judge asks for a response.

If the judge doesn't say anything right away, stand up and ask to make appearances.

Once the judge says yes, each attorney should introduce themselves and their party. "Good evening, Your Honor. Mazamir Yousefi for the State." "Good evening, Your Honor. Andrew Tran for the State."

Pet Peeve: Have your chairs pushed back beforehand so they don't make a screeching sound. That's an awkward way to make a first impression.

In some high school competitions, it is customary for the witnesses to introduce themselves, too. In that case, once your attorneys have all made their appearances, ask, "Your Honor, may our witnesses introduce themselves?" Each witness should state their real name and the witness they are portraying. "My name is Laureen Bousmail and I will be portraying Reggie Rodgers." Some teams emphasize that they are getting into character. "My name is Laureen Bousmail and today I ***am*** Reggie Rodgers." Some teams like to add a few words describing their witness. "My name is Laureen Bousmail and I will be portraying the scuba dive leader, Reggie Rodgers." All these approaches are fine.

If you have had your witnesses introduce themselves, your timekeeper and/or bailiff should also introduce him or herself.

Once you finish appearances, turn to preliminary matters.

10.3 Preliminary Matters

"Preliminary matters" refers to the discussion you have with the presiding judge before opening statements. It is usually procedural. Some judges call it "housekeeping."

Most teams do not do this, but we recommend first giving the judge a very brief summary of the case. It should be a sentence, not a paragraph. "Your Honor, this is a wrongful death action stemming from a scuba diving accident." This is realistic and shows you can summarize the case succinctly. If the judge asks you for the "caption" or "title," it is simply the names of the parties (e.g., *Allen v. Neptune Underwater Expeditions*).

There is no precise recipe for what you should include in the preliminary matters. It depends on the case and what you want to accomplish. But keep your preliminary matters brief. Limit your preliminary matters to no more than four items. If you are going second, don't repeat something the other team has already addressed. If the other team covers everything in your top four, come up with something else. It creates a bad impression if the other team has a nice pretrial dialogue with the judge and you say nothing.

WAR STORY

We once saw an attorney announce that she had eleven preliminary matters. The judge showed a look of horror and said, "Pick your top three."

Here are some things you may want to cover during your preliminary matters.

Exhibit numbers. In most Mock Trial competitions, the exhibits are prenumbered. You may want to clarify with the presiding judge that all exhibits will keep those numbers regardless of the order in which they are introduced at trial. That way judges aren't confused when the first exhibit you introduce is, say, Exhibit 7.

> Your Honor, all exhibits are pre-marked. May they retain their original marking regardless of the order in which they are introduced?

Movement. You will want to know where you are allowed to move and stand during speeches and examination of witnesses. Some teams ask the judge their preference. This is a poor strategy. Many judges will not have a preference, so if instead you ask for a specific outcome—*your preference*—there is a decent chance the judge says yes. Even if you don't have a strong preference, you might induce the judge to go along with something that makes the other team uncomfortable.

> Your Honor, may we have permission to move freely during opening statement, closing argument, and examination of witnesses?

For one, and only one, issue during pretrial, you may make an even stronger statement as to what should take place.

> Your Honor, it is our understanding that in this jurisdiction we are able to move freely about the well during openings and closings. Is that the Court's understanding as well?

Movement will often be the most important thing to you. When it is, exercise this option here. If another issue is more important, save this approach.

Whatever the judge says as far as movement—make sure to do it during the trial. Some allow free movement throughout trial. Some want you to seek permission to ever leave the counsel table. Some will allow you to move freely *except* when you are approaching witnesses. Write down what the judge said so you remember it. It is annoying to a presiding judge who gave you permission to move during pretrial if you still ask during trial. It is even more annoying if they *declined* to give you permission up front and then you forget to ask at the appropriate time.

Sequestration of witnesses. In some competitions you may ask that all witnesses are constructively sequestered. "Sequestration" means they are not present for the opening statement and testimony of other witnesses, and thus they cannot be questioned about those portions of trial. "Constructive" means pretend. In real life, a sequestered witness cannot be present in the courtroom. In Mock Trial, we want everyone to learn and see their teammates perform, so we pretend that the witnesses were not present before they testify. Note that sequestration does not apply to parties (plaintiff, defendant) or a party's designated representative (a real person representing a corporate party, such as a CEO appearing on behalf of her company).

> Your Honor, pursuant to Rule 615 of the Federal Rules of Evidence, we move for the constructive sequestration of all witnesses, except of course the parties themselves.

Be strategic about whether you want witnesses sequestered. For some cases, it is beneficial to have your expert listen to other testimony and comment on it. In other cases, you may not want an opposing witness to have that option. Whatever happens in your particular case, remember it and have your witnesses act accordingly. Witnesses cannot comment on something that occurred when they were constructively sequestered unless that same information is also in their witness statement or the attorney tells them what occurred prior to asking them to comment on it. "Dr. Wright offered her opinion that the shooter was left-handed. Do you believe that is possible?"

Constructive sidebars. In real life, the jury would not hear objection arguments that involve substantive information or that involve a dispute as to whether certainly prejudicial material will be admitted during trial. Either the jury would leave the courtroom and then the judge would speak with the attorneys, or the attorneys would approach the bench so they could discuss the issue outside of the jury's earshot. In Mock Trial, however, we want the jury to hear everything because the jury is scoring the attorneys. So, we ask for constructive sidebars. This allows everyone to pretend the jury does not hear things it should not hear.

> Your Honor, we ask for constructive sidebars—in other words, that we treat all objection arguments as though they are outside the presence of the jury.

If you do not address sidebars during pretrial, you can still bring it up when you are arguing something that would be prejudicial for the jury to hear. "Your Honor, may we be heard in a constructive sidebar?"

Swearing of witnesses. In real life, all witnesses swear an oath when they take the witness stand. In some Mock Trial competitions, witnesses swear a similar oath to abide by the rules of the competition. In other competitions, you might decide to skip that step and ask that all witnesses be assumed sworn.

> Your Honor, pursuant to Rule 603 of the Federal Rules of Evidence, we ask that all witnesses be assumed to have sworn an oath.

Permission to use an exhibit or demonstrative aid in opening statement. You should not show an exhibit to the jury until it has been admitted into evidence. However, you can seek an exception from this general rule if you have a "good faith belief"—a reasonable expectation—that the exhibit will be admitted during trial.

> Your Honor, may we use Exhibit 2 in our opening statement? It's a photo of the knife found at the crime scene. We have a good faith belief it will be admitted during the direct examination of our first witness, the officer who found it.

Read stipulations. Stipulations are facts agreed to by both parties. In Mock Trial, many cases come with prewritten stipulations. You may want the jury to hear that stipulation before the trial starts.

> Your Honor, may we read stipulation number three? [Wait for the judge to say yes.] "All searches and interrogations were Constitutional."

There are pros and cons to doing this during pretrial. It saves time, and it can alert the jury to a key fact in your case. However, it may sometimes be more impactful to read the stipulation during a direct or cross-examination to highlight a key point. Don't do both—stipulations only need to be read once. That said, you can bring it up an additional time if needed to make or respond to an objection.

Technically, the jury is not present during the preliminary matters, so if you want the jury to hear a stipulation, wait until your case-in-chief. For example, the prosecution might read a stipulation that the defendant is left-handed right before calling the CSI who will testify that the attacker was left-handed.

Point out key legal issues. Mock Trial cases often have unusual procedural issues. For example, in most Mock Trial cases, civil trials are bifurcated (meaning the trial is only about liability, not damages). This is unusual in the real world, so the scoring judges may expect you to argue damages—and score you down for not doing so—if you don't point out in preliminary matters that the trial has been bifurcated.

> Your Honor, we want to note that this jurisdiction has an unusual definition concerning negligence. It does not include a duty element. We wanted to raise this now so the Court is aware of the reason we will omit that element during our opening statement.

Point out key rules issues. Many Mock Trial judges volunteer in multiple tournaments. If there is a quirky rule in your competition, point it out. For example, if your tournament prohibits visual aids, you might point that out. Don't waste one of your limited preliminary matters to address a rule that can easily be addressed during trial. For example, some tournaments prohibit re-direct examination (and most prohibit re-re-direct examination). If that is the case in your tournament, and the judge asks if you have re-direct, respond with "Your Honor, re-direct examination is not permitted in this jurisdiction." Use "jurisdiction" as opposed to "tournament" or "competition." You want to avoid using any language that creates the impression that you are not in the middle of a real trial.

> Your Honor, we want to note that this jurisdiction has an unusual rule concerning rebuttal. Any rebuttal time must be requested at the beginning of trial. So we are requesting now that all unused time from our closing argument be reserved for rebuttal.

Presenting a bench notebook. You want to make sure the judges have a copy of all rules, exhibits, and witness statements. Some tournaments provide this to the presiding judge. In competitions that do not, you may be allowed to provide one. If given the option, take it. Create a separate notebook for each judge in the round (presiding and scoring). Include a roster of your team members' names, as well as the aforementioned items. It should look nice and neat. Such notebooks make first impressions also. Be careful not to have anything in or on the notebook that identifies your school. This is generally a rules violation as the judges are not supposed to know who is competing in front of them.

> Would the Court like a bench notebook? It has a copy of all rules and case materials.

One final consideration: Who should handle the preliminary matters? Some teams like to have the attorney who is not opening or closing handle preliminary matters. This has some advantages. It gives that attorney extra face time with the judges, which can help increase their scores later in trial. It also divides the workload more evenly among the lawyers. Other teams like to have the opener handle preliminary matters because it flows nicely from preliminary matters to opening statement. Some teams like to have their closer handle preliminary matters to identify that person as the lead attorney. All these approaches are acceptable, though we recommend assigning preliminary matters to the person who will make the best first impression on judges. This means choosing the attorney who is the most personable, professional, and confident.

11

Pretrial Arguments

In real trials, lawyers can make a "motion in limine." A motion in limine is a request, usually before trial, that the judge exclude a specific piece or kind of evidence. For example, the defense might ask the presiding judge to exclude evidence of the defendant's confession because it was obtained unconstitutionally. Or the prosecution might ask the presiding judge to exclude evidence that the prosecution's eyewitness has a prior felony conviction. This is similar to an objection, except the lawyer makes the motion before the jury hears the evidence at all. This way the jury never hears the potentially inadmissible, prejudicial evidence.

Most Mock Trial competitions at the high school and college levels do not have motions in limine. But a few do, including California's High School Mock Trial competition and many Empire Mock Trial tournaments. Tournaments usually refer to motions in limine as "pretrial arguments."

Pretrial arguments are different than the "pretrial matters" that occur in almost all competitions. Pretrial matters occur quickly before the trial starts. (See the previous chapter for more information.) When competitions include pretrial arguments, they are very important. Pretrial arguments generally receive a separate score. They affect whether certain evidence is admitted. And because they occur at the start of trial, they affect judges' impressions of which team is stronger.

11.1 How Pretrial Arguments Work

In competitions featuring pretrial arguments, the case packet includes a pretrial issue that each party must argue. In law school competitions, teams can decide which motions in limine to raise. In high school competitions, teams do not choose which pretrial argument to make.

The case packet almost always includes supporting law each party is allowed to use during its arguments. That law can consist of Constitutional amendments, statutes, and "precedent." Precedent is past legal cases where courts have analyzed similar issues. Precedent will generally include some cases that are helpful to each side. Attorneys use the similarities and differences between those past cases and the current case to argue for the result they want in the current case.

The "moving party" speaks first. The moving party is the party that brought the motion. For example, if the defense moves to suppress (exclude) the results of an allegedly illegal police search, the defense attorney argues first. She explains why the judge should *grant* her motion. The judge will often interrupt the attorney with questions. There is generally a time limit for the moving party's argument.

Next, the "responding party" argues. In the previous example, the prosecution is the responding party because they are responding to the defense's motion to suppress. The prosecution explains why the judge should *deny* the defense's motion. Again, the judge usually interrupts with questions. The prosecution usually has the same time limit as the defense.

In some competitions, both parties get a short rebuttal. In some, only the moving party gets a rebuttal.

Pretrial arguments do not involve any witnesses or objections. The lawyers argue to the judge and respond to the judge's questions.

11.2 Structure

Like opening statement or closing argument, a pretrial argument should always follow a carefully constructed order.

First, the introduction should state your party, your requested relief, the evidence at issue, and a numbered summary of your arguments. Requested relief is simply what you want the judge to do. The evidence at issue is what a party is trying to exclude or admit. The numbered arguments are the subpoints you will later use to argue that the motion should be granted or denied. You need at least two subpoints and never more than three. The introduction should be as succinct as possible while still conveying the significant details. The introduction for the moving party should look like this:

> The defense moves to exclude all statements Ms. Croddy made February 15, 2020, in the back of a police car. First, this was a custodial interrogation without Miranda warnings. Second, the officer tried to prevent Ms. Croddy from exercising her Sixth Amendment right to a lawyer.

The introduction for the responding party should look like this:

> The State asks the Court to deny the defense's motion because introduction of the defendant's statement would not violate the defendant's Miranda rights. First, the statement was not made while the defendant was in custody. Second, the statement was not elicited by an interrogation.

The State's introduction is less specific about the evidence at issue, calling it the "defendant's statements" rather than "all statements Ms. Croddy made February 15, 2020, in the back of a police car." The party going second benefits from the judge already knowing the basic facts. When you agree with the other side's characterization, you can omit longer descriptions and summaries and focus more on your argument. Of course, if you disagree with the moving party's summary, you can say so.

Second, offer the court a factual background. "Your Honor, may we give the Court a brief factual background?" Many judges will say yes, and you will get to a summary of the relevant facts. Some judges will say no because they already know the facts and want you to skip to the arguments. It's win-win for you. If they say yes, you get to show off how well you can summarize the facts. If they say no, you look good for moving on seamlessly, and you now have more time for your arguments.

If you are the responding party and you want to give a factual background, make sure you explain why. Otherwise, the judge will think you are wasting time and being repetitive. "The defense gave their version of the facts, but there are a few facts they left out. May we give a brief factual background?" If given permission, don't repeat what the other side said—focus on what was left out or what you disagree with.

The factual background should give the judge everything they need to decide the motion in your favor—and no more. It needs to be short. Here is a factual background used by a state champion:

> My client, Lee Croddy, is a popular political commentator. On February 15, 2020, one of his fans, Remi Montoya, broke into a government official's home and took government documents. The prosecution has charged Ms. Croddy with aiding and abetting the burglary. Their evidence includes a statement made by Ms. Croddy in the back of a police car. The statement we seek to exclude is, quote, "I told the kid to go down there and get those documents."

Like an opening statement, the pretrial argument should introduce facts that sound neutral but are intended to persuade. For example, here the factual background could have referred to Remi Montoya as the person who received private instructions from the defendant right before she committed the burglary. That makes it sound like the burglar was following the defendant's orders. Instead, the factual background calls Remi Montoya "one of [the defendant's] fans." This sets up the defense's argument that Remi Montoya was a crazed fan of the defendant who was acting on her own.

Third, deliver your arguments. These should match your subpoints promised in the introduction. Repeat the numbering from earlier. "First, this statement was made during a custodial interrogation without Miranda Warnings." The argument section should follow this logical structure: conclusion-rule-analysis-conclusion. This is the same argument structure lawyers are taught to use on law school exams and real-life arguments. Start with the conclusion. Explain the law that leads to that conclusion. Analyze why that law, when applied to the facts of this case, requires the outcome you want. Then repeat your conclusion.

Fourth, deliver your finish. With closing arguments, we want a longer conclusion that includes a new concept or argument. With pretrial arguments, we want a short conclusion that summarizes our position and requested relief.

> Because the statement was made as part of a custodial interrogation without *Miranda* warnings, and because the officer tried to prevent Ms. Croddy from exercising her right to a lawyer, we ask the Court to grant our motion and exclude Ms. Croddy's statement.

You can be even more succinct if you are running low on time:

> For these reasons, we ask the Court to grant our motion and exclude Ms. Croddy's statement.

How long should your pretrial argument be? It needs to be significantly shorter than the time limits because you will need time to answer the judge's questions. Ideally, you should be able to deliver your pretrial argument in half the allotted time without speaking quickly. Sometimes that's not possible because the facts are complicated, and the time limits are short. But your prepared remarks should never be longer than two-thirds of the time limit.

11.3 Using Precedent

The case packet will usually include summaries of about ten prior real cases. These case "precedents" are an important part of your pretrial argument. If a prior case had the same outcome you are seeking, you argue why that case is similar to this one. If a prior case had a different outcome than what you are seeking, you "distinguish" that case: you argue why that case is different from this one.

Before we explain how to do that, let's discuss some background about the American legal system. When judges decide legal issues, they do not start from scratch. They consider what other judges have done before when faced with similar issues. If the prior case decisions come from a higher court in their jurisdiction, they are required to follow those decisions. This is called "binding authority" because the judge is bound to follow it. For example, if the Minnesota Supreme Court decides an issue, the Minnesota lower courts must follow it. The highest court is always the United States Supreme Court. All judges need to follow the rulings of the United States Supreme Court. This system is called "stare decisis," which is Latin for "to stand by things decided."

If the prior decision was not from a higher court, then the judge in your case is not required to follow it. For example, a Minnesota trial court judge is not bound by the prior decisions of a Texas trial court judge. But you can still argue that the judge should choose to follow the other court's decision because it is logical. This is called "persuasive authority."

You probably will not need to do legal research to find these prior cases because almost every Mock Trial competition that has pretrial arguments includes the permissible cases in the packet. These are the only cases you may use. It might look like this:

> *Miranda v. Arizona* (1996), United States Supreme Court. Ernesto Miranda was arrested and questioned at the police station about a kidnapping and rape. Police never informed Miranda of his right to have an attorney present. After two hours of interrogation, Miranda gave a written confession. At trial, the confession was admitted despite an objection from Miranda's attorney. The jury found Miranda guilty. On appeal, the Supreme Court of Arizona affirmed the conviction and held that Miranda's Constitutional rights were not violated because he never specifically requested an attorney. The United States Supreme Court reversed Miranda's conviction, holding that, under the Fifth Amendment, a defendant's statements during a custodial interrogation are inadmissible in a criminal trial if law enforcement failed to inform the defendant of the right to remain silent and the right to speak with an attorney before the interrogation started. The Court explained: "if a person in custody is to be subjected to

> interrogation, he must first be informed in clear and unequivocal terms that he has the right to remain silent. For those unaware of the privilege, the warning is needed simply to make them aware of it—the threshold requirement for an intelligent decision as to its exercise. More important, such a warning is an absolute prerequisite in overcoming the inherent pressures of the interrogation atmosphere. It is not just the subnormal or woefully ignorant who succumb to an interrogator's imprecations, whether implied or expressly stated, that the interrogation will continue until a confession is obtained or that silence in the face of accusation is itself damning, and will bode ill when presented to a jury. . . . The Fifth Amendment privilege is so fundamental to our system of Constitutional rule, and the expedient of giving an adequate warning as to the availability of the privilege so simple, we will not pause to inquire in individual cases whether the defendant was aware of his rights without a warning being given.

Typically, each case will include the case name, the year, the court, the facts, the holding, and the rationale. In this example, the case name is *Miranda v. Arizona.* That means the defendant, Mr. Miranda, was appealing the lower court's ruling. His opponent was the State of Arizona. You can refer to the case as "*Miranda v. Arizona*" or, with famous cases like this one, simply as "*Miranda.*"

The case was decided in 1996. The year is important because, when two cases conflict, the more recent case controls. For example, there are cases before *Miranda* that have different conclusions, but *Miranda* overrules them because it is more recent.

The court that decided *Miranda* was the United States Supreme Court. This makes the case the most powerful precedent available (unless it is contradicted or overruled by a more recent United States Supreme Court case).

The holding is simply the court's decision. Here, the holding is that "under the Fifth Amendment, a defendant's statements during a custodial interrogation are inadmissible in a criminal trial if law enforcement failed to inform the defendant of the right to remain silent and the right to speak with an attorney before the interrogation started."

The rationale is the court's explanation for the decision. In this example, the long quote is the rationale. (The actual *Miranda* rationale is much longer, spanning multiple pages, but Mock Trial cases usually summarize the cases.)

So how do we *use* precedent to help our argument? Start by asking yourself, "Was the result of this previous case the result I want the court to reach in this case?" If you are seeking to exclude a confession in your case, then yes, you want the same result as *Miranda*. Your job is to explain why the facts in your case are similar to the facts in Miranda and therefore require the same outcome. For example, you might argue:

> Your Honor, this interrogation was unconstitutional. In *Miranda v. Arizona*, the Supreme Court excluded a defendant's confession under very similar circumstances. In *Miranda*, the police interrogated the defendant for two hours without telling him he had a right to a lawyer. In this case, the police interrogated my client for three hours without telling him he had a right to a lawyer.

If you are the prosecution seeking to admit a confession, then no, you want a different result from *Miranda*. Your job is to explain why the facts in your case are different from the facts in *Miranda* and therefore require a different outcome.

> Your Honor, this interrogation was Constitutional. The defense relies heavily on *Miranda v. Arizona*, but the circumstances there were quite different. In *Miranda*, the defendant was in custody. He had been arrested, and he gave his confession in a police station. Here, the defendant was not in custody. He had not been arrested. And he gave his confession voluntarily in his own living room after inviting the officers in and offering them iced tea.

There are always ways to distinguish cases that are bad for your position. For one thing, no two cases are the same. But more importantly, case authors choose pretrial arguments that fall in between past cases (if your case were truly identical to one of the case precedents, there wouldn't be anything to argue). Look hard and find ways to distinguish cases with unfavorable outcomes.

For every case cited in the packet—even those you do not plan to discuss in your argument—you should, at a minimum, know (1) the name, (2) the year it was decided, and (3) the holding. Having this basic knowledge will allow you to address arguments the other side makes and also respond to any questions from the judges about the cases.

11.4 Answering Questions

Answering questions from the judge is the hardest part of pretrial arguments. It is also the most fun. Here are some tips on how to do it well.

Relax. Don't panic. The fact that the judge is questioning your argument does not mean she disagrees with you. She is looking to have a discussion, which gives you a chance to show off.

Listen carefully to what the judge is asking. Make sure you understand the judge's question. Wait until the judge is finished, even if you think you know what the judge is saying. Never interrupt a judge. This is not like cross-examination. You are not trying to "control" the judge. The judge is in charge. Anything you do that steps on the judge's toes will result in a lower score.

Start your response by answering the judge's question. Failing to do so is one of the most common mistakes that mock attorneys—and real attorneys—make. If the judge asks about something that is later in your outline, do not tell the judge you will get to that soon. Do not tell the judge that they are asking the wrong question. Do not just return to your prepared remarks. Do not try to dodge the question because it goes to one of your weak points. *Answer the judge's question.* If the question calls for a yes or no, start with a yes or no, and then explain. "Yes, Your Honor, the interrogation was longer than the one deemed unconstitutional in Miranda, but the difference here is that the defendant was represented by counsel. . . ."

You might wonder, How can I possibly answer the judge's questions intelligently, clearly, and persuasively . . . if I have almost no time to think? The key is preparation. Think about what questions a judge is likely to ask. Have your teammates and coaches ask you questions in practice. Make a list of every question a judge might ask. Prepare both sides of the case, even if you are only arguing one side; this will help you identify arguments or questions a judge might raise. If you do all of that, you will have answers to almost every question a judge might ask. And if a judge asks a question you have not prepared, your preparation with all those other questions will give you the foundation to answer a new one.

When asked a question, avoid saying, "That's a great question." If you say that repeatedly, it wastes time and makes you look nervous. If you don't say it repeatedly, it implies that other questions posed to you were not great, which can rub a judge the wrong way. This tip is particularly important when there are multiple judges asking questions.

Some judges will toss you "softballs," which are easy questions that allow you to make your key arguments. Don't assume that every question is a trick or trap. When you do get hard questions, stand your ground. Many judges are assertive when asking questions. They may try to box you into a corner. They may express skepticism about your position. They are testing you! Do not change your position just because the judge is expressing disagreement. If you respectfully, but forcefully, maintain your position and explain why you are correct, you will be rewarded for standing firm under tough questioning.

Finally, once you have finished answering a judge's question, pivot back to your prewritten argument. You may have covered a future part of your presentation when you were answering questions. If so, when you get to that point either skip over the section or, if it is important, touch on it briefly and reference the judge's earlier question.

The most important thing to remember about judges' questions is that they are not a problem. They are an opportunity. Anyone can deliver prepared remarks. The best pretrial attorneys separate themselves by giving clear, concise, persuasive responses to judges' questions.

11.5 Performance

Speak slowly. Speaking slowly shows confidence. It also helps listener comprehension. Pretrial issues are complicated, and while the presiding judge is probably familiar with the facts and law, the scoring judges may not be. Speaking slowly gives them a chance to understand. In addition, if you speak slowly with your prepared remarks, it allows you to speak slowly when you are responding to a judge's questions. Everyone will be used to you speaking slowly, which means you will have extra time to think about your answers without the judges realizing you are stalling to gather your thoughts.

Speak loudly. It shows confidence.

Be dynamic. Speak with passion, use your hands for gestures, and use your face to demonstrate emotion. However, a pretrial argument should not be delivered with the same passion as if you are speaking to a jury in closing argument. Pretrial arguments take place outside the presence of the jury, so you need to pretend as though the jury is not there. Judges focus more on the facts and the law than do jurors who are more likely to get caught up in the emotional aspects of a case. Making an emotional appeal will irritate the judge or make them uncomfortable, but you still need to engage the audience, so don't be monotone.

Use a conversational tone. You want to speak *with* the judge, not *at* the judge. If you appear conversational with the judge, the scoring judges will be impressed.

Look at the presiding judge. Continue eye contact throughout the presentation, but be especially careful not to break it until you have finished your introduction. As soon as you look away or glance down at an outline, it's a pause that invites the judges to jump in with questions. Questions are good, but you want to speak freely long enough to set the tone and make a good impression.

11.6 Teamwork

In some competitions, the attorney who does the pretrial argument does only the pretrial argument. Make sure that attorney is still included in team practices, scrimmages, and social events. They are a vital member of the team. They will often have insights about how to improve the trial presentation, and the witnesses and trial attorneys may have ideas about how to improve the pretrial argument. Besides, this year's pretrial attorney might be next year's opener, or vice versa. It is important for every team member to see all parts of the trial.

12

Team Scores

Some competitions have judges award a "team score" in addition to scoring the individual functions of the trial. It provides a chance for judges to reward or penalize things done as a team. It is also sometimes used as a tiebreaker if everything else is equal. The good news is that if you go to a competition with a team score, you don't need to do anything differently. All the things you would do to earn a good team score are things you want to be doing anyway!

The most important thing for the team score is, as you'd expect, teamwork. Help one another with visual aids. No one should be setting up their own easel. If someone is getting ready to impeach, someone else should be ready to hand over the witness's affidavit. Demonstrate cohesion by referencing back to the theme in multiple aspects of the trial.

Also, little things can make a big difference. Keep your counsel table clean. It makes you look organized. Use a "team color" used to accent your professional attire (ties, jewelry, etc.). Push in your chair if you step away from the counsel table. Make sure your supplies all function properly and look professional.

If a co-counsel needs help with an objection, help them. You can write on your pad so they can see your suggestion. Or they can lean over and get your advice. But don't make it look like you lack confidence in your teammate. If the judges see your teammate arguing an objection—and see you frantically trying to get your teammate's attention—judges will assume you doubt your teammate's ability to handle the issue on their own. That is a bad look.

You will spend hundreds of hours in practice. Don't waste that massive investment of time by trying to save a few cents and using equipment that will fall apart during trial. Everything you do will impact your scores. Even if a judge doesn't directly score down a trial function, those subconscious likes and dislikes can be reflected here.

Finally, have fun. If both teams are prepared and professional (and following the advice in this book), the round will be close. If the judges can't differentiate between teams based on technical skills, the team score may come down to which team they felt was more enjoyable to be around. If you are having fun, the judges will have more fun scoring you.

13

Other Roles

Most of this book focuses on attorneys and witnesses, but there are other roles vital to team success. This chapter covers timekeepers, bailiffs, alternates, and captains. These roles are often unscored, but we have seen them make a major difference in competition.

13.1 Timekeepers

Most competitions require all teams to provide a timekeeper. In some competitions, the role is called "clerk." This person times both your team and the opposing team. Timekeepers should display notecards to their teammates counting down the time remaining. Sometimes the denominations on the cards are dictated by tournament rules. If you can't have less than a "1 Minute" card, you can turn that card sideways to convey 30 seconds left.

When a competitor runs out of time, the timekeepers inform the judges. The best way to do this when the *opposing* team runs out of time is to stand and interrupt, saying: "Excuse me, Your Honor. Time has expired." Don't just hold up a sign that says "Time" or "Stop." By standing and verbally interrupting, you will force the attorney or witness to stop speaking. We strongly advise that your team *not* run out of time. But if it happens, just hold up the "Time" card, which indicates time has expired.

Sometimes the two timekeepers in a round have different calculations. When this occurs, the judges typically split the difference, or go with the calculation giving the competitor more time to finish the presentation. You should communicate with the other team's timekeeper throughout trial to make sure your calculations are the same.

Timekeepers should dress professionally. They should be friendly. Even when calling time on the other squad, they should sound more apologetic than gleeful.

Although timekeepers do not have to have another role on the team, most competitions require the person to be on the team roster. Serving as a timekeeper can be a great role for alternates. It gives them something to do and a great seat to watch the action. Because they are on the roster, they can also speak with the team during breaks and share observations. A timekeeper usually has the best vantage point of the judges and can pass along the reactions they see.

13.2 Bailiffs

A few competitions have a bailiff position. The bailiff announces the start of the trial, swears in witnesses, and maintains order in the courtroom. If the bailiff role is scored, make sure you make an impact during the trial.

Start by approaching the presiding judge beforehand and introducing yourself as the bailiff for the round. Get the judge's name and pronunciation. Ask the judge if you may give a short reminder at the start of trial regarding courtroom rules. Introduce yourself to the jurors. These first impressions may help increase your score.

When the judge is ready, announce the start of trial. "All rise! Honorable Judge ____ presiding."

Give a short reminder of courtroom rules. This might include no eating or chewing gum. This may include a reminder to silence cell phones. The point is to sound authoritative and professional.

When each witness testifies, you will swear them in. Most competitions will provide instructions about what to say, but they usually take the form of, "Raise your right hand. Do you solemnly swear to abide by the rules of the Mock Trial competition?" In real life, witnesses swear or affirm to tell the truth. In Mock Trial, the witnesses are pretending to be other people, so they can't tell the truth. For this reason, many competitions "assume the witnesses have been sworn" to avoid this exercise.

As bailiff, you should always be loud, confident, and concise. Dress professionally. Some bailiffs will remain standing all trial.

13.3 Alternates

Most successful teams have alternates, also known as understudies. These students are prepared to play a role (or multiple roles) if another student is unavailable.

It is easy to take an alternate role for granted and think you will not have the opportunity to perform in competition. But students get sick, or quit, or have scheduling conflicts. You never know when you might be called upon to step up. Additionally, alternates play an important role in team practices by covering parts for people who are missing and contributing their ideas and observations.

WAR STORY

In 2012, Professor Bernstein's UC Irvine team had an understudy, Mazamir Yousefi, who was going to travel with the team to a big competition. She found out as she was boarding the flight to New York that a teammate had become unavailable. Mazamir would be serving in two brand new roles. But because she had been practicing hard in another witness role, she had developed the Mock Trial skills to make her successful in any witness role. Maz ended up winning witness awards that weekend and never looked back. She would eventually win national awards as an attorney and witness in college and law school, and at time of publication she was an attorney at one of the most prestigious law firms in the world.

Being prepared as an alternate is a great way to show your teammates and coaches that you are ready to take on responsibility.

13.4 Captains

Every team, whether coached or not, should have one or two student captains.

Captains do not need to be the strongest competitors on the team. They do not need to be the attorneys giving the closing arguments. The captains need to be dedicated, reliable, and passionate. They need to be good leaders.

Captains help set the practice schedule and keep practices productive. They help newer members learn their roles. Captains help resolve intra-team disputes. They often help coaches or other team leaders decide the rosters and roles. They lead by example—being punctual, professional, and prepared.

Captains can also be liaisons with the coaches. Sometimes team members are more comfortable talking with their peers than their adult coaches. Captains should determine when those conversations should remain between teammates, and when they should involve a coach.

During competition, captains need to keep the team confident and relaxed. If the team is winning, captains need to keep the group from growing complacent. If the team loses a trial, captains need to keep the group focused on performing their best in the next trial.

14

Objections

An objection is an attempt to stop your opponent from asking a question, giving an answer, or admitting an exhibit. The next chapter discusses the substantive rules governing which evidence is permitted at trial and which is objectionable. This chapter focuses on the mechanics and strategy of objections.

Making and responding to objections are crucial parts of Mock Trial. A proper objection can disrupt your opponent's examination, prevent them from offering evidence that hurts your case, and allow you to show off your skills. The best teams use objections as a chance to shine.

Making and responding to objections is also challenging. Unlike an opening statement or direct examination, you won't be able to plan out exactly what objections you want to make and when. The other team is not going to email you a script of all their questions and answers a week before trial. Instead, you will need to learn the rules of evidence and practice objecting so you can be ready for anything the other side throws at you.

Be mindful that whether any particular objection is sustained or overruled, it's not likely to have a major impact on scoring. The caveat is that it can become a big deal if you let it throw you off your game or if you appear annoyed with the presiding judge. Whether you're making or responding to an objection, if you lose, you lose. Further arguing the point is unlikely to result in a different ruling, but it is likely to negatively impact your score.

In preparing for objections, you must understand your competition's "rules of evidence," but also its competition rules and/or "rules of procedure." For example, many competitions do not permit objections during opening statements or closing arguments. Thus, if you make an objection during those aspects of the trial, it will reflect poorly on you even if the objection has a sound legal basis. Similarly, the case packet might state that certain exhibits are (a) already in evidence, (b) are stipulated that they are admissible and may not be objected to, or (c) are deemed to be authentic but are subject to objections on other grounds. You need to know which status applies to each exhibit.

When an objection is made, the opposing attorney and witness should stop speaking. The objecting attorney states their position as to why the evidence is improper. The attorney seeking to admit the evidence is given a chance to respond. Generally, the presiding judge gives the objecting attorney the chance for a brief reply. The judge then states a ruling. If the objection is "overruled," the examination continues or the piece of evidence is admitted into the record. If the objection is "sustained," the attorney needs to move on or try to elicit testimony that would cause the judge to reconsider.

An entire book could be written about just Mock Trial objections. In fact, some former mockers have done just that. *Winning Objections* is an excellent text for those who want to dig deep into this area.[1] Before digging into the intricacies of objections, however, you need to know the basics. And, before you practice making basic objections, you need to learn whether you should be objecting in the first place.

14.1 How to Object

In most competitions, only the attorney who is handling the cross-examination may object to the direct examination, and vice versa. Although most competitions do not allow objections during openings and closings, those that do generally require objections to be made by the attorney doing the opposing opening or closing. In other words, no "tag teaming" is allowed.

How do you make an objection?

First, stand up. Don't stand up halfway. Stand up all the way. This shows respect to the judge and communicates confidence.

WAR STORY

Don't just stand up. Stay up. You have to remain standing until the judge has finished ruling. Professor Bernstein recalls one instance when the judge wanted to teach a law student a lesson. The attorney stood up and said, "Objection, hearsay." While the other side was responding,

1. *Winning Objections: A Mock Trial Guidebook*, by Brian Pilchik, Amanda Mundell, and Emily Miller (2020) is available at WinningObjections.com.

the attorney who made the objection sat down. The judge looked at him and said, "Counsel, stand up while an objection is pending." He did. "Your objection is overruled. ***Now*** you can sit down."

Second, say, "Objection."

Third, state the grounds for the objection, such as hearsay, relevance, or foundation.

Sometimes your opponent's evidence will violate multiple rules of evidence. It is permissible to state multiple grounds for your objection. "Objection, hearsay and improper character." But do this sparingly, as it will often confuse judges. When one ground is significantly stronger, keep it simple and just state that. If that ground is overruled, let it go. Immediately re-asserting a new objection to the same question looks desperate.

For some grounds, it can be useful to state the rule number. We recommend citing the rule number for any of the prejudice-based objections, such as misleading, cumulative, unduly prejudicial (Rule 403), improper character evidence (Rule 404), improper method of proving character evidence (Rule 405), improper subsequent remedial measure (Rule 407), improper expert opinion (Rule 702), and ultimate issue (Rule 704).[2] For most grounds, though, it does not make sense to cite a rule number. For example, real life attorneys don't cite a rule when objecting to hearsay, relevance, foundation, lack of authenticity, speculation, etc.

Most of the time, those are the only steps to making an objection: Stand up, say "objection," and state your grounds. Notice that you do not keep talking to explain your objection. For example, don't say, "Objection, relevance. The officer's training on blood spatter is not relevant because. . . ." This is called a speaking objection, and many judges will score you down for adding this explanation without permission.

If the objection is not self-explanatory, there is a fourth step. Say: "May I be heard." If the judge says yes, you should—briefly—explain the basis for your objection. If the subject is sensitive and your competition is presumed to have jurors, ask to be heard "outside the presence of the jury." If you're trying to keep the jury from hearing something, and you

2. These numbers correspond to the *Federal Rules of Evidence*. Some state competitions use the rule numbers corresponding to their own state's rules of evidence. Other competitions, especially at the middle school level, have a shortened list of objections with their own numbering system. If you are going to cite the numbers, use those applicable to your competition.

discuss it in front of the jury while making the objection, it defeats the purpose of the objection.[3]

Use speaking objections rarely, though. Most objections are self-explanatory (and if most of your objections are not self-explanatory, you are probably objecting too often or at the wrong times). Judges don't like it when attorneys unnecessarily ask to be heard.

Sometimes it is appropriate to add a few words to identify which evidence you are challenging. Suppose the eyewitness testifies, "The defendant was standing over the victim and smiling. He wanted to kill the victim." The witness has testified to three different facts: the defendant was standing over the victim; the defendant was smiling; and the defendant wanted to kill the victim. To clarify your objection, you could say, "Objection, speculation as to what my client was thinking."

There are some objections where an extra phrase or request can increase the likelihood of winning an objection. For example, instead of just saying, "Objection, narrative," say "Objection, narrative. I ask that the direct proceed in a question-and-answer format." Because proceeding in a question-and-answer format is the way things are supposed to work, the judge may sustain the objection without thinking too hard about whether the witness was, in fact, narrating. Similarly, instead of just saying: "Objection, argumentative," say" "Objection, argumentative. I ask that the witness be allowed to finish her answer."

When making or responding to objections, look only at the presiding judge. It is tempting to look at opposing counsel because you are debating with them. Don't do it. Don't even tilt in their direction. Doing so looks personal and unprofessional. Listen and respond to opposing counsel's comments, but otherwise pretend they do not exist. You might feel tempted to look at the jury to make sure they understood your point. Don't do it. The whole point of objections is to make sure the jury doesn't hear inadmissible evidence. In real life, the jury often leaves the room when attorneys argue objections, or the attorneys approach the bench so the jury cannot hear. Look only at the presiding judge. This admonition is true when making objections and when responding. Looking at the presiding judge makes you appear professional and helps you keep eye contact, making your statements more persuasive.

---

3. In Mock Trial, there are rarely people in the room portraying jurors. Everyone just pretends there are. So, when you ask to be heard "outside the presence of the jury" you are just demonstrating that you know how it would work in the real world. This can earn you a higher score. However, if you ask to be heard outside the presence of the jury, don't forget to ask if you may presume you are back in the presence of the jury when your argument or professional statement is completed.

There will be instances where evidence would ordinarily be objectionable, but a competition rule makes it admissible. For example, the case might include a map with no foundation for its accuracy—but the case includes a stipulation that the map is admissible. When your opponent offers the map into evidence, you can't object to it because the other side will say, "this is stipulated as admissible," and it will look like you don't know the rules. But if you don't object to the map, the judges might think you missed an obvious objection. The solution is to briefly explain why you aren't objecting. When the judge says, "Any objections?" you simply say, "No, Your Honor. We've stipulated that this exhibit is admissible." Or: "No, Your Honor, this exhibit was deemed admissible prior to trial." As usual, don't cite to the "competition rules." If you say something has been admitted or deemed admissible, your judge will be able to connect the dots and you have avoided breaking the illusion that you're in a real trial.

14.2 When to Object

It is important that objections be made timely. When you are objecting that a question is improper (calls for speculation, calls for a narrative answer, calls for hearsay, etc.), try to get your objection on the record *before* the witness answers. If there is no time to do so, make the objection as soon as you can and "ask that the objection precede the witness's answer." If the objection is then sustained, ask that the witness's answer be stricken from the record.

If you are objecting to a witness's testimony, object as soon as they testify to something objectionable. If possible, object when the witness is about to say something objectionable. "I saw blood on the defendant's hands. I assume he got the blood by. . . ." The witness is about to speculate. You can object before the jury hears the inadmissible testimony. "Objection, the witness is about to speculate about how my client allegedly got blood on his hands."

If you are objecting to an exhibit, object when opposing counsel offers the exhibit into evidence. Don't object when they show you the exhibit, when they hand it to the witness, or while they lay foundation. None of those things are objectionable. But when they offer the exhibit into evidence, that's when you object. The judge should ask if you have any objections, and that's when you stand and object.

You can also object if opposing counsel attempts to use an exhibit or show it to the jury without first offering it into evidence. "Objection, this exhibit is not in evidence."

If you offer an exhibit, and the opposing side's objection is overruled, the judge should also say "Exhibit X is admitted." If the judge forgets this step, it is your job to remind them. Simply say: "Your Honor, for purposes of the record, is Exhibit X admitted?"

Note that you don't need the judge's permission to object. You have a right to interrupt the opposing attorney or witness to ensure that only admissible evidence is presented at trial. However, that right only extends to stating the grounds for the objection. If the basis for the objection is not obvious, you may seek permission from the judge to elaborate on why you have objected.

14.3 Whether to Object

Now that you know *how* to object and *when* to object . . . you need to figure out if you *should* object.

Generally, you should object only when—but not always when—the opponent has asked a question, offered testimony, or offered an exhibit that violates the rules of evidence. But most situations are more complicated. Does their evidence obviously violate the rules of evidence, or is it a close call? Does this judge seem receptive to this type of objection? Does your opponent seem strong on the rules?

Whether to object is a judgment call that comes with experience, based on many factors. You might read the rest of this section and think, "How could I ever consider all those factors at once?" The answer is practice and experience. If you have ever played video games or sports—or have gotten really good at anything that requires quick decisions—you can relate. When someone plays video games, they must react to what's happening on screen and then remember which buttons to push on the controller and in which order. When someone swings a tennis racket, they have to watch the ball, decide whether to hit a backhand or forehand, decide where they want the ball to go, set their feet, swing the racket, and hit the ball at just the right angle. The first time we do these things, it's overwhelming. Too many things are happening at once. But with practice, all these tiny decisions become routine and automatic.

Here are some factors to consider when deciding whether to object:

How clearly does the opponent's evidence violate the rules? Is there a strong response available to the opponent? If you are clearly correct, obviously it is a much better situation for objecting. If your argument is a reach, you should be less eager to object.

How important is the evidence? If the evidence is harmful to your case, or crucial to your opponent's case, you should be more likely to object. If the evidence is trivial, you should be more likely to let it go.

Does your team plan to introduce similar evidence? If so, you probably don't want to object to the evidence because your argument could be used against you later.

Do you plan to cross-examine on this evidence? Usually, if you can get an objection sustained on your opponent's direct examination, object. But if that evidence forms a significant portion of your cross-examination, it may not be worth it to object.

How many objections have you already made to this examination? How many objections do you anticipate making to the remainder of the examination? You don't want to object too often. As we've discussed one of the keys to winning rounds is to be likeable. Making lots of objections interrupts the proceedings and can annoy the judge. If you have already made lots of objections, be more hesitant before making another. If you anticipate objecting later in the same examination—especially if you anticipate objecting to something more important—be more hesitant before objecting to this evidence.

Has the judge already sustained multiple objections to this examination? If so, the value of another sustained objection is diminished. Also, the cost of an overruled objection is higher—it might make jurors feel like this examination was a wash, when in fact you were winning by getting multiple objections sustained. If you have already damaged your opponent's direct with objections, be cautious before objecting again. It gives your opponent a chance to turn things around.

Is the other team's examination effective and engaging? If you can disrupt the flow of a really good direct, you should generally do it, even if the objection is only 50-50 to get sustained. On the other hand, if their direct is boring, why object? A good rule of thumb: if your opponent is beating themselves, don't interrupt.

Is this a particularly vulnerable moment for opposing counsel? If the opponent is low on time, a sustained objection can be crippling. If it feels like the last question of an examination, or even a question close to the end, a sustained objection will hurt. It will be on the judges' minds right before they write down a score. If the opponent is doing a re-direct examination, a sustained objection can leave them with no questions prepared—and may force them to end their examination on a sustained objection. These situations should make you more likely to object.

How comfortable do you feel with objections and the rules of evidence? How strong does your opponent seem on objections? Winning the objection is helpful. But sounding better than your opponent is far more important. If you think you will sound more prepared and persuasive than your opponent, you should object more. It gives you a chance to distinguish yourself from the opponent. If you think your opponent might have an edge when it comes to objections, object less. Don't give them a chance to show off.

What do you know about the judge? Has the judge been sustaining or overruling objections? Has the judge been sustaining or overruling objections on *these grounds*? Every judge is different. All the attorneys at your counsel table should be working together to decipher the judge's preferences. "She likes hearsay objections. She overrules relevance objections."

Has the judge started looking at you as opposed to the attorney conducting the examination? If so, the judge may expect you to object. If you know what objection the judge is fishing for, make it.

Is your team winning or trailing? If you think you are behind, an objection gives you a chance to catch up.

As you can see, there is a lot to think about when deciding whether to object! If you are just starting out, you can simplify the analysis: *Do I have a convincing argument that my opponent is violating the rules of evidence?* As you become more experienced and comfortable in the courtroom, you will evaluate objection decisions more quickly and thoroughly.

Years ago, the prevailing wisdom was, "Find something to object to, even if you're wrong." Most successful teams have abandoned this advice. Objecting to a strong opponent, especially when you are incorrect, allows them to distinguish themselves. As a result, most high-level trials feature very few objections. For example, the 2015 Top Gun final round has some of the best advocacy you will see, and there was only one objection all trial.

Let's Get Real: With real jury trials, be even more hesitant to object unless the issue is important ***and*** you think will win (at trial or on appeal of that point). The jurors will start to doubt your credibility if you are getting overruled. And, even when your objection is sustained, the jurors might think you are hiding evidence from them.

14.4 Responding to Objections

The best defense to an objection is to avoid drawing it in the first place. You want to make your own presentations bulletproof. Avoid anything that might prompt a good objection. You want to keep the other side sitting down silently. You can do that by phrasing your questions carefully. Instead of asking, "How often *does* the defendant come into your store?"

ask "How often *have you seen* the defendant come into your store?" The former calls for speculation, but the latter is unobjectionable. You can make it harder for the other side to object by focusing on evidence that is clearly admissible. And you can make it harder for the other side to object by laying foundation before eliciting testimony or offering an exhibit. For example, if you are offering a document that qualifies under the business record exception to the hearsay rule, lay the foundation before offering it:

Q. Was this document prepared in the ordinary course of your business?

A. Yes.

Q. Was it made at or near the time of the transaction?[4]

A. Yes.

Note that you can't stop opposing counsel from objecting. No matter how good your questions and answers are, they can still make incorrect objections. But if they make incorrect objections, that is great news for you! Now you get to show off your courtroom skills by defeating their objections. By avoiding objectionable content, you put yourself in a win-win situation. If they object, you can defeat their incorrect objections and look unstoppable. If they don't object, you get to present an uninterrupted examination that looks flawless.

But what should you do when the opponent objects? Here is how to respond:

First, you don't need to stand up. Presumably, you are already standing since it's your direct or cross. The one exception is if opposing counsel is cross-examining your witness and they object to the witness's answers. Usually this situation involves a nonresponsive objection. In that case, stand up just as you would if you were the one objecting.

Even though opposing counsel raised the objection, look at the judge when responding.

The judge will usually invite you to respond. "Counsel, how do you respond?" Stay calm. Speak loudly. Speak slowly. And be brief. Tell the judge why the evidence is admissible. "Your Honor, this testimony is relevant to bias. It shows the witness is friends with the plaintiff." Do not

4. Ordinarily, we use open ended questions during direct examination, but in situations like this, it's important to use the specific phrasing that conforms to the exception. It would sound unnatural for the witness to say them, so the attorney does so. Note: Even though these questions call for a yes or no answer, they are not leading because they do not suggest the answer.

get rattled by the objection. If you've prepared properly, you should have seen the objection coming. You know why the evidence is admissible.

Pet Peeve: Sometimes the judge will invite you to respond without saying, "Counsel, would you like to respond?" Instead, the judge will look at you, gesture to you, or say, "Counsel?"—all of which indicate their invitation for you to respond. If you they do that, and you then say: "Your Honor, may I be heard," they will be annoyed because you aren't reading their signals.

Occasionally, judges will rule without giving you a chance to respond. This happens a lot in real life, so when your trials are judged by real-life judges or trial lawyers, it will happen more often. If the judge overrules the objection without asking for your response, great. Keep going with your examination. If the judge sustains the objection without asking for your response, don't say "May I be heard?" This will generally draw a terse, "I've ruled, counsel." If it was a form objection—leading, calls for narrative, compound—just rephrase the question. *You can often score points with judges for showing them how easily you adapt to a sustained objection!* If the objection was to lack of foundation, lay the foundation (if possible). *You can often score points with judges for showing them how easily you can lay foundation.* If the objection was substantive—relevance, hearsay, character—you have a decision to make. Can you offer the evidence in a different way that will overcome the objection? If so, do it. If not, or if the evidence is less important, just move to a new topic.

Pet Peeve: If you have an objection sustained against you, and you need to move on to a new topic, do not say, "I'll move on." This means, "I was defeated." Everyone knows you lost the objection. You don't need to take out an ad in the paper.

If you notice that the presiding judge is ruling without inviting a response, you need to jump in faster. When the objection is made, immediately ask to respond before the judge rules. Also, make a mental note for when it's your turn to object. If the judge is sustaining objections without letting the other side respond, that should make you more likely to object.

When the judge gives you a chance to respond to an objection, what should you say? Responses are not an explanation of why you're asking the question. They must address the specific issue raised in the objection. For many objections, there are "magic words" to use in the response.

Relevance

Opposing Attorney: "Objection, relevance."

You: "This question is probative on the issue of ________."

or

"This goes to the witness's credibility, which is always relevant."

Shorter is better tends to apply to all objection responses, but especially for relevance. If you need 45 seconds to explain why something is relevant, chances are it isn't.

> **Pet Peeve**: Don't start responses to relevance objections by saying, "This is very relevant" or "This is highly relevant." Just explain why it's relevant.

Hearsay

Opposing Attorney: "Objection, hearsay."

You: "This is not hearsay because ______________."

or

"This statement falls within an exception to the hearsay rule because ______________."

Leading

Opposing Attorney: "Objection, leading."

You: "The question is not leading because it does not suggest the answer."

or

"I'll rephrase."

Beyond the Scope[5]

Opposing Attorney: "Objection, beyond the scope."

5. In the real world, both sides can call the same witness during their respective case-in-chief. In Mock Trial, only one side may call any given witness. Accordingly, the initial cross-examination generally does not need to be within the scope of the initial direct (all subsequent re-directs and re-crosses must be within the scope of the examination that immediately preceded them). If your competition rules do not

You: "Mr. Walker opened the door to this line of questioning by asking the witness about ___________."

Speculation

Opposing Attorney: "Objection, speculation."

You: "It's not speculation. The question was phrased, 'to your knowledge. . . .'"

or

"It's not speculation. Professor Clark is an expert and this is within her field of expertise."

Asked and Answered

Opposing Attorney: "Objection, asked and answered."

You: "It was asked, but it was not answered."

or

"I previously asked about X, this question is about Y."

You need to listen carefully to the objection made in order to fill in the blanks in the above phrases correctly.

It is often useful to say, "That goes to the weight, not the admissibility." That means that opposing counsel's objection addresses how much weight the jury should give the evidence, not whether the jury should hear it at all. This is a common response for relevance objections, foundation, and expert credentials. For example, if someone is objecting to an expert's qualifications, this response indicates the concern may impact the weight the judge or jury should give to the expert's opinion, but the expert meets the basic standards for the opinion to be offered.

You should prepare your objection responses as much as possible. For every question you ask and every answer you elicit, you should be able to succinctly state the relevance. For every question you ask and answer you elicit, you should be able to identify the foundation that permits it. Any time you ask a question about someone else's statements or a document, you should have a hearsay response ready. Any time you ask a question about someone's previous behavior, separate from the core

---

limit initial cross to the scope of the initial direct and someone mistakenly makes that objection, state: "Your Honor, in this jurisdiction, witnesses cannot be recalled. For that reason, the scope of the initial cross-examination is not limited to that of the initial direct." Be prepared to show the judge the rule if the other side disagrees. Note the reference to "this jurisdiction" rather than "this competition." You always want to act as if it is a real-life trial rather than a game.

incident of the case, you should have a character response ready. And so on. When you practice for months, you can prepare for virtually any reasonable objection—good objections *and* bad objections. It can be fun to have a practice where everyone, including other witnesses and timekeepers, gets to object. Doing so can prepare attorneys for responding to wacky objections. It can also lead you to stumble on good objections your team's attorneys have not thought of.

When dealing with an objection that has multiple grounds, start with the one you know you can win. This gives you momentum heading into the grounds that present a closer call. If your opponent didn't cite the rule number, and you can, you'll have instant credibility.

Once an objection is overruled, re-ask your question. Don't ask the witness if they want you to re-ask, just do it. It emphasizes that you won the debate, and, even if the witness remembers the question, the judge may not.

> **Pet Peeve**: There is no more boring moment in a Mock Trial than this: *Would you like me to re-ask the question? Yes, please re-ask the question. Okay, I will re-ask the question. . . .* Jurors will score you higher if they are awake.

Even if you respond perfectly to an objection, some Mock Trial judges will sustain bad objections "just to see how you deal with it."[6] That's okay. Remain calm. Either adjust your question to get the evidence you want or move confidently to the next topic. Losing an objection is rarely a big problem as long as you react well.

Always remain respectful of opposing counsel. Sometimes your opponent will make a bad objection, and you will be excited to showcase your courtroom superiority. Don't be snarky or condescending. No one likes a bad sport. We have seen rudeness by a team that was right create sympathy for a team that was wrong.

WAR STORY

Professor Bernstein had a student at UC Irvine who was a little too confident when responding to an objection. The other team objected to Irvine's direct examination. The judge looked confused by the objection and asked the attorney to explain. The attorney gave a long, convoluted

6. There are even more Mock Trial judges who will say they intentionally sustained a bad objection to cover up what they later realized was a bad ruling.

answer and the judge looked even more confused (but she didn't say anything). She looked at the UC Irvine attorney, who said, "Your Honor, I didn't understand the objection, either." The judge chuckled and overruled the objection. The presiding judge scored the UC Irvine attorney very well—but the scoring judge gave him a 6 for being rude. Always remember your scoring judges, and always err on the side of being polite and professional.

14.5 Arguing Objections

Some objections are resolved quickly. Form objections rarely require much discussion. But some objections involve more debate, especially those involving relevance, hearsay, character, or expert testimony. The judge may permit you to argue back and forth a few times before they make their ruling.

Here are some tips for arguing objections. First, the physical setup is the same: Remain standing. Look only at the judge. Speak slowly, clearly, and loudly.

Ask to be heard. "May I be heard?" Or: "May I respond?" When an objection is raised, judges will usually give the other side a response. After that, you probably need to ask to respond—unless the judge looks at you or otherwise indicates they want you to respond.

Don't just repeat yourself. If you have nothing new to add, you probably don't need to be heard. An exception is if opposing counsel didn't respond to your argument, or if opposing counsel misconstrued or misunderstood your argument. Then you may need to repeat it.

Use rule numbers and the language of the rule. Doing so gives you credibility and makes your argument more persuasive. For example, don't say, "This is a present sense impression." Instead, say, "This qualifies under the present sense impression exception to the hearsay rule. Under Rule 803(1), the declarant was describing an event immediately after observing the event." Remember, your goal is not merely to win the objection. Your goal is to score points. We have seen plenty of situations where the attorney who lost the objection *ruling* won the objection when it came to scoring points.

Listen to the judge. If the judge indicates a preference for a certain argument, use that argument even if you prepared or prefer a different argument. If the judge seems skeptical of an argument, see if you can make a different argument. If the judge seems ready to rule in your favor, don't get in the way. We have seen too many attorneys turn a win into a loss by talking too much. "When you are winning, shut up" is advice that will serve you well in Mock Trial and real courtrooms. To put in another way, "When the court is leaning your way, let it fall."

In addition to making arguments based on the rules, rely on common sense and fundamental fairness. "Your Honor, the defense opened the door to this line of questioning when it asked. . . ." Judges almost always allow one side to do what the other did. "Your Honor, the prosecution is challenging the methods used by our expert. But these are the same methods used by their expert. They can't have it both ways."

Let's look at what an objection argument might involve:

Prosecution: What does the report say?

Defense: Objection, hearsay.

Judge: Counsel, your response.

Prosecution: Your Honor, this is a business record.

Defense: Your Honor, they have not yet laid the foundation that this report was created during the regular course of operations for this company.

Judge: Sustained.

The judge will usually, but not always, give the objecting attorney the last word. When given the opportunity to speak, you should usually take advantage of it. Many teams will say, "I stand on my objection." This is acceptable, but rarely ideal. In the above, the other side claimed they met an exception to the hearsay rule, and the attorney was able to point out that although an exception existed, the opposing side had not yet elicited the testimony needed to fall within that exception.

Be mindful of the fact that some responses from the other side lead their way into new objections from you.

Prosecution: How many times did the defendant shoot the victim?

Defense: Objection. Calls for speculation.

Judge: Counsel, your response.

Prosecution: Your Honor, the witness knows how many shots were fired because he spoke to the medical examiner.

Judge: Anything further.

Defense: Yes, Your Honor, I'd add the grounds of hearsay.

What do you do when the other side made a solid argument and the testimony actually is admissible? It depends. When evidence is offered for a limited purpose, ask that the jury be instructed on that point. For example, out of court statements can be admissible when they are "not offered for the truth of the matter asserted."

Prosecution: What did the neighbor tell you?

Defense: Objection. Hearsay.

Judge: Counsel, your response.

Prosecution: Your Honor, we are not offering the statement for its truth, but rather to show its effect on the listener.

Judge: Anything further.

Defense: Your Honor, based on that response, we'd ask that the jury be instructed that they are only to use the statement for that limited purpose.

But what if you're really stuck? Let's say you forgot about an exception, or you were making the objection for other strategic reasons. What do you do when, based on the other side's statements, it's clear the evidence is admissible? You could "stand on your objection" but we advise against that. The objection is a loser. Standing on it only makes it look like you don't realize it's a loser. Rather, say you "withdraw the objection." This gives you credibility in the future when you stand your ground and fight even after the other team has given a response.

Of course, you want to avoid situations that require withdrawing your objection! That is simply making the best of a bad situation that is of your own doing. This is why we suggest objecting only when you believe you are correct.

14.6 Voir Dire

The term "voir dire" comes from French and Latin, and it means "to speak the truth." It's pronounced either "vwahr deer" or "vhawr dy-er." If that's not confusing enough, it has two meanings in our legal system. Voir dire refers to the process of questioning potential jurors to make sure they are fit to serve on the jury. You won't be selecting jurors in Mock Trial, so you can safely ignore that meaning. Voir dire also refers to the process of questioning the other side's witness to determine whether there is an adequate foundation before they give certain testimony.

This arises most often with expert witnesses. Suppose the prosecution calls Dr. Garcia to the stand to testify as an expert in blood spatter. The prosecutor asks Dr. Garcia some background questions about her field of expertise and her credentials, and then the prosecutor asks for her conclusion about the blood spatter in this case. You are the defense attorney, and you think the prosecutor has not satisfied the Rule 702 requirements for an expert conclusion. You object: "Objection, lack of foundation for expert opinion under Rule 702." The judge might overrule your objection, sustain it, or allow you and the prosecutor to debate the issue before making a ruling. Or the judge might ask if you want to voir dire. That means the direct examination would pause and you would question the witness to support your objection. You may also attempt to initiate voir dire by saying: "Prefatory to making an objection, may I voir dire the witness?" In this instance, the process proceeds as discussed below, but, at the conclusion of the voir dire, you state the grounds for your objection.

If a judge asks if you want to voir dire, you should say yes if you can find even a couple questions that will support your point. Voir dire is a powerful way to interrupt your opponent's direct exam, discredit the witness before they offer a conclusion, and even exclude some of your opponent's evidence.

Here is how to voir dire the witness. First, treat this as cross-examination. Stand up and move to wherever you will stand while conducting your cross. Next, ask a few questions that support the grounds for your objection. Once you have the answers you want, turn to the judge and repeat your objection. Here is how it might play out:

Prosecutor: What is your conclusion?

You: Objection, lack of foundation for any reliable principles and methods.

Judge: Would you like to voir dire the witness?

You: Yes, Your Honor.

[You stand and move to spot for cross-examination]

You: Good evening, Doctor.

Witness: Hello.

You: You conducted a blood spatter analysis, correct?

Witness: Yes.

You: You used a new method for conducting that analysis?

Witness: Yes.

You: It was invented two years ago, wasn't it?

Witness: Yes.

You: That method has not been approved by any national scientific organizations, has it?

Witness: No.

You: Hasn't been subjected to peer review either?

Witness: No, not yet.

You: Your Honor, the defense objects to any conclusion based on this untested, unapproved method. Rule 702 requires that any opinion be based on reliable principles and methods, and this method doesn't meet that standard.

Following your statement, the other side will either respond and try to get the evidence in or withdraw the question and move on. (If it's the latter, you win that objection by default.) Judges will usually overrule objections to an expert's credentials or methodology because, in a Mock Trial, they want each side to be able to present their expert's conclusion. But you can still score a lot of points by voir diring the witness.

Voir dire usually occurs in Mock Trial when the judge invites you to voir dire. You can also request it. In the example above, you would say, "Objection, lack of foundation for any reliable principles and methods. May I voir dire the witness?" Make sure, though, that your competition permits voir dire before asking to do so. Also, when it is permitted, it almost always counts against your cross-examination time. Keep it brief.

Sometimes, though, the judge will ask if you want to voir dire and there are no questions you can ask to support your objection. This occurs when the witness has adequate foundation for their opinion, but opposing counsel has not yet established it. There, you can say, "Thank you, Your Honor, but I am not seeking to voir dire the witness. I am not objecting that the witness is unqualified. I am objecting that counsel has not laid a foundation for their qualifications. I would ask that the foundation be laid before the opinion is offered."

In real life, voir dire is also permitted on other foundational issues. For instance, if you are challenging whether an exhibit meets the business records exception to the hearsay rule, the judge might allow you to voir dire on that specific issue. In Mock Trial, judges almost never offer or permit voir dire on issues unrelated to experts.

Remember that voir dire always occurs outside the presence of the jury. The whole point is to establish whether the evidence is admissible before the jury sees it. Of course, in Mock Trial the jury of scoring judges doesn't actually leave the room during voir dire. This is important when the voir dire covered the same questions you had planned to ask during cross-examination. You don't want to repeat the same questions because it will bore the judges. But you don't want to skip those questions because technically they are not on the record and you want to be able to argue those facts in closing argument.

There is an elegant solution. "Your Honor, may we presume that the jury has heard the voir dire? That way we can avoid repeating the same questions and answers on cross-examination." Not only does this permit you to use the testimony in closing argument, but it tells the judges that you know the rules. You can make this request after the judge has ruled on your voir dire, or at the beginning of your cross—whichever you prefer.

14.7 Standing Objections

When the judge overrules your objection, and opposing counsel continues down a line of questioning that you believe is inappropriate, a "standing objection" may be used. A standing objection treats it as if you are objecting to all questions on a particular topic without you having to repeatedly make an objection that is going to be overruled.

The phrase to use for a standing objection is: "In light of your ruling, we would request a standing objection to any further questioning regarding ___________."

This is rare in Mock Trial, and we would only advise using it if you can tell the judge is experienced and knowledgeable.

14.8 Offers of Proof

An offer of proof is made to explain something to the judge or to make a record for appeal. In the first instance, a common time for an offer of proof is in response to a hearsay objection. The judge may not be able to rule on the objection without knowing what the witness is going to say. The attorney may ask to "make an offer of proof" with respect to the witness's expected answer or use the shorthand: "May I proffer?"

In the second instance, the judge has already ruled, and you disagree with the ruling. You make an offer of proof to potentially change the judge's mind, but mostly to preserve the record for appeal. If an appellate court cannot see and evaluate the evidence that was kept out, it's unlikely to find reversible error. So, following the adverse ruling, the attorney states: "In light of the court's ruling, may I make an offer of proof?

An offer of proof may be done by way of professional statement or in question-and-answer format. The former is just the attorney representing what the excluded evidence was or what it was expected to be. Question and answer format looks just like direct or cross-examination, but occurs outside the presence of the jury. The former is faster; the latter can be more impactful.

In Mock Trial, there is no appellate court. So, why would you make an offer of proof? The same reason you do anything and everything—to score points.[7] Making an offer of proof demonstrates that you know how things work in the real world. The more real you make things look and seem, the more points you're likely to earn.

If you make an offer of proof, keep two things in mind. First, it counts against your time limits, so decide if it's worth it. Second, keep in mind that—unless the judge reverses their ruling when you're done—it's not part of the trial record. So, your team cannot reference the information obtained from it during closing arguments.

14.9 What to Do After a Ruling

Don't say thank you after a ruling. If you lost, it sounds disingenuous. If you won, it sounds cocky. Use "the nod" instead. The nod is an acknowledgement of the ruling. If the ruling was bad, it says, "I realize I can't win them all. Watch how I get around it." If it was a good ruling for you, it says, "Thank you for applying your vast legal knowledge to that issue; we both know I can't praise you for it aloud, so I'll just nod."

Most Mock Trial judges will err on the side of letting evidence in, so don't be upset if your objection is overruled. You might still have increased your score.

Conversely, if your objection is sustained, listen *very* closely to the next questions asked. Often, attorneys are so busy patting themselves on the back for the sustained objection they fail to realize the opposing attorney snuck in the exact same information by asking the same question a slightly different way.

Finally, never, *ever* appear unhappy with a ruling. If you sit down and start whispering to your cocounsel or scribbling frantically on your legal pad, the judges will all assume you are complaining about the ruling. In real life, such conduct tells the jury that the objection loss was a big deal—you don't want them to think you lost an important ruling. In Mock Trial, it will just look unprofessional and risk earning ire from the judge in later rulings—or worse, in their scores.

7. As with all advanced techniques, before making an offer of proof confirm it is permitted under the rules of your particular competition.

15

Rules of Evidence

If you control the rules of evidence, you control the courtroom. You can present clean and persuasive direct and cross-examinations, disrupt your opponent's directs and crosses, exclude evidence critical to your opponent's case, and look more knowledgeable than your opponent.

"Evidence" is the legal word for "proof." It's the testimony given by the witnesses and the exhibits admitted into the record (that's why it's often called "offering an exhibit into *evidence*"). Evidence is how we prove the facts necessary to convince the jury that our theory is correct. Opening statements and closing arguments are important, but they are not evidence. An opening tells the jury what the evidence is expected to be, and a closing summarizes for the jury what the evidence actually was.

Suppose you want to prove that, in 2019, the Cal-Berkeley football team defeated the Stanford football team (Judge Nelmark went to Stanford Law School, while Professor Bernstein went to Berkeley).[1] You could call an eyewitness who was at the game. You could call all 48,904 fans who attended the game. You could call a witness who didn't attend the game but spoke to someone who did. You could introduce a photo of the scoreboard or a video recording of the game. You could offer a newspaper article about the game. You could call a football expert who would testify that Cal likely won because it had superior coaching, players, and heart. You could call an eyewitness who believes Cal probably won because she saw their fans after the game, and they seemed happy.

All these examples would constitute evidence of who won the game. But because we want trials to be fair, reliable, and efficient, the law restricts which evidence is permitted. The rules would allow an eyewitness to

1. Judge Nelmark would like readers to know that Professor Bernstein's choice of 2019 is not coincidental. It was the first time in a decade that you *could* prove Cal beat Stanford in football.

testify, "I was there, and I saw Cal win the game." That's probably reliable testimony. If there is something unreliable about the testimony—if the witness has memory problems or prior perjury convictions or a reason to lie about the result—then cross-examination can expose that unreliability to the jury. But what about the witness who didn't see the game but spoke to someone who did? Or the witness who is guessing about the winner based on fan reactions? That is less reliable, and the rules of evidence will often exclude that testimony. Efficiency is important, too. Trials take the time of judges, court staff, and jurors. Would it be persuasive to hear from all 48,904 fans? Probably. Is that a good, efficient use of everyone's time? No way. The rules wouldn't permit that many witnesses because the trial would never end.

All evidence is permissible except that which is excluded by the rules. So, the default is that everything is allowed unless the opposing side makes an objection and can identify the rule mandating exclusion. In the real world, objections are also important because even if the judge disagrees and allows in the material, objections preserve the potential error for review by an appellate court. As judges are often told in pre-round training sessions, there is no appellate court in Mock Trial!

You might wonder, why would the case problem include inadmissible material? For starters, it helps differentiate the best teams. They can demonstrate their ability to identify which evidence is actually admissible. In addition, sometimes evidence is admissible if you are using it for one purpose but not admissible for a different purpose. Often, whether evidence is admissible in trial is about more than the evidence itself; it has as much to do with how well each side makes its argument and, in a case with a pool of witnesses to choose from, which witnesses are selected.

The rules of evidence take time and experience to master. First, you need to learn the rules themselves. Then you need to apply them to the facts of your case. Finally, you need to practice. A lot. Learning the rules isn't like cramming for a history test, where you can earn an "A" just by memorizing names and dates. You need to become so comfortable with the rules that you can apply them in an instant; you can listen to the opponent's direct and immediately know when to object.

One word of caution before you dive in: the rules of evidence will be interpreted differently by every presiding judge. This happens because evidentiary rulings are often discretionary, and reasonable minds will differ. In baseball, some pitches are clearly balls, some are clearly strikes, and the ones right on the edge of the strike zone require interpretation from the umpire. It's the same with real trials and Mock Trial. Different smart, knowledgeable judges can hear the same evidence and reach different conclusions. And, of course, some judges don't know the rules as well as others; if you are going to be a trial lawyer, you need to be able to win trials even when the judge is imperfect.

All of this means that you need to be flexible. This book will explain how the rules work. But you will need to listen carefully to your presiding judge and figure out how they apply the rules in their courtroom.

15.1 Which Rules of Evidence Apply to Your Competition?

Every jurisdiction has its own set of evidentiary rules. Federal court has different evidentiary rules than state court. The rules of evidence in Iowa, where Judge Nelmark presides, are different from the rules of evidence in California, where Professor Bernstein practiced.

Every Mock Trial competition has its own set of rules of evidence. Most high school and middle school competitions use a highly simplified version of their state's rules of evidence. College Mock Trial is governed by the Midlands Rules of Evidence (because all American Mock Trial Association cases take place in the fictional 51st state of Midlands, where the citizens have a wide variety of accents and there is a surprisingly steady murder rate—about one per year). The Midlands Rules of Evidence are very similar to the Federal Rules of Evidence. Almost every interstate law school competition relies on the Federal Rules of Evidence.

For the purposes of this book, we will use the Federal Rules of Evidence. But make sure to check your competition's rules. They may not recognize several real-life objections, and they may define certain rules differently from the Federal Rules.

WAR STORY

When Judge Nelmark was a high school competitor in the State of Iowa High School Mock Trial Semi-Finals, he objected that opposing counsel was being "argumentative." The competition rules at that time had an objection for "badgering the witness," but not "argumentative." As a result, his team's 20-point victory and spot in the State Championship turned into a disqualification loss. Really. Judge Nelmark would like you to know that his "illegal" objection was ***sustained***. Not that he's still bitter or anything. But, in all seriousness, know your competition's specific rules.

15.2 Form Rules

Some rules are not designed to restrict the evidence the jury hears, but rather just the way it is presented. Imagine a witness takes the stand and begins testifying. There are no questions. She just starts talking. For two hours, the witness presents nothing but relevant, important facts. All the evidence is admissible. But our legal system thinks this is a bad way for the jury to *hear* the evidence. Without questions from the lawyer, the jury might not know why each piece of information matters. Without questions from the lawyer, opposing counsel does not know what information is about to be elicited—which makes it hard to object before the testimony has already been heard. Most importantly, it's hard for the jury to listen to a person speak, nonstop, for an entire direct examination.

The rules that govern the way evidence is presented are called form rules, and if they are violated we can raise "form objections." This section covers the most common form objections.

15.2.1 Leading

A leading question is one that suggests an answer. "You went to the store, right?" Under Rule 611(c), a leading question is allowed only in three situations: (1) on cross-examination, (2) with a hostile witness, and (3) on preliminary questions. In general, there is no reason to lead a witness on direct exam. If the other team is leading their witnesses on other than preliminary background information, object.

Many judges mistakenly think that any yes/no question is leading. For example, "Did you go to the store?" is not leading, but some judges think it is. The presiding judge in your round is always right, regardless of what the rules state. If you are the attorney performing the direct examination, try to avoid "Did" or "Were" questions. And if you encounter a judge who thinks yes/no questions are leading, adjust your questions immediately. In addition, start objecting to the other team. Chances are, they won't be able to adjust their questions easily.

15.2.2 Compound

Compound questions ask two different questions at once. "Isn't it true that you found no blood in that room, and you found no hairs, either?" This should be two separate questions because the answer to each question could be different. One way to spot compound objections is to listen to conjunctions, such as "and," in the question. If you hear a compound question, object. Opposing counsel can do little except concede and rephrase.

Just because a question involves multiple facts does not make it compound. "You own a red Chevy truck?" is not compound. Yes, it involves multiple facts. But it can be answered with a single answer—either the witness owns a red Chevy truck or they do not.

Similarly, a question that "links" to the previous answer is not compound. "After you found the body, did you call anyone?" is permissible. The first clause is restating the witness's testimony; the second clause is the only question. Note that some judges might prohibit this question on the basis that counsel is testifying, but it's not a compound question.

15.2.3 Asked and Answered

As much as repetition is an effective tool for persuasion, you can't keep repeating the same question. If opposing counsel asks a question, gets an answer, and then re-asks the same question to the same witness, that question is objectionable. Note that the question must have truly been answered. If the witness is being nonresponsive, don't object asked and answered. It will likely draw the response from opposing counsel that: "The question has been asked, but it has not been answered." This underscores that the witness was being evasive.

The asked and answered rule does not apply if different lawyers ask the same question. You can't prevent your opponent from asking a question on cross simply by asking it during your direct. Nor does the rule apply with different witnesses. Asking a question to one witness does not prohibit you from asking the same question to a different witness.

15.2.4 Argumentative

You can ask questions that establish facts, but you may not make arguments or draw inferences. For example, on cross-examination, you can ask: "You told the police you *didn't* see the shooter's face?" and "You told this jury you *did* see the shooter's face?" But you cannot ask, "Were you lying then or lying now?" That doesn't seek any facts. It is just looking to argue and name-call. The question, "Do you expect the jury to believe that?" is a classic argumentative question. It does not seek information. It is only meant to smear the witness.

If a lawyer characterizes a witness's testimony, that is argumentative. Suppose the witness gives an answer and the lawyer responds, "That's hard to believe." You can object argumentative.

The line between argumentative questions and permissible questions is often blurry. You will need to develop your own style of asking questions and listen carefully to how the judge controls the trial and what they are willing to let you get away with.

15.2.5 Badgering

Attorneys cannot berate or intimidate witnesses. If opposing counsel is nasty or rude to your witness, you can object badgering. If the attorney is standing right next to your witness and screaming, you can object badgering. If the attorney interrupts your witness, you can say, "Objection, badgering. My witness should be allowed to complete her answer."

WAR STORY

If opposing counsel is being intimidating by getting too close to a witness without permission, it might be "badgering." It might be "argumentative." It is never, as then-competitor Nelmark once said during a Mock Trial practice in the midst of football season, "encroachment."

15.2.6 Assumes Facts Not in Evidence

You cannot ask a question that assumes information that has not yet been established. You cannot ask a witness, "When did you first meet the defendant?" until you have established *that* they met the defendant.

15.2.7 Vague

Questions must be specific enough that the jury understands what is being asked. This is a good objection to break flow. If the attorney doesn't specify a time or place, a vague objection can be effective. For example:

Q. Did you see the defendant the month before the murder?

A. Yes, three times.

Q. What was the defendant's demeanor?

You: Objection, vague as to time.

Form objections can be effective when you are facing a more experienced opponent. They can't show off their evidentiary knowledge very easily because the issues are so simple.

15.3 Substantive Rules

Substantive rules of evidence affect which evidence the jury gets to hear. You can use substantive objections to prevent your opponent from presenting the evidence they want to present. It is often hard to get judges to sustain a substantive objection, but when you do it's often more destructive to your opponent's case—and their scores.

15.3.1 Relevance

Only relevant evidence is admissible. This is to prevent the trial from becoming unnecessarily long and to make sure the jury isn't distracted or prejudiced by information that does not matter.

Under Rule 401, relevant evidence is "any evidence tending to make the existence or nonexistence of a fact necessary to the resolution of the action more or less probable." In simpler terms, evidence is relevant if it helps the jury determine the outcome of the case. If one element of the charge is that the defendant is the one who shot the victim with a rifle, it would be relevant to know if the defendant owned a rifle. Obviously, that fact does not resolve the issue because you can own a rifle without shooting someone, and you can shoot someone without *owning* the gun that shot them. But ownership of the rifle is relevant to determining the defendant's guilt.

Relevance has a famously low bar. In other words, evidence need not be very important to be admissible under Rule 401.

Relevance objections tend to be very unwise. They are easy to defeat because the bar for relevance is so low. They give the opponent a chance to argue their case—without using up any time for closing argument. If the relevance of the testimony was unclear to the judges, you have given your opponent a chance to clarify. The best teams rarely object to relevance.

Some teams like to make relevance objections during the introductory questions of the other team's character witnesses. Their goal is to disrupt the direct and prevent the character from establishing likeability. If the witness is giving long answers with utterly irrelevant information, then a relevance objection may be successful and effective. But if the witness's "character answer" is fairly short, a relevance objection is more likely to annoy the judges, who may be enjoying the witness's answer. And these kind of relevance objections are especially unwise if your team's character witnesses have similar introductory questions.

15.3.2 Unfair Prejudice

While relevancy is necessary for the admission of evidence into the record, it does not guarantee admission. Relevant evidence may be excluded under Rule 403 if its "probative value is substantially outweighed by its prejudicial impact." This occurs, in simpler terms, when an item of evidence has a legitimate purpose for being admitted but it also has an illegitimate purpose whose danger far exceeds the value of the legitimate purpose.

Suppose, for example, the prosecution in a murder case wants to admit a particularly gruesome photo of the victim. The photo certainly has probative value: it helps prove that the victim is in fact dead, and it may indicate the manner of death. But these facts may be established through other means—description by eyewitnesses or experts. And the photo also carries a strong prejudicial effect. Viewers are likely to be upset by the grisliness of the picture. They may become so angry that they are more likely to convict—even though the horrific nature of the crime probably has little to do with whether the defendant is the perpetrator. Such evidence is thus often excluded because its probative value is far outweighed by the danger of its prejudicial effect.

Just because a fact is bad for your case does not make it *unfairly* prejudicial. Presumably, all the facts offered by your opponent are bad for your case. To win a 403 objection for unfair prejudice, you need to show that the jury is likely to misconstrue the evidence or give it too much weight. The general standard for prejudicial effect is whether the evidence is likely to inflame the passions of a reasonable person (i.e., whether it is likely to make a rational person act irrationally).

Objections based on "unfair prejudice" are rarely successful. The standard—the prejudicial effect must "substantially" outweigh the relevance—is hard to meet. Mock Trial cases rarely include facts that are sufficiently prejudicial that they need to be excluded. Avoid this objection, especially in a bench trial. Judges are probably more able to think logically in the face of potentially prejudicial evidence than lay jurors—and even if they aren't, judges think they are.

15.3.3 Authenticity

Exhibits must be authentic to be admitted. Under Rule 901, "To satisfy the requirement of authenticating or identifying an item of evidence, the proponent must produce evidence sufficient to support a finding that the item is what the proponent claims it is."

For documents, you need to establish that the exhibit is the original or a fair and accurate copy of the original.

For media exhibits—photos, audio recordings, video recordings—you need to establish that they fairly depict whatever you are trying to depict. Suppose Exhibit A is a photo of a person standing by a lake. If you are trying to establish that the photo shows what Lake Wanaka looked like in 2021, you need a witness to testify that she was familiar with Lake Wanaka and this photo accurately depicts how it looked in 2021. The witness doesn't need to identify the person in the photo. On the other hand, if you are introducing this as a photo of the victim, the witness needs to testify that she recognizes the person in the photo as the victim. The witness does not need to be able to identify the lake. In either case, the witness does not need to be the person who took the photograph (though this is another common misunderstanding by judges).

Sometimes Mock Trial cases involve tangible exhibits. For example, Professor Bernstein's Gladiator and Trial by Combat cases generally have one tangible exhibit per year, such as ski masks, lead pipes, necklaces, (fake) cocaine, and bullet shell casings. To authenticate a tangible exhibit, a witness needs to testify that the exhibit is the item in question ("This is the mask I collected from the defendant's trunk") and that it is in "substantially the same condition" as when it was collected. Authentication often means establishing a chain of custody: who had the exhibit from the time it was collected and confirmation that the exhibit has not been altered.

Many Mock Trial cases will stipulate that some or all exhibits are authentic. Make sure you know whether you need to lay foundation for authenticity and whether you can object if your opponent does not.

15.3.4 Foundation for Personal Knowledge

A witness cannot testify to a fact until we know how they know that fact. For example, a witness cannot take the stand and say, "My name is Bob Williams. The defendant shot Ms. Park." How does the witness know that? We need to establish that the witness saw the shooting before the witness says that's what happened. That information—establishing how a witness knows something—is called foundation for personal knowledge.

When opposing counsel attempts to elicit testimony without laying foundation, object. There are multiple ways to phrase it:

"Objection, lack of foundation for personal knowledge."

"Objection, lack of foundation."

"Objection, foundation."

If it is not clear from the context, you can also identify what foundation you think is missing. Suppose the witness testifies, "The house was at 10 Main Street. It was worth two million dollars." If you want to challenge only the foundation for the second half of the answer, you can object, "Objection, lack of foundation for the value of the house."

There are three common *incorrect* responses to a foundation objection. (1) "Your Honor, I was going to ask that next." That's not how it works. Just like you need to lay the foundation for a house before you build the actual house, you have to lay the foundation for a witness's observations before you offer the observations. (2) "Your Honor, this is in the witness's affidavit." It is not enough for the foundation to exist in the witness's Mock Trial statement. It has to be stated on the record in trial before the witness can testify to it. (3) "Your Honor, the witness testified to ___, so we can assume that ____" If you have to assume the foundation, you haven't laid the foundation. When opposing counsel makes an improper response like this, you can respond, "Your Honor, we need to hear that from the witness, not from counsel. We ask that proper foundation be laid."

If the judge sustains a foundation objection against you, don't sweat it. Just lay the foundation. Ask the witness how they know the fact. Establish the missing foundation. Then re-ask your question. You don't need to ask permission to lay foundation. Just do it. You can often increase your score by laying foundation and making it look easy.

If the judge sustains your foundation objection against the other team, remain alert. If opposing counsel tries to re-ask their original question without solving the foundation problem, renew your objection. "Objection, the same foundation still hasn't been laid."

Earlier we said relevance is generally a poor objection. *Foundation is generally the best objection.* It is easier for judges to sustain because they don't feel like they are excluding the evidence, just asking the other side to lay a little more foundation. It doesn't let opposing counsel show off because there are no rule numbers to cite or fancy legal knowledge to repeat. If they didn't lay the foundation, they didn't lay the foundation. The consequences of a sustained foundation objection can be disastrous for the opponent. Their best-case scenario is they successfully lay foundation. But that burns their time. Their worst-case scenario is they struggle to lay the foundation. Or they elicit inadmissible evidence that allows you to object on other grounds.

Let's Get Real: In Mock Trial, making the other side burn some of their limited time by laying foundation is useful. In real jury trials, if you're constantly requiring the other side to back up, the jury will likely feel you are wasting their time, which is bad for your client. If foundation can be easily laid, it's probably not worth objecting to. If the foundation cannot be laid, it's a different analysis because you may be able to keep the evidence out entirely.

You will find that foundation objections often reveal hearsay objections:

Q. When did the defendant marry the victim?

You: Objection, foundation.

Judge: Sustained.

Q. Do you know when the defendant married the victim?

A. Yes, I spoke to someone who attended the wedding.

Q. So when did the defendant marry the victim?

You: Objection, the witness's knowledge is based purely on hearsay.

Judge: Sustained.

15.3.5 Speculation

A witness can only testify to what they know. They cannot guess. The legal term for guessing is "speculation." Speculation involves information a witness cannot know with any certainly.

If the question is asking for speculative information, you say, "Objection, calls for speculation." If the question is fine, but the witness supplies speculative testimony, say, "Objection, speculation."

The most common speculation occurs when a witness tries to testify to what someone else was thinking. "Why did the defendant go to the store?" Object speculation. The witness cannot tell us why someone else decided to do something. "How did Mr. Trujillo feel about the defendant marrying his daughter?" Object to speculation. The witness is being asked what someone else thought. Notice that both questions would be proper if they were adjusted slightly. "Did the defendant tell you why he went to the store?" "Did Mr. Trujillo tell you how he felt about the defendant marrying his daughter?" Those questions might draw different objections (e.g., hearsay), but they don't involve speculation. The witness knows what they were told. (The hearsay objection in this instance can likely be defeated if the testimony is offered by the State because statements from a party opponent in the case are not hearsay. More on that later.)

Witness testimony is also speculative if a witness tries to testify about events they didn't actually observe. Most good teams avoid this testimony, but be alert and object if they try to introduce it.

Sometimes witnesses will speculate when estimating or offering an opinion. Consider the following questions about a car accident:

About how tall was the pedestrian?

How fast was the car going?

When you interacted with the driver after the accident, was he drunk? Each of these requires some guesswork, but they are not equally admissible. Under Rule 701, a lay witness (nonexpert) is allowed to testify to matters within their "rational perception"—things they saw, heard, tasted, felt, smelled. We call these lay witness opinions. For example, even assuming the witness did not pull out a tape measure, most people can still estimate the height of another person they saw clearly. The question about height is fine, and nearly every judge would allow it.

Some judges would allow a lay witness to estimate a car's speed. Some would exclude that estimate as speculative. Your safer bet is probably to soften the witness's answer. "Had you seen cars driving on this road before? From what you observed, was the defendant driving faster or slower than most of the cars you usually see on this road?" Most judges would allow this question because we trust people to give this general estimate, even if we don't trust them to offer a miles-per-hour conclusion.

Most judges would sustain a speculation objection to the question about whether the driver was drunk. A layperson cannot testify that another person was drunk. But sometimes a slight change in phrasing makes all the difference. "Jimmy *was* drunk" will be sustained as speculative in most trials. "Jimmy *seemed* drunk" will usually be permitted. This is because most people are familiar with the common symptoms of drunkenness, so saying that someone *seemed* drunk is generally admissible if you can establish foundation for the witness's opinion.

Speculation and lack of foundation are often confused because they are very similar. Testimony lacks foundation for personal knowledge when counsel has not established that the witness knows the answer. Testimony is speculative when we know the witness doesn't know the answer. A lack of foundation problem can be cured by laying more foundation. Speculation cannot be cured; it's just inadmissible.

15.3.6 Character Evidence

Under Rule 404, character evidence—also known as propensity evidence—is "evidence of a person's character or a trait of character for the purpose of proving action in conformity therewith" on a particular occasion. In other words, character evidence is when a party tries to prove that a person did something by using evidence of the kind of person they are—their *character.* "Jimmy is a violent person, so he probably killed the victim." "Susie is a liar, so she probably lied to you today."

Character evidence takes two forms. One is a witness's opinion about a person's character. This requires foundation for the opinion. "I have known Tom for ten years, and he is very peaceful." The other is prior behavior. "I once saw someone swing a golf club at Tom's head. He dodged the five-iron and gave the guy a hug."

Under Rule 404, character evidence is generally inadmissible. Trials are supposed to be about what people did during the events in question, not what they have done in the past. We don't want juries to convict someone of a crime just because of other things they've done in the past or the kind of person we think they are.

Let's look at an example. Shawna is on trial for murder in 2021. The prosecution alleges that Shawna shot and killed Greg with a sniper rifle from half a mile away. At trial, the prosecutor tries to admit Shawna's criminal record—specifically, her previous convictions for (1) illegal possession of a firecracker in 2020 and (2) murdering Bob in 2016. Let's consider each.

First, the firecracker conviction should be excluded because, even though it is recent, it is irrelevant to whether Shawna murdered Greg. But what if the prosecutor argues that the firecracker conviction "shows what kind of person Shawna is—the kind of person who ignores the law"? Shawna's attorney should respond: "That would be character evidence. Rule 404 prohibits the prosecution from arguing that a person's prior misconduct makes future misconduct more likely." The evidence should be excluded.

What about the previous murder conviction? To most of us, this seems very relevant—if she did it before, she might do it again. But the law thinks jurors are unable to give such evidence its appropriate weight. The law fears that jurors will look at Shawna's prior conviction for the same crime and think, "Once a murderer, always a murderer"—and ignore all other evidence. To counter this tendency, Rule 404 bars the prior murder conviction if the prosecutor's purpose is to show "action in conformity therewith."

We say character evidence is "generally" inadmissible because there are several exceptions. We will focus on the two most common categories of exceptions here. You should also review the exceptions for a victim or defendant in a criminal case (Rule 404(a)(2)) and habit evidence (Rule 406).

The first major category of exceptions to the character evidence ban comes from Rule 404(b). This rule says that evidence of a person's wrong, crime, or act "may be admissible for another purpose, such as proving motive, opportunity, intent, preparation, plan, knowledge, identity, absence of mistake, or lack of accident."

Let's go back to Shawna's murder trial. If Shawna's 2016 murder of Bob involved a sniper rifle fired from 400 yards away, that information would probably be admissible in the 2021 Greg murder trial. The prosecution could credibly argue, "We aren't using this under 404(a) to prove that Shawna is the type of person who commits murder. Instead, we are using this evidence under Rule 404(b). This shows her knowledge of how to operate a sniper rifle and her ability to hit a target from great distance.

Those are rare skills, and they help prove that the defendant could and did commit this crime."

This concept is crucial: *the same evidence can be inadmissible when offered for one purpose, but admissible when offered for another purpose*. This means you need to be creative when thinking about whether you can use certain evidence.

Study the permissible uses in Rule 404(b). For example, if Shawna claimed at trial that, "Yes, I did pull the trigger, but I didn't mean to hit Greg," her prior accurate shootings with the sniper rifle would help prove her "lack of mistake or accident."

The second category of character evidence exceptions comes from Rules 608 and 609. This rule only applies to witnesses. Because juries need to determine whether witnesses are telling the truth, we have special rules for witnesses that allow attorneys to present evidence that reveals the witness's character. Under Rule 608(a), a party can present evidence that a witness has a reputation for being dishonest. A party may also call a witness to testify that, in their experience, another witness is generally dishonest. Once a witness has been attacked as dishonest, the other party may present similar evidence—reputation or another witness's opinion—that the witness is truthful. Rule 608(b) allows an attorney to cross-examine a witness about their prior instances of dishonesty.

Rule 609 is similar, but it relates to criminal convictions. Note that criminal arrests, charges, accusations, and trials do not qualify under this rule—only convictions.

Under Rule 609(a)(1), a witness's felony conviction is admissible as long as the judge does not think it is unfairly prejudicial. A felony is any crime that was *punishable* by more than a year in prison. The witness did not actually have to be sentenced to more than a year for this exception to apply. If the prior crime carries a sentence of up to three years in prison, but the witness was only sentenced to six months in prison, the crime is still "punishable" by more than a year. The rationale for this rule is that felonies are the most serious crimes in our society. A felony conviction may offer insight into the witness's morality and character, and the rules reflect the view that the jury is entitled to learn such information.

Under Rule 609(a)(2), a witness's conviction for a crime involving dishonesty is admissible. Notice that, unlike the felony exception, the judge does not need to evaluate if the evidence is unfairly prejudicial. It is admissible, period, because the law thinks that when a witness has committed a crime of dishonesty, the jury should know that. A crime of dishonesty is one where we can tell simply from the elements of the crime that dishonesty was involved. This includes fraud and perjury. It would not include murder or robbery. Those are terrible crimes, but they do not necessarily involve dishonesty.

You should read the entirety of Rule 609 to understand the restrictions on this evidence. There are two main principles to remember here. If the conviction (and the witness's release from prison) was more than ten years ago, the law generally prohibits evidence of the conviction. The idea is that people change over time, so this evidence is less reliable. Also, crimes committed as a juvenile are almost never admissible. The rationale is similar: people do dumb things when they are young, but they may have matured as adults.

As you can see, character evidence is complicated. There are exceptions, exceptions to the exceptions, and exceptions to those exceptions. Many real-life lawyers struggle with the character rules, so make sure not only to prepare carefully, but also be ready to explain the rules clearly. Being right is only valuable if you can persuade the judge that you're right.

15.3.7 Hearsay

No evidentiary topic confuses law students and attorneys as much as hearsay.

At its heart, the hearsay doctrine attempts to exclude unreliable evidence from the trial record. The idea is that witnesses should only be allowed to testify to information of which they have personal knowledge—things they saw, heard, did, felt. Kate can testify, "I saw Ben shoot Andrew." We allow Kate's testimony because we're not worried about whether it is reliable. If it's unreliable—maybe she is lying, maybe she wasn't wearing her glasses—then we expect the other party to show that unreliability during cross-examination. The other attorney can just cross-examine Kate: "You didn't have a good view?" "You hate Ben, don't you?" and so on.

Consider the difference, though, if Kate instead testifies, "Andrew told me that Ben shot him." The participants are the same, the underlying fact (that Ben shot Andrew) is the same, but now we have no way of determining the reliability of the testimony. Sure, we can cross-examine Kate—but that will only tell us if Kate is reliable, not if Andrew is reliable. The person whose reliability we care about here is Andrew, since it's his account of what happened that is being presented. In this second example, we are relying on secondhand information. The hearsay doctrine says such secondhand information (hearsay) is inadmissible unless one of a limited number of exceptions applies (Rule 802).

As you approach issues of hearsay, try to remember the aforementioned rationale for the exclusion of hearsay evidence: the inherent unreliability of secondhand information. Think about why the court should or shouldn't trust these potential pieces of hearsay evidence.

Learning hearsay has two essential components. First, you must learn what qualifies as hearsay and what does not. Second, if a statement does qualify as hearsay, you must learn whether an exception makes it nonetheless admissible. Remember—if it's hearsay without an applicable exception, it's inadmissible.

15.3.7.1 Definition of Hearsay

Before we dive into hearsay, you should know some basic terminology. Take the following example:

> Attorney: Where were you?
>
> Witness Janessa: At football practice.
>
> Attorney: Who was there?
>
> Janessa: Vik, Shoyeb, and me. Andrew was supposed be at football practice, but he was at Mock Trial practice.
>
> Attorney: How do you know he was at Mock Trial practice?
>
> Witness Janessa: Shoyeb told us, "I saw Andrew at Mock Trial practice instead."

In this example, Janessa is the "witness." She is repeating a statement, "I saw Andrew at Mock Trial practice instead." The statement was made by Shoyeb, which makes him the "declarant." The people who were there to hear the statement were Vik and Janessa.

You should memorize the following definition of hearsay:

> Hearsay is an out-of-court statement
> offered to prove the truth of the matter asserted.

Let's split the definition into three parts. Hearsay is (1) an out-of-court (2) statement (3) offered to prove the truth of the matter asserted. To determine if something is hearsay, simply determine if it meets that definition. If so, then it's hearsay. If not, then it's not hearsay.

Is it a statement? Hearsay is about excluding certain types of information and the threshold question is whether something counts as a statement. We don't use our everyday definition of statement, but rather the legal definition. Under Rule 801(a), a statement is "(1) an oral or written assertion or (2) nonverbal conduct of a person, if it is intended by the person as an assertion."

The first clause of the definition is the most common type of statement—an assertion that is either written down or spoken aloud. Assertions are statements that claim something is true. In the above example, Janessa testified, "Shoyeb said, 'I saw Andrew at Mock Trial practice instead.'" Shoyeb is asserting where Andrew was. It is either true or false.

Contrast that example with words that are not assertions. "What time is it?" This seeks information but does not assert any information. It is neither true nor false. It's just a question. Or: "Bring me a water bottle." It does not assert anything. This is neither true nor false. It's just a command. Thus, neither of these examples can be hearsay.

Sometimes hearsay does not involve any words at all. If a person intends to communicate an assertion without speaking or writing, that's still hearsay. The most obvious example would be a nod in answer to a question—the person says nothing, but clearly intends to communicate a "yes." Thus, that nod is hearsay. Be careful, though. The communication must be intended as an assertion. If Kunal is nodding to the beat of the latest Top 40 single, that's not hearsay because he doesn't intend to communicate a "yes." So, is a nod hearsay? It depends on the context. If you are the attorney, your job is to argue the facts that support your position.

The final requirement of a statement is that, under Rule 801(b), it must be made by a human declarant. If a witness testifies that the dog was growling, the growl is not hearsay because there is no human declarant. If the witness says, "I know it was five o'clock because I checked my watch," the statement is not hearsay because the witness is just reporting what the electronic device showed. That distinction holds true whether the witness was looking at a clock, thermometer, Fitbit, etc. Note that this analysis gets more complicated when it's not just the witness reporting an observation but rather an attempt to enter into evidence a printed document containing information created by a machine. In such cases, it depends on how the document was generated.

Forgetting to evaluate whether a supposed hearsay statement is actually a statement is one of the most common attorney errors. Students immediately go to the exceptions when such exceptions are unnecessary. You can skip the tough arguments if you can point out that the statement isn't actually a statement and therefore it's not hearsay.

Was the statement made out-of-court? This prong of the hearsay definition is usually the easiest. One caveat: The phrase "out-of-court" really means "outside of this particular trial." In other words, statements made in another court or during another trial qualify as "out-of-court" statements even though they were made in a court. A transcript from another trial can still be hearsay. Why? Because the parties in this trial may not have had an opportunity to cross-examine the declarant to see if they are reliable.

Is it being offered for the truth of the matter asserted? This third part of the definition concerns the purpose of the testimony. It forces us to answer the question: Why are we trying to admit the evidence in the first place? If the attorney is trying to prove that a fact is true because someone once said it was true, that means the statement is being offered for the truth of the matter asserted.

Consider this example:

Attorney: Where was Matt on Sunday?

Witness: On Monday, Matt told me he was at the Giants game on Sunday.

The attorney is offering this statement to prove that Matt was at the game on Sunday. The statement asserts that Matt was at the game on Sunday. In other words, the statement is being offered to prove the truth asserted by the statement. This statement is almost certainly hearsay.

Contrast this with the same statement in other context, used for another purpose:

Attorney: Do you know if Matt was still alive on Saturday?

Witness: He was. On Monday, Matt told me he was at the Giants game on Sunday.

Notice that both the witness's testimony and Matt's statement are the same as in the above example, except now the attorney is offering that testimony to prove a very different proposition. Before we wanted to know where Matt was; now we simply want to know whether Matt was alive. In this instance, the attorney is not offering the testimony to prove the truth of the matter asserted (that Matt was at the Giants game). Rather, the statement is being used to show that Matt was alive—if he made a statement on Monday, he wasn't dead the preceding Saturday! In other words, we don't care if Matt's statement is true—we only care that Matt made a statement at all. Thus, the attorney is not offering the statement to prove the truth of the matter asserted. This statement could not qualify as hearsay.

Let's Get Real: Judge Nelmark had a hearing where one attorney was fresh out of law school and the other had been in practice more than 20 years. The case involved recordings of out-of-court statements. When the young attorney offered one into evidence, it drew a hearsay exception. Judge Nelmark asked the young attorney if he was offering the document for the truth of the matter asserted. The young attorney confidently said: "Yes." No hearsay exceptions were offered, so Judge Nelmark sustained the objection. Soon, the shoe was on the other foot, and Judge Nelmark asked the experienced attorney if he was offering the recording for its truth. He also said: "Yes." Again the document was excluded. There are two takeaways from this story. First, even experienced attorneys lack understanding of the hearsay rule. Second, pay attention to your presiding judge. If the other side's answer does not achieve the desired result, try something different when you're asked the same question.

Consider the next example on your own before looking at the explanation below. The attorney is cross-examining the same witness, the defendant accused of killing Matt. Does the italicized statement constitute hearsay?

Attorney: You had motive to kill Matt, didn't you?

Defendant: No.

Attorney: Isn't it true that you told Matt not to go to the Sunday game without you?

Defendant: Yes, I did say that.

Attorney: In fact, you said that if he went without you, you would kill him?

Defendant: Yes, I said that.

Attorney: Did you talk to Matt on Monday?

Defendant: Yes. On Monday, *Matt told me he was at the Giants game on Sunday.*

Let's break it down to see if this is hearsay. Matt (1) made a statement (2) while out of court. The only issue is whether it is offered to prove the truth of the matter asserted. What is the truth being asserted by the statement? That Matt was at the game on Sunday. Is that why the attorney is offering the testimony into evidence? No. The attorney is offering this to prove that the defendant had motive because the defendant thought Matt was at the game on Sunday. Notice that whether Matt was actually there is irrelevant because the statement is being offered for the effect on the listener (in this case, the defendant), not for the truth of the matter asserted.

There are several reasons why an attorney might offer testimony other than to prove the matter asserted. These are called "non-hearsay" purposes. Remember that the non-hearsay purpose must still be relevant. Here are three examples:

- A police officer testifies that she received a call from dispatch, reporting a homicide at a certain address. The words from dispatch are not offered to prove that a homicide occurred, but to explain the officer's subsequent action in heading to the scene of the alleged crime.
- A doctor is sued for malpractice after giving medication to which the victim was allergic. If the victim testifies, "I told the doctor I was allergic to that medication," that is not offered to prove that in fact the victim was allergic, but rather to show the doctor knew it. This shows the doctor's negligence in administering the drug anyway.
- A defendant is charged with killing a victim at an abandoned lighthouse. A witness testifies, "I told the defendant the victim would be at the lighthouse that night." This is not hearsay because it is not offered to show that the victim was at the lighthouse. Instead, it shows the defendant knew where to find the victim, which makes the defendant a more likely suspect.

Similarly, impeachment is not hearsay because it is not offered to prove the truth of the matter asserted. Suppose Errol sees a car accident and tells the police officer the red car hit the blue car. At trial, Errol testifies that the blue car hit the red car. The lawyers could introduce Errol's previous statement as impeachment. This is not being offered to prove the truth of the matter asserted by the first statement—that, in fact, the red car hit the blue car. Rather, it is being used to show that Errol has made inconsistent statements about this issue, which goes to the credibility of his trial testimony. If you are trying to impeach a witness and the other side objects hearsay, you can respond, "Your Honor, this isn't hearsay. It's impeachment."

15.3.7.2 Other Statements That Are Not Hearsay

Certain statements look like they should fit the definition of hearsay but are not treated as hearsay.

The most common and most important example is "statement by a party opponent." Under Rule 801(d)(2) of the Federal Rules of Evidence, statements by a party opponent are considered "exempt" from the definition of hearsay. In other words, these statements otherwise meet the definition of hearsay, but the law has decided not to treat them as hearsay. For example, if the State charges Ms. Rhodes with robbery, the prosecutor can introduce anything Ms. Rhodes has said and it's not hearsay. There might be other objections to statements Ms. Rhodes has made, but hearsay is not one of them. This is a powerful rule for prosecutors in criminal cases.

The party opponent "exemption" does not go both ways. The defense attorney cannot use the party opponent rule to introduce Ms. Rhodes's statements because she is not the defense's party *opponent*.

The party opponent rule also extends to anyone authorized to speak on behalf of the party opponent. That usually includes statements made by their employee, agent, lawyer, or coconspirator. Suppose that a politician sues *The New York Times* for defamation, alleging that the newspaper published a false article about the politician. At trial, the politician's lawyers could introduce any statements by *The New York Times* editor or the reporter who wrote the story, and the defense would not be able to exclude their statements as hearsay because they are employees of the defendant. Note that in a criminal trial, the defense cannot invoke this rule. For example, the defense cannot say that police officers are agents of the State and therefore their statements are admissible under Rule 801(d)(2). In a criminal trial, the defense has no party opponent for the purposes of the hearsay rule.

Defense attorneys in criminal cases should be careful not to object hearsay to the defendant's statements. It can be tempting to make the objection because your client's statements otherwise fit the definition. Not only is it a losing objection, but it also is the worst kind of losing objection. If the prosecutor says, "This is a statement by our party opponent," there is literally nothing (correct) you can say in response. Don't put yourself in a position where you have to withdraw the objection.

Another category of statements that are not treated as hearsay are certain prior statements of a witness. Under Rule 801(d)(1), the parties can introduce a witness's prior statements if they were given under oath and are inconsistent with what the witness has said at trial. These are called "prior inconsistent statements."

Under a different subsection of Rule 801(d)(1), the parties can introduce a witness's "prior consistent statements" under certain circumstances. Suppose that an alibi witness testifies at trial that the defendant was with him during the time of the crime. The prosecutor argues or implies that the witness has only concocted that fact to protect his friend. The defense could then introduce the witness's statements about being with the defendant if they were made *before* the witness knew the defendant was being accused of murder. These prior consistent statements tend to suggest the witness is telling the truth because they were made before the witness had a reason to lie.

One final category of statements that look like hearsay but are not: verbal acts. These are sometimes referred to as "words of independent legal significance," and they do not have to be verbal statements. Suppose Steve signs a document agreeing to sell 100 apples to Tim at a certain price. The document is not hearsay. It's a contract. The words create a binding legal promise. The contract technically does not meet the definition of hearsay because it is not an assertion. The contract is neither true nor false. It is a statement of what the parties have agreed to. Other examples of verbal acts include slander, words that demonstrate someone has joined a criminal conspiracy, and bribery. This verbal acts rule occurs very rarely in Mock Trial and, because most judges don't understand it, use it only as a last resort.

15.3.7.3 Exceptions to the Hearsay Rule

The idea behind the hearsay rule is that our legal system distrusts second-hand information. Thus, hearsay is generally inadmissible. But there are exceptions to the hearsay rule because some statements are made under circumstances that the law deems more reliable.

Let's look at one example to illustrate how hearsay exceptions work. Suppose Stan sues a candy bar manufacturer because its product causes people to get red spots on their back. At trial, Stan's lawyer calls a doctor to the stand. The doctor testifies, "I am Stan's doctor. Last year, he called me and said, 'I just ate a candy bar, and now I have red spots. What should I do?'" The lawyer for the candy bar company objects hearsay. These statements are definitely hearsay: the plaintiff is using Stan's statements that he got red spots after eating the candy bar to prove that, in fact, he got red spots after eating the candy bar. But the judge should overrule the objection because statements made to a doctor for the purpose of diagnosis or treatment are an exception to the hearsay rule. Why? Because the law presumes that people have a reason to be honest with their doctors. If you lie to your doctor when they are trying to diagnose or treat your condition, it can go very badly for you. Of course, some people lie to their doctors ("How often do you drink?"), but the law says that statements to our doctors are sufficiently reliable that they should be admissible in court.

If a statement qualifies as a "hearsay exception," it does not mean that the statement is not hearsay. Quite the opposite; to be an exception to hearsay, it must be hearsay. Rather, it is an exception from the rule that otherwise renders the hearsay inadmissible (Rule 802). Why does this distinction matter? It affects how you phrase your argument in court. If you were Stan's lawyer, and the defense objected hearsay to the doctor's testimony, you should not respond, "This isn't hearsay because it falls under the Rule 803(4) exception, statement made for medical diagnosis or treatment." Instead, you should say, "This is hearsay. But it is admissible because it falls under the Rule 803(4) exception, statement made for medical diagnosis or treatment." Indeed, nearly every response to a hearsay objection should be (1) "This is not hearsay because . . ." or (2) "This meets an exception to the hearsay rule because . . ."

There are more than 25 specific hearsay exceptions in the Federal Rules of Evidence. We will highlight a few of the most-used hearsay exceptions.

Rule 803 lists more than 20 exceptions that apply regardless of whether the declarant is available. In other words, the declarant might be dead, or the declarant might be down the street having a sandwich. The circumstances under which they made their statement are considered so reliable that you can have another witness come to court and repeat their words.

Present Sense Impression, Rule 803(1)

You must demonstrate that (1) the declarant makes a statement (2) while observing an event or immediately thereafter, and (3) the statement describes the event. The rationale is that people are unlikely to lie if they are describing an event as it happens.

Excited Utterance, Rule 803(2)

You must demonstrate that (1) an exciting event took place, (2) the declarant was still under the stress of that event, and (3) the statement relates to the event. Once the declarant is no longer under the original stress of the event, their statements are no longer considered excited utterances—even if they later become upset again and make a statement about the event.

This rule is often confused with the present sense impression exception. But there are important differences. Present sense impression requires an immediate statement; an excited utterance can occur minutes or even hours later if you can prove the declarant has remained under the duress of the event the whole time. On the other hand, an excited utterance must be about an exciting event. A present sense impression can be about anything, even the mundane.

Then-Existing Mental, Emotional, or Physical Condition, Rule 803(3)

Rule 803(3) is a powerful hearsay exception and the most underused in Mock Trial. "A statement of the declarant's then-existing state of mind (such as motive, intent, or plan) or emotional, sensory, or physical condition (such as mental feeling, pain, or bodily health). . . ." That means the following statements would all qualify under this exception:

"My head hurts." (pain)

"I am happy." (mental feeling)

"I have cancer." (bodily health)

"I hate Jimmy." (motive)

"I want to kill Jimmy." (motive/intent)

"I am going to kill Jimmy." (plan)

"I am going to the movies tomorrow." (plan)

Statements for Purposes of Medical Diagnosis or Treatment, Rule 803(4). Discussed above.

Records of Regularly Conducted Activity ("Business Records"), Rule 803(6)

You must demonstrate that (1) the record was made at or near the time of whatever event is reflected in the record; (2) the record was made by someone with knowledge; (3) the record was kept in the course of a regularly conducted activity of the business; and (4) making the record was a regular practice of that activity. The idea behind the business records exception is that if a company routinely keeps records of its activities, those records are probably trustworthy. This exception might encompass receipts from a hardware store, a hotel guest log, or a doctor's notes from a patient's visit.

The definition of "business" is broad: any "business, organization, occupation, or calling, whether or not for profit."

The foundation for the business records exception can be established by calling the person who made the record *or* the person who keeps the records—called the custodian. For example, you do not need to call the cashier from the hardware store, the hotel desk clerk, or the doctor who wrote the notes in the chart if the custodian is available or otherwise attests to the requirements of the exception.

Rule 804 lists five more hearsay exceptions that apply only when the declarant is unavailable. The law considers these exceptions slightly less reliable, so if the declarant is available to testify in court, you need to call them to the stand so they can be cross-examined. If you can prove they are not available, then you can use their hearsay statements if they meet one of the five listed exceptions.

Rule 804 is very specific about what constitutes unavailability. You cannot just say, "Sorry, Judge, Susie plays bingo on Tuesdays, so she won't be here." You can show unavailability by proving that the declarant is dead; seriously ill; can no longer recall the subject of the statement; refuses to testify despite a court order; or is protected from testifying because of a privilege (e.g., a spouse cannot be compelled to testify against another spouse).

A common misconception is that unavailability is its own exception. Just because someone has died does not mean all their statements are suddenly hearsay exceptions. Unavailability is just the first requirement to unlocking the Rule 804 hearsay exceptions. These exceptions include:

Former Testimony, 804(b)(1)

An attorney must show that the testimony (1) was given as a witness at a trial, hearing, or deposition, and (2) and is now offered against a party who had an opportunity and similar motive to develop the testimony by direct or cross-examination.

Suppose Paul sues Delia because her pet rattlesnake bit him. Before trial, Paul's lawyer deposes Nat, their neighbor. A deposition is a formal question-and-answer session where a witness takes an oath to tell the truth, and lawyers for all parties in the case ask the witness questions. Paul's lawyer asks Nat what he saw, and Nat says, "I saw Delia let her snake loose. Then I saw it bite Paul." Nat dies before trial.

Either side can use Nat's deposition testimony. First, Nat is unavailable because he's dead. Second, he gave testimony under oath. Third, it would be offered against a party who had the chance to question the declarant. Notice that Paul can still offer Nat's testimony at trial even though Delia's lawyer did not ask any questions; she had the *opportunity* to ask questions but chose not to.

Dying Declaration, 804(b)(2)

An attorney must show that (1) the declarant thought he was about to die and (2) he made a statement concerning the cause or circumstances surrounding that death. This exception applies even if the declarant survives. The premise is that people want to die with a clear conscience so if they *think* they are dying imminently, they are more likely to tell the truth.

Statements against Interest, 804(b)(3)

Attorneys must show that: (1) the declarant made a statement; (2) it is against his financial, personal, or legal interests; and (3) a reasonable person would not make such a statement unless it was true. Basically, this assumes that people will not say something seriously detrimental to their own welfare or reputation unless it's true.

15.3.7.4 Hearsay within Hearsay

Sometimes you will encounter instances of hearsay within hearsay, or "double hearsay." A report is written by the doctor but contains statements from the patient complaining of chest pain. Those statements from the patient contain multiple levels of hearsay: (1) the doctor says that (2) the patient says that she has chest pain. Or a witness testifies, "Bert told me that Ernie told him that Oscar is a grouch." The statement contains multiple levels of hearsay: (1) Bert says that (2) Ernie says Oscar is a grouch.

When you have multiple potential layers of hearsay, the statement is only admissible if there is an argument for admitting each level of potential hearsay. That rationale can be that the statement does not meet the definition of hearsay, or it can be that the statement qualifies as an exception to the hearsay rule. In the first example above, you might argue that the doctor's record qualifies under the business records exception and the patient's statements qualify under the statements for medical diagnosis exception. That would make all aspects of the statements admissible.

15.3.8 Expert Testimony

There are special rules for expert witnesses. You can't just watch a lot of *CSI* episodes and then testify in court that you think the defendant's blood matched the blood at the crime scene.

15.3.8.1 Requirements for Giving an Expert Opinion

To have your witness give their expert opinion, you need to lay proper foundation.

First, you must qualify your witness as an expert in their subject matter. According to Rule 702, the witness must have "knowledge, skill, experience, training, or education" sufficient to demonstrate their expertise. Notice the rule says "or," not "and." The witness does not need to satisfy all these factors.

Rule 702 also has certain requirements for the expert's opinion. It must be based on "sufficient facts and data." In other words, the expert needs enough information about this case. It doesn't matter how impressive the DNA expert is; they cannot offer an opinion about whether the blood at the crime scene matches the defendant's DNA if the defendant's DNA was never tested. Their opinion must also be based on "reliable principles and methods." This means the DNA test that was used has been proven reliable. Reliability can be shown by saying it has a low error rate; it has been approved by other experts; or that it is commonly accepted by law enforcement or scientific organizations. Finally, the expert must attest that they applied those reliable methods to the facts and data of the case at hand.

If your opponent fails to establish any of these foundational elements before offering expert conclusions, object "lack of foundation" or "improper opinion."

15.3.8.2 Experts and Otherwise Inadmissible Information

Experts often must rely on information they are told. An accident reconstruction expert probably did not see the car crash take place. They base their conclusions on evidence they gather. That can include measurements and physical evidence from the crash site and statements from eyewitnesses. But what if those statements from eyewitnesses are hearsay?

Rule 703 says that experts may rely on underlying facts and data made known to them if they are of the kind "reasonably relied upon by experts in the particular field." That includes evidence that is otherwise inadmissible, such as hearsay. An accident reconstructionist can rely in part on statements from eyewitnesses. A doctor can rely on a medical chart created by another doctor. This ability to use information obtained from others allows the expert to give an opinion even if some of the facts they relied on would not normally be admissible.

Although the expert's opinion may be admissible, can the expert testify to those inadmissible facts? According to Rule 703, the answer is no—"unless their probative value in assisting the jury to evaluate the expert's opinion substantially outweighs their prejudicial effect." In English: The otherwise inadmissible facts only get admitted if they really help the judges understand the conclusion. Note that this is sometimes called a "reverse 403 test" because it uses the opposite of the weighing in Rule 403. There, the prejudicial impact must substantially outweigh the probative value.

However, there is a special rule for cross-examination. Under Rule 705, you may always cross-examine an expert on any facts they relied on when forming their conclusion—even if those facts are inadmissible, such as hearsay. The rationale is that you are not offering these facts for their truth, but rather to undermine the witness's conclusion. If the accident reconstructionist was told the red car hit the blue car, but she reached the opposite conclusion, the jury should know that her conclusion was contradicted by some of the facts she learned.

15.3.9 Best Evidence

Rule 1002 is known among trial lawyers as the Best Evidence rule: "To prove the content of a writing, recording, or photograph, the original writing, recording, or photograph is required, except as otherwise provided in these rules or by law." In other words, if you want to prove the content of an out-of-court exhibit, and that exhibit is available, you need to admit the exhibit. For example, if you are trying to prove what a newspaper article said, you should not do so by calling a witness who read the article and asking them what they recall. You have to admit the article.

15.3.10 Scope

In Mock Trial, on direct and cross-examination, you may cover any admissible information. On re-direct, you are limited to the scope of whatever was covered on cross-examination. On re-cross, you are limited to the scope of whatever was covered on re-direct examination. If re-re-direct is allowed, it is limited to the scope of the re-cross. And so on. The goal is to promote efficiency. Lawyers don't get to explore entirely new topics on re-direct or re-cross.

16

General Tournament Tips

16.1 Judges Meetings

Before a round begins, most competitions have a Judges Meeting. This training is designed to prepare someone to score a round, even if they have never participated in a Mock Trial competition before.

Some Judges Meetings are open to the public. If they are open in your competition, it is wise to send someone to see what rules and scoring criteria are being emphasized. Sometimes tournaments tell judges that a certain piece of evidence should be admitted or that impeachments should be handled a certain way. That can be useful to know.

Usually, the Judges Meetings are the same every round. So if you go to the Judges Meeting for round one, you can probably skip the later Judges Meetings.

You should also see if a training presentation or other instructions for judges are posted online. If so, get it in advance and use it to your advantage in preparations.

Coaches are often required to attend Judges Meetings in case they are needed to judge rounds. Coaches are not assigned to judge their own teams but are frequently enlisted to judge other rounds.

WAR STORY

During one of then–law student Nelmark's first assignments as a tournament representative, he was paired with Dr. Sara Zeigler. The two of them—who would go on to become AMTA's fourth and fifth presidents—could find no rule allowing them to penalize a team's coach who had hidden in the bathroom so he could not be assigned to judge a round. To remedy "Bathroom-Gate," such a rule was passed at the next board meeting.

16.2 Captains Meetings

Some competitions have a mandatory Captains Meeting before each trial. The captains will select witnesses (if there is a choice in witness selection), share the order and gender of their witnesses, and show the other team their enlargements and demonstrative aids.

You will typically only be allowed to have one or two team members in Captains Meetings. The location of the Captains Meeting might be quite far from where the round is taking place. You will want a system in place for the Captains to immediately relay information to the rest of the team, who will be in the trial room waiting for the round to start. In preparing supplies and getting mentally prepared, it's very helpful to know who will be testifying. We recommend texting your teammates the key witness information (selection, order, and gender) and anything unusual ("Heads up: they said they are going to object to our demo as hearsay, so Susie should start preparing a response"). We recommend taking photos of the other team's demonstrative aids and texting them to your teammates. That way everyone has plenty of time to review before trial.

Most competitions allow teams to challenge the use of any demonstrative aid that invents facts outside the case packet. Usually, you must do so before leaving the Captains Meeting. Make sure to raise any challenges at that time because afterward that it will probably be too late. If the demonstrative aid is unclear, ask your opponent how they intend to use it. A demonstrative aid might be permissible for one purpose but impermissible for another.

Make sure to show your demonstrative aids to the other team during Captains Meetings. Many competitions will prohibit you from using anything in trial that you did not show to the other team beforehand. If your demonstrative aids are large, you may prefer to bring an 8.5 x 11 version to Captains Meeting and send the full-size version to your courtroom so your teammates can fully set up for trial.

It is important to determine the gender of the witnesses who will be testifying. Since the names of the characters are gender-neutral (so that they may be more easily portrayed by any student regardless of gender), you won't know whether to use "Mr." or "Ms." (or other) in speeches unless each gender is clarified. It is amazing how many times the wrong title is used—sometimes even after the witness has testified or is sitting at the counsel table right in front of the judges. Don't mess this up. It's distracting to judges, and it makes it look like you're not paying attention.

16.3 Tabulation Rooms

The Tabulation Room or "Tab Room" is where the ballots are added and the pairings for each round are determined. Typically, timekeepers are asked to bring the ballots to the Tab Room at the end of the round. Before the competition begins, make sure your timekeepers know where the Tab Room is located.

The adding of ballots is fairly straightforward. Determining the pairings for each round is much harder. Most competitions have some form of "power-matching," which means teams doing well are paired against other teams doing well. The American Mock Trial Association has its Tabulation Manual posted online. By 2020, it was 58 pages. It is *not* necessary to learn the tabulation rules to compete.

WAR STORY

The first AMTA Tabulation Manual was written by UW-Milwaukee coach Brad Bloch. Judge Nelmark extensively revised it when he became AMTA's Tabulation Director. While serving as a representative at an AMTA Tournament, he was faced with repeated (false) accusations that the pairings were being done incorrectly. He finally stated: "That book you keep coming up and telling me I'm interpreting incorrectly? I wrote it." That is not to say Judge Nelmark is infallible when working in a Tab Room.

WAR STORY

While working in the Tab Room at a high school mock trial tournament, then-college student Nelmark once added the ballots correctly, and still got the result wrong. One team was "CC" and the other was "CCC." The results got reversed on the pairings cards, impacting the power matching in the next round. He still feels bad about it. The tournament (wisely) switched to using all three-digit number designations in the future.

Some Tab Rooms are completely open. Some are limited to only coaches and/or only at certain times. If you are permitted to have someone visit the Tab Room, take advantage of the opportunity. The volunteers in the Tab Room work hard and do the best they can to avoid mistakes, but they are not perfect. Double check the math on each of your ballots. Competitions that permit teams to review their ballots after each trial often have the rule that if you fail to spot or report an error within a designated time period, the recorded result is considered final. Make sure each side's total score is correct, and make sure the correct team has been declared the winner.

17

Advice for Specific Competitions

17.1 "Live Witness" Competitions

In almost every Mock Trial competition, the attorneys and witnesses are teammates from the same school. You and your teammate can prepare your direct examination in detail, often for months. Our advice for those competitions is covered earlier in the book.

Some competitions, though, use a format where the attorney meets the witness for the first time right before trial. They usually have 15–20 minutes to prepare together. This format has different names, such as "live witnesses," "woodshed witnesses," and "guest witnesses." Sometimes the live witnesses are members of a different team in the competition. In that case, the witness's points count for the witness's team and the attorney's points count for the attorney's team. Sometimes the tournament host provides the witnesses, in which case only the lawyer is being scored.

When you meet your direct examination partner 15–20 minutes before trial, your strategy for preparing the direct changes a lot! You cannot rehearse every question and answer.

For *witnesses* competing as live witnesses, remember your goal is to score points for *your* team. Yes, you also want to help your directing attorney. Working together should increase both of your scores. But your primary goal is to score points for your team.

First, develop your witness personality as you would in a normal competition. Figure out how you will portray that personality within the first few questions. Assume you will get the standard first few questions: Please introduce yourself. Where do you live? What do you do for a living? Second, know the facts inside-out. Such knowledge is always important, but especially when you don't know exactly what your lawyer will ask you. Third, work together with your directing attorney. That means focusing on the facts that support the attorney's theory of the case. Insist that the attorney ask the introductory questions that allow you to tell your story and showcase your personality. Finally, do not invent facts. Sometimes the attorney from another team will want you to push the boundaries so they have stronger facts to argue. Don't do it. You will be the one who pays the price if there is an impeachment.

For *lawyers* who direct examine a live witness, there are three ingredients for success: writing the direct, preparing the witness, and performing well during trial.

When writing the direct, you need to write questions that can only be answered one way. Questions like, "What happened next?" or "Describe the car" are dangerous. You risk the witness giving you too much information, which can bury your most important facts and bore the jury. You risk the witness saying something objectionable. Instead, ask tighter, close-ended questions.

What was the date of the accident?

What time of day?

Where did the accident take place?

Why were you there that day?

How close were you to the accident?

How well were you able to see the accident?

How many cars were involved?

What was the make and model of each car?

These aren't leading questions because they do not suggest the answer. They start with our journalist words: what, where, why, and so on. But they aren't fully open-ended, either. They direct the witness to specific information.

When writing the direct, use lots of headlines and transitions. Usually this helps the jury follow your direct. Here, it will also help your live witness follow the direct.

When writing the direct, keep it as short and simple as possible. We want it to be short because that helps us minimize the chance that something goes wrong. With an unrehearsed direct—and someone you have barely met as a witness—the risk of something going wrong is much higher. We want it to be simple because not every witness you get will be an all-star. If you ask the witness to adapt to a complicated theory or to give too many unusual answers, the risk of something going wrong gets much higher.

At the tournament, you will need to prepare the witness in a very short amount of time. Organize that time carefully. Start by building trust with the witness. If the witness is being scored, ask the witness if there is anything they need to showcase their character. Then tell the witness your team's theory of the case. The witness will be able to answer individual questions more helpfully if they know and understand your overall strategy.

Practice some of the questions. Emphasize the importance of answering the question asked. If the question is, "Did you see the accident?" the answer isn't, "Yes, it was on July 5th, at the corner Main and Washington." The answer is, "Yes." Explain that you will ask the follow-up questions: "When was the accident?" "Where did the accident take place?" This allows you to control the timing and flow of the direct and to avoid objections. It allows the witness to answer questions with confidence because they know how much information to give and when to stop.

Once the witness takes the stand, *listen*. Listen carefully to the witness's answers. You have a plan for what you want to ask and what you want the witness to say. With a live witness, you will always have to adjust your plan. Listen to the witness's answers and follow up. Did they use a vague pronoun? "You said 'they.' Who were you referring to?" Did they see the defendant twice? "Let's take those one at a time. When was the first time you saw the defendant?" Speak slowly. Don't interrupt the witness. Don't assume the witness said what you were expecting. Listen and respond. Doing so will make your performance engaging and easy to follow.

17.2 One-on-One Competitions

There are one-on-one Mock Trial competitions at the high school level (Gladiator), college level (Trial by Combat), and law school level (Top Gun). These invitation-only events are limited to the best competitors in the United States (and sometimes even outside the United States).

To succeed in these one-on-one events, you must master the skill discussed above: direct examining live witnesses. Achieving mastery takes practice.

Get comfortable improvising more than you would in a normal competition. The college and law school one-on-one events provide the case only 24 hours ahead of time. Very few competitors can memorize their directs, crosses, and speeches in 24 hours. Instead, memorize the introductions and finales to your opening and closing. If you know your structure—especially your roadmap—you can deliver the rest. For direct examination, know the main point of each chapter. For cross-examination, memorize as much as you can, but definitely know the main point of each chapter.

Above all, scrimmage. Practice the one-on-one format against your teammates, program alumni, or other competitors. Follow the format of your tournament, especially the preparation time and specific in-trial time limits. Being able to prepare a case quickly is a critical component of these events. Figure out what you need to improve, and then practice that skill.

17.3 Competition Levels

17.3.1 Middle School

Middle school, called "junior high" in some states, generally consists of grades 6–8. It is the youngest age where competitive Mock Trial exists. Some elementary schools conduct a mock trial, but it is usually more like a play where students read their parts instead of drafting their own content.

There is no national governing body for Middle School Mock Trial and not all states have programs. The programs are typically run by or affiliated with state or local bar associations. In some states without a middle school program, teams of middle school students students are allowed to enter the high school competition.

Middle School Mock Trial generally follows the same format as the higher age groups. The case packet and rules might be somewhat simplified, but a round will look and feel much the same as competitions for higher age groups. At the highest levels, Middle School Mock Trial competitors will perform like real attorneys. It's amazing!

Because most middle school students will not have done Mock Trial before, you have to start with fundamentals. And then practice. And then practice again. Middle School Mock Trial competitions can be won just by looking smooth and confident in the courtroom. However, it takes hundreds of repetitions to reach this level.

Middle School students are typically 11–14 years old. Thus, they are filled with hormones. This can make coaching very challenging. Some days the students might be focused and well behaved. Some days, they might be so hyper, you can't get anything done. Other days, they might be sullen or tired. If you are going to coach at this level, you have to be willing to roll with it.

Here are our top three tips for Middle School Mock Trial:

- Set as many practices as you can. The team needs time to prepare for competition even if some practices are not especially productive. Additionally, middle schoolers generally will not work as hard outside of group practices as older students. Thus, content development and attorney/witness practice may have to happen during team practices.
- Work on the fundamentals of objections. Some middle school teams have smooth presentations but look like a deer in headlights when they need to go off script.
- Memorize as much as possible. Simple content that can be presented without notes will score better than complex content being read.

17.3.2 High School

In the United States, most states have High School Mock Trial programs, as do a number of territories. The programs are typically run by or affiliated with state bar associations. Each state program runs independently and has its own case, though they do sometimes collaborate and swap materials from year to year. For example, the case of *Jamie R. Killian v. R.A.G.E. Enterprises & Chris Schultz* was originally written by then–college student Nelmark for the Iowa Middle School Mock Trial Program, but was subsequently adapted and used by a middle school program in Indiana and high school programs in Michigan, Hawaii, and the Commonwealth of the Northern Mariana Islands.

Most high school programs have a spring season, with the case coming out sometime in the fall semester and the state champion being crowned shortly after Spring Break. Most programs operate on this timetable because they want their champion to be able to compete for a National Championship at a tournament held in May each year.

The National High School Mock Trial Championship ("NHSMTC") is an independent nonprofit organization that hosts a tournament for the winners from each state. The first one was held in Des Moines, Iowa, in 1984 with teams from Illinois, Iowa, Minnesota, Nebraska, and Wisconsin. In 2019, the competition included 42 state champions as well as teams from Guam, the Commonwealth of Northern Mariana Islands, and South Korea. The case for the NHSMTC is not released until all the state high school tournaments are completed. So, competitors must prepare for the championship on a very tight timetable.

There are many invitational competitions for high school teams. Some of the most prominent include Empire, Providence Cup, NorCal,

Beach Ball, and tournaments hosted by college programs. These are often excellent practice for your official state competition.

Gladiator is the one-on-one high school Mock Trial World Championship and is run by Professor Bernstein. Students compete without cocounsel, playing the roles of attorneys in half their trials and witnesses in the other half. Founded in 2015, Gladiator has included students from most states and five countries.

Here are our top three tips for high school Mock Trial:

- Scrimmage as much as possible. In our experience, coaches tend to avoid scrimmages because they are afraid other teams will steal their ideas. The value of practice and repetition for your team is almost always worth any risk of someone taking some ideas.
- Focus on witness performances. In our experience, high school teams often forget to develop witness personalities, so doing that can help differentiate you.
- Emphasize the rules of evidence and objection practice. This is an area where even top high school teams can struggle because making and responding to objections requires thinking on your feet. Knowing the rules of evidence and being able to articulate them during objections and responses can help set you apart.

17.3.3 College

Since its founding in 1985, the American Mock Trial Association (AMTA) has governed College Mock Trial throughout the country. AMTA now has more than 700 competing teams from more than 400 colleges and universities. The AMTA case alternates between criminal and civil.

AMTA hosts regional tournaments throughout the country. At these events, 20–30 teams compete for bids to the next level—Opening Round Championship Sites (ORCS). At each of the eight ORCS, six teams receive bids to the National Championship Tournament (NCT). No more than two teams from each school can qualify for the NCT. The 48 teams are divided into two divisions. All teams compete in four rounds (two plaintiff/prosecution and two defense) with the winners of each division facing off in a fifth round that determines the champion.

The AMTA season is long. The case comes out in August. Regional tournaments are generally in February. ORCS are in March. Following ORCS, a new case is released for the NCT, which takes place in April.

Because the AMTA season is long, many teams will compete with the same case at multiple invitational tournaments before the official competition season starts. Some teams go to five or six invitational tournaments. This fact changes the game significantly.

Unlike Middle School, High School, and Law School Mock Trial, it is hard to win in College Mock Trial simply because your content is better. Good content helps, of course. But over a six-month season with the same case, every competitive team tends to figure out the superior theory and lines of questioning. It's difficult to wow the judges with original material because, by regionals, other teams are probably using similar ideas. Similarly, it's difficult to surprise your opponent because by regionals and ORCS, every competitive team has seen or heard about nearly every strategy. Thus, in College Mock Trial, we recommend placing increased importance on other areas that score points.

Here are our top three tips for College Mock Trial:

- Practice your public speaking. Make sure you sound natural. College Mock Trial tends to breed a polished style—that sounds fake. You can beat teams who speak like that if you speak clearly and confidently while sounding natural.
- Avoid objectionable material. Top college teams tend to be strong on the rules of evidence. Don't give them a chance to object to you.
- Strategize how your witnesses will handle cross-examination. This means preparing for different questions in detail. The longer season with the same case allows you to be more detailed in your preparation.

Trial by Combat is the College Mock Trial one-on-one national championship, founded by Professor Bernstein. It is co-hosted by his law school, UCLA, and Drexel University Kline School of Law. This competition accepts 16 students from among the more than 6,000 who compete each year.

17.3.4 Law School

Law School Mock Trial is fundamentally the same as the other levels of Mock Trial. Students are competing in a trial simulation and scored by practicing lawyers. There are dozens of invitational tournaments and at least two well-known competitions with regional tournaments that feed to national tournaments: the National Trial Competition, hosted by the Texas Young Lawyers Association and sponsored by the American College of Trial Lawyers, and the Student Trial Advocacy Competition, sponsored by the American Association of Justice. Generally, the same skills are rewarded in Law School Mock Trial as in other levels.

But Law School Mock Trial has the most differences from the other levels. Witnesses are not scored. This means there are virtually no "big" character portrayals, accents, costumes, etc. Trials may be longer even though each side only calls two witnesses. Teams often have a total time limit for all of the trial functions. This means each individual part—opening, direct, cross, etc.—can be considerably longer than its high school and college counterparts, which allows for far more detail. Each invitational tournament has its own case. This means teams are not constantly honing the details of the same case all year. There is greater value and reward for original strategy because other teams will not have time to steal it or prepare for it.

Here is our advice for Law School Mock Trial:

- Hone the ability to improvise and adapt. Because the competitors are soon to be actual lawyers, the judges demand real-world attorney skills. Practice dealing with the unexpected in scrimmages.
- Ditch the showy witness portrayals—but don't ignore your witnesses. Some former college competitors arrive in law school and portray their characters in the same fun, flashy way that scores tons of points in college. Such portrayals risk annoying the law school judges, who want realistic portrayals. It also risks annoying invitational hosts, who may not invite you back. But don't take the opposite approach, either. Too many law school teams ignore their witness performance. A boring witness leads to a bored jury. Make sure your witness speaks with energy and passion. Make sure your witness speaks like a real person. If they do, your directs will score higher than your opponents'.
- Focus more on performance skills than your opponents. Law school teams have better theories than college and high school teams (which makes sense, since the competitors are getting professional training to be lawyers). They have studied the rules and thought out the appropriate objections and responses. But they seem to focus less on practicing their delivery. If you practice your performance skills, you can separate your team from your opponents.

18

Competing Virtually

In 2020, the pandemic closed courthouses and campuses. But Mock Trial, which had always occurred in person, didn't stop. It went virtual. For more than a year, Mock Trial competitions at every level were conducted using online platforms like Zoom.

Mock Trial is better in person. Talking to a jury is more fun than talking to a camera. Convening with your friends and teammates—whether it's traveling across the country or simply meeting at the courthouse—is a special part of Mock Trial that is lost online. Still, Mock Trial on Zoom was pretty great. Tens of thousands of students were able to compete. Teams and students that struggled with travel costs could suddenly afford participation. Graduates who had moved far away could now coach their alma maters. No matter where the tournament was being held, judges could be recruited across the country.

It is too soon to predict if virtual competitions will continue. Perhaps some events will remain online because it is less costly for hosts and teams. Perhaps teams will use Zoom for scrimmages. And, of course, there is the unfortunate possibility that Mock Trial will be forced back online in the future.

This chapter explains how to win virtual Mock Trial competitions. During the pandemic, Judge Nelmark presided over and scored multiple virtual competitions, including regional and national championship rounds. He also presided over countless real-life remote hearings using the GoToMeeting platform. During the pandemic, Professor Bernstein's law school teams set an all-time record for most wins in a season. This is their advice for competing virtually.

18.1 Content

Most of your content should remain the same online. You still need a great theory and theme. You still need dynamic attorneys and memorable witnesses.

We recommend only two substantive changes when competing virtually. First, aim for shorter performances. Online, judges have even shorter attention spans than they do in person. Zoom is exhausting, and judges can easily toggle between watching trial and surfing the Internet, checking their email, and getting a snack from the kitchen. We have suggestions later in the chapter for keeping judges engaged online. But you still want to keep every speech and witness examination as short as possible. We found that judges reward brevity with big scores.

Second, on cross-examination, avoid questions/topics that allow a witness to fight with you. Witness control is harder online. Our usual moves for grabbing the judges' attention on cross—moving around the courtroom, performing with more energy than the witness—are either unavailable or less effective. Since witness control is harder online, you should be a little more reluctant to choose cross-examination topics that give the witness a chance to argue.

18.2 Setup

18.2.1 Sitting v. Standing

The most important question for online Mock Trial is whether, as attorneys, you should sit or stand. Most competitions will tell you either is fine. But there is a right answer.

Stand. Or, more specifically, stand when presenting an opening statement or closing argument. Stand when conducting a direct or cross-examination. Sit when stating appearances, addressing preliminary matters, and objecting to your opponent's examinations.

Standing allows you to perform more powerfully. In person, one step to the right or left is often weak (you need bigger movements). Online, one step to the right or left catches everyone's attention. Even more powerful is a step toward the camera. And even when you are not moving laterally or backward/forward, your head and shoulders will move more—and convey more emotion—if you are standing.

Additionally, standing makes it easier to have good posture and speak in a loud clear voice. Standing also helps you maintain eye contact, as discussed later in this chapter. It is not coincidental that the attorneys on the college and law school national champions stood for their performances.

Witnesses should remain seated unless advised to stand by the judge or referring to a physical demonstrative (as opposed to something shown on the screen).

18.2.2 Background

For attorneys, we recommend a plain, monochromatic background. We have seen teams compete online while standing in mock courtrooms and even real courtrooms. They think it makes their performance look more realistic or grand. In reality, it ends up distracting judges. They have things they can look at other than the people performing. Worse, it makes the attorneys look small, dwarfed by the size of the courtroom.

We have seen attorneys compete in offices or libraries so they can show books behind them. We have seen attorneys compete with beautiful flowers or giant American flags by their side. All of these decorations distract from the attorney performing.

For witnesses, we recommend the best background that your competition (and budget) permits. In the American Mock Trial Association online trials, top teams used their backgrounds to identify and enhance their characters. Winemakers had wine bottles and vineyard photos behind them. Doctors had labs or medical degrees behind them. Teams were creative and, when tastefully done, were rewarded with points.

In any setup, make sure there is nothing that changes in the background. No moving objects. No fans. No blinking lights. No windows with light coming through. Anything that catches a judge's eye pulls their attention away from you. For this reason, also do not use any "virtual" backgrounds. As you move, a virtual background can make the edges of your image fuzzy.

18.2.3 Cameras

We recommend that attorneys compete with two devices. The first is a laptop. Use the internal camera when seated. Laptop cameras are not always as good as external cameras (such as webcams), but they are certainly sufficient when you're sitting at the laptop, less than two feet away.

When you stand up to perform, the laptop camera is not ideal. For one thing, laptops tend not to have the highest quality cameras. (Of course, technology changes fast, and we could imagine that this statement becomes outdated.) But the other reason is camera angle. Unless you are going to move your laptop to eye level—and do so without disorienting the judges—you will want a second camera.

Specifically, you want an external camera that connects to your laptop. Switch to the external camera when standing. A webcam is ideal, but if you are looking to save money, just use your smartphone. Modern smartphones have excellent cameras and, while not as sharp as webcams, they are generally much better than your laptop's internal camera.

Mount the external camera on a tripod. Set it at eye level. It tends to be the most flattering and professional view.

WAR STORY

In one of the first online competitions, Professor Bernstein's student Jack Eyers accidentally set the camera too low right before his closing argument. After the closing, the team said, "Hey, your closing was great, but why did you stand in one place the whole time? What happened to the movement you had planned?" Jack, "I couldn't move. To keep my head on camera, I basically had to do the splits." The closing was 12 minutes.

18.2.4 Lighting

Make sure you are lighted from the front. This will allow judges to see your face. Even if you have adequate lighting from the front, avoid competing with additional light behind you, including that from a window. If you are lighted from the back, you will look like a silhouette. Judges will not be able to see your facial expressions, and your ability to connect with them will suffer.

Depending on your location, natural light may provide sufficient front lighting. If not, you might want to invest in an extra light source. In fact, it's ideal to have one available, just in case. You never know when you'll end up competing on a day when it's rainy and dark outside.

18.2.5 Location

Your location does not need to be fancy. In 2020 and 2021, multiple national champions competed from their bedrooms or living rooms.

Your location *does* need to be quiet. If you are competing with family, roommates, or nearby televisions making noise in the background, that can be distracting. This is particularly true if your roommate walks behind you wearing only a towel, as happened in one recent online competition.

Look for a location that will be quiet (or arrange for others to be elsewhere or quiet during your trials). Pets can add a moment of levity to a real-life hearing, but those attorneys are not being critiqued on their performance. In Mock Trial, anything unexpected has the potential to throw you off your game. Leave your house if necessary to find a more secure and predictable location.

WAR STORY

That said, always make the most of what you have. Audrey Shepard, a college student at UCLA, won an All-American Attorney Award and the Trial by Combat national championship with chicken sounds coming from her backyard and other animal sounds coming from her next-door neighbor. She grew accustomed to joking about it with judges.

Of course, some things are out of your control. If there are sirens or honking cars (or clucking) in the background, don't sweat it. Pause, smile, maybe crack a joke, and keep going. Everyone realizes the challenge of competing virtually.

18.2.6 Space

You do not need as much physical space as some might guess. In fact, if the area behind you is too large, it will make you small by comparison. We recommend you set up the camera so that you have exactly as much standing space as you need, but no more.

How much standing space do you need? Imagine the floor is a three-by-three tic-tac-toe board.

7	8	9
4	5	6
1	2	3
	Camera	

Each of these squares is separated by one regular footstep. Start in front of the camera and have a teammate or coach watch you online and tell you when you are as close as possible without being too close. The jury should be able to see your face, part of your shoulders, and (depending on your height) maybe half your torso. Stop there. That is the 2 spot. Take one step backward. That is the 5 spot. One step to *your* right is the 4. One step to your left is the 6. One step back is the 8.

You might think that one step is not enough. After all, in the "Performance" chapter we recommended large movements across the courtroom. But one step on video looks gigantic. Later in the chapter, we will discuss how much time to stand in each of these locations.

Some teams like to compete with all members in the same room. This is permissible, but the audio/video setups should be for individuals. In other words, don't have one far off camera showing the whole team. Doing so makes it impossible to show the necessary facial expressions of a single competitor. Even having the camera pulled out to show an attorney and witness at the same time detracts from the judges' appreciation of your performance.

Similarly, having a camera that pans or zooms to cover different competitors is also distracting. The laptop camera and the external camera should each remain stationary. While you do not need a separate laptop for every team member, you will want to have one for each person who is appearing on screen at the same time. As different competitors use it, make sure to adjust the external camera (before the person is on camera) so it remains at eye level. In this scenario, pre-mark your tripod for different competitors so it can be readjusted quickly.

18.2.7 Audio

Laptop microphones are fine while sitting. But when you stand up and perform in front of a camera, the laptop does not always pick up the sound very well. We recommend an external microphone.

A microphone does not need to be expensive. Our choice is a wired lapel mic that plugs into your laptop and clips onto your lapel. Place it as close to your head as possible so it will really pick up the sound.

Some people used wireless lapel mics. These are fine, too, but we prefer the wired lapel mics because (1) they are less expensive; (2) they are at least as reliable, and maybe more reliable; and (3) as explained earlier, you will not be moving more than a few steps during your performance. Some prefer wireless earbuds. These are also fine. We prefer the lapel mic because it is less physically distracting for the audience.

Test the audio to make sure it's coming through loud and clear. Not every judge will have a good speaker system. If the volume on their end is high, it's easy for them to turn it down. But, if the volume is maxed and they are still straining to hear, it's likely to hurt your score.

WAR STORY

Make sure you are muted during breaks in trial. In one law school trial, a team accidentally kept their mics on at break . . . and proceeded to make personal comments about the other team's attorneys. After about 30 seconds, one of the scoring judges said, "Excuse me, you might want to mute yourselves." You can guess how the judges scored the trial.

18.2.8 Internet

The most reliable Internet connection is always a hardwired connection. If you can connect your laptop directly to the router, that will usually provide the smoothest performance. If Wi-Fi is the only option, keep your computer as close as possible to the router and turn off or disconnect other devices that may be relying on your Internet.

Have a Plan B in case your Wi-Fi goes down during competition. This might be using a mobile phone hot spot or having another location to which you could quickly travel. Download the software application (for example, Zoom) on your phone just in case you need it. Write down the Meeting ID and password/access code so you have them handy.

18.2.9 Plug In

We know this is obvious, but several competitors had problems because they forgot to plug in their power cords and their batteries drained to zero during trial. Plug in your laptop. Make sure your external microphone, your smartphone (if you're using it for a camera), and any other technology that you need (and that cannot be easily plugged in) is fully charged at the start of trial.

18.2.10 Settings

Practice competing online using all the same online platform settings you will use in competition. Note that settings vary among online platforms. Just because you are a rock star at using Zoom does not mean you understand whatever other platform your competition is using.

After you've perfected the settings, write them down, and then double check them immediately before competition. This is always a good idea, but it's especially important if anyone else has access to your laptop. Having a filter that makes you look like a cat may make you go viral, but it will also likely cost you the round. Also, make sure to check the name that appears when you log in. This can sometimes be reset automatically if you have other devices connected to Wi-Fi. Have a teammate verify (from a different computer) that everything is appearing as you want it to.

The number one problem Judge Nelmark has seen in real online hearings is someone being unable to hear or be heard. (Attorneys are just as guilty of this as the parties.) Typically, after everyone has waited for what feels like an eternity, the person discovers that they had the wrong microphone selected, or that the volume was off, or that the hearing was being broadcast in a different room due to an errant Bluetooth activation.

Such glitches will generally not be counted against your time limits, but they create a bad first impression.

18.3 Attorney Performance

The best advice we can give for attorney performance online is to play big. You need far more energy for online performances than in-person performances.

Deeksha Kohli was one of Professor Bernstein's top competitors. In person, she was vivacious, loud, and dynamic. Sometimes judges thought she was too much. But when the world went virtual in 2020, Deeksha got to compete in the first online Law School Mock Trial tournament. During practice, she and Professor Bernstein discovered that her normal level of energy was not enough over Zoom. For the first time, she had to be extra dynamic. Competitors who were not as naturally energetic in person had to be *way* more energetic online.

Don't forget to change volumes. If you use a lapel mic, you will be able to whisper and judges will still hear it. That can be very effective.

Hand gestures are different online. Because the jury can only see the top half of your body, and maybe less, your gestures need to be higher. The gestures should be at chest level, shoulder height, or eye level. Make sure to practice keeping your gestures within the frame of the camera. This will feel unnatural at first, but you will grow comfortable with it.

Because these gestures are so commanding—they will be right in front of the judges' face—use them a little more sparingly than you would in person. A little will go a long way.

Maintain the physicality you would in the courtroom. Turn your body when pointing. Bend your knees. Reach for something when reenacting a scene.

Use your eyes. Most of the time look directly at the camera. *Do not look at the judges appearing in the corners of your screen. That does not give them eye contact!* You are seeing their eyes, but they are not seeing yours. The only way to simulate in-person eye contact in an online tournament is to look directly at the camera.

You can also use your eyes to create drama and a sense of place. Let's say you are telling us that it was hard for the eyewitness to see because the streetlight was out. Raise an arm and point to where the streetlight was. And look at the streetlight. Of course, there is no streetlight in your living room. But these miming gestures create a sense of reality for the judges. This is especially effective when you have a plain monochromatic background as discussed earlier. A good rule of thumb is that if you want something to seem real to the jury, you need to actually look at it. This is doubly true online.

Where should you stand?

7	8	9
4	5	6
1	2	3
	Camera	

Spend more than 80 percent of your standing time in the 2 and 5 spots. The 5 spot is centered and a comfortable distance from the camera. The 2 spot will add emphasis to your performance and really connect you to the audience. For transitions or change of pace, move to the 4 or 6.

For an occasional dramatic moment, you can use the 8 spot. For example, it can be useful to step back to the 8 if you are talking about an eyewitness who could not see well or if explaining that something happened long ago. But keep your time in the 8 spot brief. You will look small, and it will be hard to maintain jury attention.

18.4 Witness Performance

Witness performance requires less adaptation online. You will be seated. Look at the camera the entire time unless you are looking away for a specific purpose. For example, if you become emotional, you can look into the distance. But almost all your lines should be delivered to the camera.

Keep your energy up. Judges lose focus on online more easily than in person, so you need to use your voice, gestures, and body language to keep their attention.

18.5 Exhibits and Demonstrative Aids

18.5.1 Admitting Exhibits

Many attorneys authenticated exhibits by sharing them on screen "constructively" outside the jury's presence. In other words, they asked the judge if they could pretend the jury could not see the exhibit until admitted. This sped up the process of admitting exhibits.

Some tournaments, or even individual judges, had a different procedure, requiring attorneys to lay a foundation for the exhibit without the jury seeing the exhibit until it was admitted. It is not difficult. Instead of the mark-show-ask-give steps we use when introducing an exhibit in person, we ask the witness to open a certain exhibit in their electronic notebook. On direct examination, you can ask, "Ms. Park, do you see Exhibit 6 in your electronic notebook?" On cross-examination, you can phrase it to exert more control: "Please find Exhibit 6 in your electronic notebook and look up at the camera when you have it."

18.5.2 Using Exhibits

One part of Mock Trial that improves online is the display of exhibits and demonstrative aids. In person, enlargements are expensive—and not especially versatile. They are usually just a single document. Some have moving parts. Others you can write on.

Online, exhibits can be sophisticated, beautiful, powerful displays. Everyone has access to programs like Microsoft PowerPoint or (free) Google Slides. Prezi is also free, and very effective, though it takes longer to learn. You are only limited by your creativity and the rules of your competition. Here are some examples of great demonstrative aids we saw or used:

- In Trial by Combat, the first virtual College Mock Trial Competition, the winning advocate—Duke University's Sonali Mehta—created dynamic timelines that incorporated key evidence seamlessly. Of course, timelines can be done in person by creating a demonstrative aid or writing on a whiteboard. But the ease, precision, and cleanness of Mehta's digital timelines exceeded what any competitor could do in person. Over the year, other teams built on this concept and timelines became integral to virtual storytelling.
- In the law school Tournament of Champions 2020 final round, UCLA School of Law combined exhibits for a powerful impact. The case involved a grocery store that did not have allergy warnings on a sample stand containing food with peanut flour. When an allergic child got sick, his family sued the store. UCLA first admitted separate photographic exhibits depicting the sample cart, sample, and warning labels. They then shrunk the samples and warning labels and asked the eyewitness to place them on the sample cart. This kept judges entertained: items were moving across the screen. It also proved a point. Judges could see that before the day the child got hurt, the store displayed warnings next to samples. But on the day the child got hurt, there were samples—and no warnings.
- In the 2020 Empire competition, a forensic expert explained the rarity of a particular DNA match: about 1 in 25,000. In person,

we would just say the number aloud or maybe write it out. One excellent high school team had a PowerPoint slide with one gold dot and 24,999 blue dots. It helped the jury visualize the improbability.

- In the National Trial Competition 2021, UCLA School of Law designed a demonstrative aid that created a car accident, step by step, matching the witness's testimony. It started as a blank highway. Judges saw lanes added, then a center divide. A bus headed east. An SUV was driving west. Then the SUV lost control, crossed the center divide, and struck the bus. The next image was a photo of the actual bus on its side.

Some of these methods are fancier than others. Some teams used complicated technology and practiced choreography. The high school team at Empire just used a slide with dots. The key is that all these teams used the virtual aspect of competition to improve their visual presentation to judges. As you think about how you can optimize your visual presentation, here are some tips:

First, use more exhibits online than you would in person. Introducing them into evidence is faster and easier online. Displaying them is faster and easier online. And using them is more *necessary* online because our other methods of maintaining jury attention—public speaking skills, moving around the courtroom—are weakened online.

WAR STORY

One team accidentally share-screened their text messaging app, which revealed that they were cheating by talking with their coach during the trial. Another team who accidentally shared their text messages during trial revealed disparaging comments about the other team . . . and about the presiding judge! Her eyes got big, she crossed her arms, and it was clear that she saw what they had written. If the team didn't like her rulings before that moment, they ***definitely*** didn't like them after that moment. Moral: Be careful what you write and be careful what you share.

Second, find ways to change what judges are seeing. Displaying a photo on screen will increase the jury's attention . . . for about ten seconds. But we can get a lot more out of that one photo. Suppose it's the photo of a car accident. A blue car has struck a red car. When you ask the witness about the blue car, add an arrow that points to the blue car. When you ask the witness about the red car, add an arrow that points to the red car. When you ask about the damage to the back of the blue car, zoom in (or enlarge) the back of the blue car. Highlight the damage by outlining the back bumper in yellow. All these maneuvers are small and relatively easy. But they emphasize what you find important and keep jury attention by changing what they are seeing.

Third, make exhibits interactive. Instead of simply clicking to the next slide, is there a way you can have the witness move one object in the slide? Can they use their arrow to show where something happened? Use technology to tell an interactive, dynamic story.

Fourth, practice using your exhibits until the use of the technology is seamless. In person, taking a moment to set up an enlargement is expected. In a remote forum, even a small pause can cause you to lose the courtroom presence you have worked so hard to create.

Finally, use your opponent's demonstrative aids against them. In person, you can approach your opponent's demonstrative aid and gesture to it. Online, you can take a screenshot, display it, and mark on it. If you do it effectively, judges will love the ingenuity and responsiveness.

One word of caution. Usually when an exhibit is shown, it takes up most of the screen with the attorney is reduced to a thumbnail image on the side of the screen. If an exhibit is used too long, it becomes difficult to evaluate the attorney's content and how they look when they present it. Exhibits should appear on the screen no more than 30% of the time during direct, 25% of the time during cross, 20% of the time during closing, and 15% of the time during opening.

19

Coaching

Some teams have multiple coaches. Some teams are student-run. Regardless of how the team is structured, this chapter is for the person who is ultimately calling the shots.

Having someone in charge is critical. Though some things (like the practice schedule) might be set by majority vote, other decisions should not be left to a democracy. For example, a team needs a unified trial strategy. A mediocre strategy with everyone rowing the same direction is better than a great strategy with only half the team on board. Discuss. Debate. Argue. All of that is fine. But when the decision is made, the team has to support that decision.

We encourage teams to have coaches. In addition to providing knowledge about the law, public speaking, and/or the competition, coaches can resolve conflict. They can also assign parts without being personally invested. Some student-run teams are very successful, but many others struggle because the students in charge, usually upperclassmen, may end up assigning parts based on their individual desires or who their friends are. A coach can more easily focus on the big picture and assign roles based on what is best for the team. This is not to say student leaders are not important. An executive board or team captain can play an important role even when a team has a nonstudent coach.

Within a coaching staff—the term "staff" is used very loosely since few programs have paid coaches—there can be a divide and conquer approach. One coach can oversee a varsity team while the other oversees a junior varsity team. One can focus on the prosecution side of the case while the other focuses on the defense. One can focus on helping the teams develop content while the other focuses on performance skills. The ways to split up responsibilities are limitless, but the point is that having multiple coaches can be really helpful.

Let's Get Real: Some real trials are handled solo, with one lawyer doing all the work to represent their client. But on larger cases, or for cases handled by law firms, there is often a division of labor similar to Mock Trial teams. For example, at a law firm, "partners" (the lawyers who own the firm) decide which lawyers are on which case teams and what roles they will have. Within each team, there is a senior attorney who manages the case and junior attorneys who help them prepare for trial. District attorneys' offices and public defenders' offices have similar hierarchies.

A coach has three primary functions: (1) organize the team (select team members and assign roles), (2) prepare the team for competition, and (3) handle logistics such as travel and registration. For middle and high school students, the third function might be delegated to a "team parent." For college and law school team members, the third function might be delegated to a team member.

19.1 Organizing the Team

19.1.1 Selecting Team Members

If you are fortunate enough to have more students who want to participate than you have roles available, you will need to have an audition or try out to determine who gets the roles.

Note that "cutting" participants does not have to occur at the very beginning of the season. You can have multiple practices where you work on objections and other general materials. Give some assignments and see who does the work. Among students who have never done Mock Trial before, a number will not realize how much work it is. Some will drop out.

Before you do tryouts, figure out how many students you can take. Most competitions allow you to field multiple teams. We strongly recommend fielding multiple teams if allowed. For starters, that gives you an extra chance to advance in the competition. But even if your second squad does not win many ballots, it can be a great chance for students to gain experience and be better prepared for your top squad the next year.

We recommend having returning members try out. Doing so sends the message that no one has a guaranteed spot; even experienced members still need to work hard. It also helps the coaches see how much people have improved. This will help especially when assigning roles.

Always take more students than the minimum number allowed for a competition roster. While you have a limited number of roster spots for the competition, there are no limits on how many students can be part of your program. Anyone who does not get a competition roster spot can be an "alternate." Alternates are useful in filling various roles during scrimmages. They can also step in if other students quit or fall ill. Even when tournaments have a limit on the number of students that may be on a roster, the roster itself typically does not have to be submitted until shortly before the competition.

For the tryout itself, a common method is to ask students to prepare an opening statement based on a fact pattern. Don't wait for the current case packet to come out. A lot can be done before that point in the season. Rather, use the prior year's case, or a simple fact pattern you prepare for the purposes of practice. Observing students prepare and perform an opening has benefits, but it is not the only option. Some coaches let participants speak on anything. This approach is more likely to bring out students who have some public speaking skills but no background with Mock Trial.

Think carefully about what you are trying to determine during tryouts. Are you trying to measure work ethic and maybe reduce the number of people trying out? Give a longer tryout fact pattern. Are you trying to encourage more people to try out? Use a shorter fact pattern. Are you trying to improve the team's public speaking? Give students a short paragraph to memorize. That will isolate public speaking. Are you trying to find students with excellent improvisational skills? Have them pull a prompt out of a hat and start speaking in 30 seconds. *What animal makes the best pet? Should the voting age be lowered to 16? What is the most important invention of all time?*

Regardless of the method used, it's useful to have multiple people observing. More and different viewpoints can help spot potential. If people who have useful ideas are not available to observe in person, record the tryouts and have them watch on video. Video can also be nice to have later in the season to re-play and help students see how far they have progressed.

When selecting participants, keep in mind that Mock Trial is like Olympic figure skating. The students will need to be able to perform the technical elements required, but there is also an "artistry" component. As long as the student has enough intellectual firepower, you can teach the technical elements—even if they have never done Mock Trial before. You can also improve the artistry over time, but people have different natural gifts (a great voice, the "it" factor, etc.) and thus different ceilings as to how good they can be.

Ask students at tryouts why they want to join. Students simply looking to improve their resumes may not put in the time. Look for people who are passionate, who like teamwork, and who are competitive.

19.1.2 Assigning Roles

Most competitions allow students to perform on one or both sides of the case. When performing on both sides, a student can be an attorney on both, a witness on both, or an attorney on one side and a witness on the other. A benefit of having some students participate on only one side is more students can have an active role in the competition. However, be mindful of the total team roster size allowed. There is generally a limit for the total number of students for both sides of the case combined.

Resist the temptation to assign parts immediately after reading the case. When students don't know which roles they will have, they will read the entire case packet more thoroughly. Additionally, when students get roles assigned immediately, they can become territorial or complacent. Assigning roles for an upcoming practice (rather than for the whole season), can help students be flexible if something needs to be changed as the season progresses. Even if the team composition stays the same, some things may need to be tweaked. For example, scrimmages may reveal that a certain attorney/witness combination lacks chemistry.

Make clear that all roles can be changed. Sometimes a person does not put in the work necessary to keep their role. Sometimes another student outperforms expectations. Sometimes practice reveals that students are better suited for certain roles than the one they were originally assigned. If students understand from the outset that roles may change, they will be less upset when roles change.

When you do assign parts, be mindful of how practices will be conducted. If you have two teams practicing together, it generally makes sense to overlap roles. For example, a student who is an attorney on both sides of the case might direct a witness for the prosecution, and then cross that same witness on the defense. If a student plays both an attorney and a witness, she can cross that witness while being an attorney for the plaintiff and then play that witness on the defense. The theory is that by overlapping tasks, students become true experts on a particular witness.

If you have only one team, it is best to assign parts *without* overlap so you can conduct a full trial with just your team members. In other words, don't have the same student both play a witness and cross that witness. (You can't ask yourself questions.) Don't have the same student both direct and cross a witness. (You can't have an objection fight with yourself.) It's permissible to have someone do the opening for both sides, but if a student is going to give a "speech" on both sides, it usually flows better to have him do the opening on one side and the closing on the other. Among other reasons, if a student gives the same speech for both sides, they can get confused about what side they are arguing for. We've seen a resounding speech as to why someone should be found "not guilty"—given by a prosecuting attorney.

WAR STORY

Professor Bernstein once had a student get confused about the witness he was portraying. The first question of the direct was, "Please introduce yourself." The witness said, "Hi. I'm Tony Kissner. I'm a doctor." When he saw his attorney's horrified face, he realized his error. He stood up, walked a circle around the witness stand, sat down, and said, "Hi. I'm Tony Kissner. I'm a golfer." No one knows why he circled the witness stand.

With multiple teams, you must decide whether to "stack" your likely top performers on a single squad or spread them out. If your goal is to win a competition, we strongly recommend stacking. At the higher levels, a weak link or two will really stand out. Also, pairing team members with others with similar abilities is usually better for morale. Do not, however, be surprised if your B team surpasses the A team at some point in the season. Hard work and team chemistry can mean more than the talent each person demonstrates during tryouts.

When assigning parts, be mindful of the order in which the witnesses for your side will testify. Most competitions allow the team to choose this order. If the order is dictated, however, you will want to start with your weakest attorney/witness pairing progressing to your best attorney/witness pairing.

When pairing attorneys and witnesses, try to make sure one in each pair has experience. An experienced attorney can help train an inexperienced witness. Similarly, an experienced witness can make life easier for an inexperienced lawyer.

Be mindful of chemistry—both in attorney/witness combinations and in the attorney grouping for a side. If you have two alpha attorneys, putting one in charge of each side of the case can be beneficial. Beyond that, attorney roles are more fungible, so it's best to assign witnesses, and then assign the attorney roles based on what students will work best together.

Some students excel at playing one type of witness (victim, expert, police officer, etc.). Assign those parts first and build around them. Some witnesses are only good at playing characters a certain way (funny, serious, with an Australian accent, etc.). While this type of portrayal might work for multiple witnesses, it probably won't work for all of them. This is a good secondary consideration in assigning parts.

19.1.3 Structuring the Season

When you register to compete, make a note of when the case packet will be released and the dates of competitions. Rules vary by state so check with your governing body, but for middle school the case release and official competitions typically happen in the fall. For high school, the case is released in the fall semester and competition occurs in the spring. For college, the case is released at the start of the academic year, Regional Competitions happen in February and March, and the National Championship is in April.

If your team has newcomers, show them a video of the competition in which you are competing as soon as possible. Mock Trial is tough to visualize without having observed it. If you don't have access to a good video from your own competition, find a video of a high-quality trial from another competition. The American Mock Trial Association sells videos of prior championship rounds through its website at www.CollegeMockTrial.org.

Check to see what guidance your competition gives to scoring judges. Obtain a sample ballot. Look for the stated scoring criteria which are sometimes in printed handouts and sometimes in a PowerPoint shared at the Judges Meetings. Knowing what judges are told to look for can help you tailor your instruction.

Successful teams often start practicing before the case is released. These early season practices provide a great opportunity to get newcomers up to speed. They also provide an opportunity to practice objections, exhibit handling, etc. The more students learn before the case is released, the more practice can focus on case specific content after it comes out. Early season practices can use a case from a previous year or a new, basic fact pattern.

Once the case is released, start running trials early. Many teams make the mistake of working for months on their content prior to having a trial. Teams are never ready for their first practice trial. It will always be choppy. The sooner you have it the sooner the team will start to improve. Don't work too long to perfect content. It will never be perfect, but the sooner you let guest judges observe and weigh in on it, the better it will end up. As we've said throughout this book, scoring points is more about performance than content. Improving performance takes lots of repetition.

When setting out the season schedule, put a fair number of trials where you will have guest judges come in and give feedback. Coaches can get too close to their students or the case materials. A guest judge will have fresh eyes and will view things more like the scoring judges in competition. Make at least one of these practices a "dress rehearsal" not long before your competition.

While you will hone your material as the season progresses, resist the temptation to constantly change strategies. You might have a guest judge with a strong opinion or scrimmage an opponent who had a good idea. That does not mean you need to rewrite your whole case. In fact, there is value in perfecting your material and practicing delivery. A+ content with B+ delivery will usually lose to B+ content with A+ delivery.

Whether formal or informal, it's great to have an end-of-season event to celebrate the team's successes over the course of the season. Have team members vote on an MVP. It's also important to recognize those who are not yet superstars—most improved, rookie of the year, and so on. Find something positive to say about every student. Those who might not excel in the courtroom may be great teammates outside of it.

Consider one-on-one exit interviews. At a minimum, it's good to know who plans to come back the following season. It can also be a good way for coaches to get feedback on their own performance. As with the students, there is always room for coaches to improve.

19.1.4 Team Dynamics

It is crucial to set the tone early in the season and make it clear that attendance at and preparedness for practices is required. If someone comes in without their content done, it wastes everyone's time. Work with captains and other leaders to help police this.

The team needs to practice like it knows someone else out there is excellent and it will take everything they've got to catch up. However, by the time "game day" approaches, you need the opposite attitude: you're the best unless and until someone out there proves otherwise. Building confidence is critical. If you "break a team down," make sure you have enough time to build them back up. With "B" teams in particular, they will need to be propped up by you during the season, because they will probably have their hats handed to them regularly in scrimmages against the "A" team.

Most feedback at practice trials is too negative. Yes, students need to be told what they need to do to improve. But don't forget the occasional pat on the back. This keeps competitors feeling good, makes them more receptive to critique, and reminds them to keep doing the things that they did well.

That said, students need to know what they can improve. Often, humor is a good way to deliver negative feedback across without hurt feelings. If everyone can laugh at themselves, people are less likely to get bent out of shape when it's their turn to be told they stunk up the joint. ☺

For newcomers, the whole trial experience can be daunting. Although you can, and should, run trials early on, don't ask a student to master the whole process off the bat. The key is subdivision. Not the entire defense case, but one cross-examination. Not a whole cross-examination, but one pocket. Not a whole pocket, but one perfect question. Subdivide as much as you need to for a student to feel good about something and gain confidence, and then build on it.

Conflict among team members is inevitable. You're dealing with students working in close quarters for months. And, due to the nature of the activity, many of the students who sign up enjoy arguing.

A Mock Trial team is like a family. Not everyone will have the same opinions. Not everyone will want to hang out together outside of practice. But to succeed, you have to respect one another. Set personal feelings aside and focus on the common good. We have always told our teams, you don't have to like one another, but you do have to love one another.

Regardless of what level of competition you are coaching, you need a policy on intrateam dating. Intrateam dating can be problematic. If the couple stays together, other students may feel there is favoritism, especially if one of the students in the relationship is part of team leadership. If the couple breaks up, that can cause a lot of drama.

See if the school has a policy before making a decision. If you don't prohibit intrateam dating, it's almost certain to happen. Students are spending long hours together. A team becomes its own social circle. At the college level, there simply may not be time to find a romantic partner outside of the Mock Trial world.[1]

If you prohibit intrateam dating, it's still likely to happen, you're just less likely to discover it right away. In a sense, this is a choice between dealing with ill will on the front end (when students will think you are

1. This is an alternate kind of "closed-universe problem."

being unfair and invading their personal freedom) and dealing on the back end with the fallout from the end of a romantic relationship. We know of several mock trial marriages, but the average courtship is still unlikely to make it through a season. The most brutal cross-examination Judge Nelmark has ever seen was one half of a recently broken up couple crossing the other half. Professor Bernstein does not prohibit intrateam dating, but he does ask his students to let him know so he can assign roles accordingly (e.g., consider placing them on different counsel tables, make sure they are not directing one another).

19.2 Preparing the Team

19.2.1 Practices

The practice structure and schedule will vary, depending each team's goals. Most successful teams practice multiple times per week. It is good to allow around three hours for at least one (if not all) of the practices so that you have a scheduled opportunity to conduct a trial and offer feedback (from coaches and/or guest judges).

Team practices should focus on (a) scrimmaging, (b) full team discussion on issues like theme and theory, and (c) instruction from coaches. "Work time"—whether writing a speech or working with a witness to prepare questions—should occur apart from team practice. Although the students at a practice can occasionally be broken into small groups to work on something, this should be the exception rather than the rule. Students can and should work on creating and memorizing content on their own. Even if they are practicing questions and answers, they can meet as a pair. "Team practices" should focus on team activities.

It can be hard to focus for several hours. Earlier in the season, it often works best to run half the trial and then do feedback, followed by the second half and then more feedback. For dress rehearsals, do it the same way as competition, with all feedback saved for the end. The team needs to practice as if it's the real thing to build stamina. If you can't get through one full round easily, it will be very hard to do three or four rounds over two to three days.

The importance of video cannot be stressed enough. Students should rewatch their own performance to see when they talk too fast, when they use *uhs, ums*, and so on. A coach can go back to the video to highlight certain things that went poorly or well. When staring at pages and pages of notes after a trial, you might recall that you liked something, but can't recall why. If you can go back, find the moment, and play it for students, it helps lock it in.

If a student misses a practice, give thought to who should step in and play their role. It should ideally be whoever would sub in at a competition. Don't just have another attorney take on a missing attorney's parts. An alternate is Plan A. Plan B is probably a witness stepping up. If an attorney team member drops out a week before competition (it happens), and you don't have an alternate ready, you're probably going to have a witness step into that role and replace the witness. It's easier to quickly learn a witness statement than to learn the rules of evidence.

Although not every practice needs to involve running the trial, when you do run the trial, do it right. Dress in courtroom attire. Don't allow gum chewing or giggling or slouching or anything that would not occur during competition. Bad practices lead to bad habits in competition. An exception would be the occasional "silly trial" just for kicks. At such a trial, people play different parts, make off-the-wall objections, and break out humorous witness portrayals. This can be a good tension breaker. When this is done, make the plan clear in advance.

19.2.2 Guest Judges

Whether going it alone or with co-coaches, it is still important to bring in "guest judges" to preside over team scrimmages. The coaching staff will be intimately familiar with the case. A guest judge, like your scoring judges at competition, will come in with fresh eyes. Additionally, coaches can sometimes have a blind spot for certain flaws in the performance of a team member who is well liked. Someone without a personal relationship can make a more honest assessment. Finally, it's crucial to just have different perspectives. You can't predict who will judge your team in competition. Accordingly, it is important to have guest judges come in from a wide variety of backgrounds (plaintiff's attorneys, defense attorneys, prosecutors, civil litigators, real judges, nonlitigation lawyers, etc.). Make sure to bring in people with experiences different from your own.

Guest judges should provide feedback at the conclusion of the scrimmage. We also advocate giving guest judges a ballot. The completed ballot is generally not shared with team members—this is just practice and you don't want them to get discouraged—but it can be very helpful for coaches to learn what is and is not working. If, for example, multiple guest judges from different backgrounds don't like a particular witness, you can bet competition judges won't either. Change things up either by having the student play the character in a different way or switching roles and having someone else play that character. Just because parts were assigned early in the season does not mean those assignments are set in stone.

In addition to gaining valuable feedback from guest judges, their very presence can help team performance. It's tough to "turn it on" for a scrimmage when the person on the bench is the same coach the students see every practice. A guest judge makes it feel real. It also will make students less nervous when they get to competition and are arguing objections in front of a stranger.

It is important to debrief after guest judges' comments—ideally at the same practice after those comments are given. Guest judges often give feedback that should *not* be incorporated. Guest judges might not be aware of the specific competition rules. They might not fully understand the team strategy. Their feedback is extremely useful, but coaches need to be aware of the feedback to point out what should not be taken to heart.

19.2.3 Invitational Tournaments

Official programs usually have a regional tournament followed by a state championship tournament, or regional tournaments followed by a national championship. Competing in one or two tournaments is not a lot of "game time." It's like putting on a play for only two days after six months of rehearsals. To combat that and get in extra practice, many college and law schools have "invitational tournaments."

An invitational tournament looks like the "real" competition. It has ballots, winners, and trophies. Some of them are very prestigious, with teams flying in from around the country to compete. The case used will be the same one used at regionals. Invitationals are great opportunities to get experience and test out themes and theories. Great programs will spend a lot of time analyzing invitational results.

When evaluating invitationals, find one appropriate for the skill level of the team you are sending to compete there. Invitationals are sort of "dress rehearsals" on steroids. They can, and should, build a team's confidence. But, throwing a team to the wolves at an invitational the team is not ready for can be counterproductive.

Celebrate both individual and team success at invitationals. Generate as much publicity as you can. This can help raise money, recruit team members, and generate momentum for the upcoming official tournaments.

If you are thinking about attending one or more invitationals, plan early. They often fill up and, if accepted to compete, you may need to raise money for travel.

If you are reluctant to compete in an invitational out of fear that other teams will "steal" your strategies, think again. First, after months with the same case, very few strategies end up being unique. More importantly, the value your students will get from extra practice against real opponents is worth any chance that other teams see your material. Besides, your material might change after the invitational. And the risk goes both ways: you can see other team's material, too.

19.2.4 Hosting an Invitational

If there are not any invitationals within driving distance—or if there aren't enough—consider hosting your own.

Hosting a tournament can be a great way to raise money. Even if the registration fees don't vastly outweigh the expenses of hosting, you're getting experience without the cost of sending your teams to someone else's tournament.

A *lot* goes into hosting a successful tournament. Work with experienced hosts for guidance. Cap the number of teams if you must, but don't overpromise and underdeliver. Also, engage in these three steps as early as possible:

First, make sure the invitational is permitted. Some organizations (surprisingly) will not let their case be used at an invitational tournament. Others require a license fee to be paid. Once the tournament is officially authorized, the governing body may be willing to help you promote it.

Second, secure your space. Even if the tournament is being hosted on campus, rooms get booked early. Don't invite teams to an event unless you're sure you have room for them. You will need one good trial room for every two teams competing, plus (at a minimum) three extra rooms to be used for a Tabulation Room, Judges Meetings, and Captains Meetings. It is much, much easier to have separate rooms for these tasks rather than doubling up.

Third, recruit judges early. You should have at least two judges per round, and ideally three (with one judge just presiding and two scoring). Coaches can be enlisted to judge in an emergency, but at an invitational, they want to watch their teams rather than critique others. Also, keep in mind that you will get cancellations and no-shows. Recruit far more judges than you need.

19.2.5 Statistical Analysis

Although Mock Trial is a competition about public speaking, winning is a math game. *It's All About Points!* The goal is to score more points than the other team. It's a cumulative effort and parts need to be assigned (or re-assigned) with that in mind.

If your team attends “invitational tournaments,” you will get back ballots. This allows you to crunch numbers and see what is working and what isn’t. If you don’t go to invitationals, try to arrange a scrimmage with another school and give ballots to guest judges. If that is not possible, at least have judges score your own intraschool practices. (Find the actual ballot used in your competition and make copies.) Even if you don’t share the ballots with students, the scores can guide your future actions.

If you have two students performing functions at an average level, they might both get sevens in competition. Two sevens is fourteen points. That’s usually not enough to win. If you reverse their roles, and one student gets a 9 or 10, you’re immediately better off. Yes, it’s possible for the other student to get a 4 or 5, but it’s quite unlikely.

When evaluating scores, keep in mind not only your own team’s scores, but also the opposing team’s scores. Your opening statement getting a 9 doesn’t help you if the opposing attorney gets a 10. When you consider a particular witness, keep in mind their score, plus the directing attorney’s score, minus the crossing attorney’s score. If you get to choose what witnesses you use, you might reject the one where the direct score is great in lieu of one where the direct score is good and the crossing score is below average.

Make sure to consider all individual scores in context of the entire ballot. Getting a 9 is great—unless the judge is giving almost everyone else a 10. Getting a 7 is usually a bad sign—unless the judge is giving everyone else 5s and 6s. You will need a formula for normalizing the scores from any particular trial. One method is to measure each score relative to the average score given by a judge. If a judge’s average score for the trial is 7.5, then a student who scored a 9 would have a normalized score of +1.5, and a student who scored a 7 would have a normalized score of –0.5. This allows you to more meaningfully compare students from different trials.

Remember, as well, that context matters. You will generally earn higher scores, especially higher normalized scores, when facing weaker opponents. Make sure to consider “strength of schedule”—your opponent’s performance quality and their record in other trials—before giving too much weight to the scores in isolation. You can also normalize your team’s scores by comparing any particular score to the average score given to your team for the round. Even if a particular score was higher than the opposition, it may still be a weak link relative to the rest of your team.

19.3 Traveling with the Team

19.3.1 Logistics

It can be helpful to designate a team member or a team parent to handle travel arrangements. Keep in mind that even if students are old enough to drive, school policy may prohibit students from driving their own cars to off-campus events. Plus, students might not be old enough to rent cars—many rental companies have a minimum age of 25.

Many teams travel to tournaments in vans. Though crowding a team into one vehicle can be chaotic, it can also lead to some fun stories. Set luggage limits to be sure everything fits—including enlargements and other trial supplies.

Traveling on a budget can be difficult. If multiple students are crammed into a room, make sure they work out a schedule so everyone can be showered and ready by the time you need to leave the hotel for the competition site. If flying to a tournament, you will want to arrive at least a day in advance so flight delays don't prevent you from competing.

If the competition does not provide lunch, make sure you have a plan. Many of the teams will try to descend on the same fast-food restaurant over the break. With limited time, you may be better off avoiding the run-around and bringing your own food—though be sure to eat it outside or in a designated area. Or you can order delivery. Just be sure to plan ahead. Hungry teams tend not to perform very well.

19.3.2 The Coach's Role during a Tournament

First and foremost, learn and share the rules of the facility at which you are competing. This is especially important if you are competing in a real courthouse. Most have strict rules on what is permitted through security and what food and drink is permitted in courtrooms. Teams have been sanctioned for not following these guidelines. More importantly, not respecting the rules of a courthouse may result in the facility being unavailable for future competitions.

Most competitions allow coaches to observe their team's trials, but not communicate with the team until after the trial concludes. So, after months of practice, you're reduced to being a bystander. Some coaches watch all their team's rounds. Others can't stand to watch. Some would love to watch, but find it makes their team nervous. Let the team know what your plan is. If you don't watch, but video recording is permitted, have someone record the round. It is difficult to later interpret a judge's written comments on the ballot without seeing what transpired.

Be aware that even if you plan to watch a round, you might get called into service judging a different round or assisting in the Tabulation Room. If this happens, do your best to serve cheerfully. Hosts do their best to recruit judges, but it's a challenge. Recruits sometimes no-show. While you might prefer to watch your team, the other teams deserve to have their round scored. Eventually, you'll be on the other end when some other coach is asked to step in and judge your team.

In most tournaments, coaches are allowed to see ballots after each round. If this is allowed, make sure you take advantage of the opportunity. If nothing else, make sure the scores are totaled correctly. Some coaches tell their teams their scores, others keep it close to the vest. There are pros and cons to both approaches. Some teams dwell too much on past scores if they hear them. Some teams waste too much time guessing what the scores were and it's best just to tell them. In any case, resist the temptation to really shake things up after one bad ballot. Mock Trial is subjective, and the next set of judges might love what you've been practicing. If you scrap something and try something new without practicing, you might address one criticism but create more problems.

Be mindful that if your team has two rounds in the same day, there is likely to be a let-down for the second one. Students are tired from preparing for competition, but the adrenaline will likely carry them through the first round. Once it wears off, they slump. Keep snacks handy. Do some walking or listen to some music between rounds to perk them up. We have seen strong teams lose afternoon or evening trials simply because they are tired and come out flat.

Scouting—watching another team's round to prepare for possible competition against that team—is a contentious issue in Mock Trial. In competitions that don't allow it, don't do it. Even in competitions where it is allowed, some people are actively against it. The benefits of scouting are often overrated, but it can be helpful, particularly in competitions where all of the witnesses are not predetermined. Watching a round can inform you as to an opponent's theory and theme, its witness choices, unusual objections, and unusual lines of cross-examination.

Regardless of whether you scout, your focus should be on "doing what you do." If you shake things up to try to respond to the other side, you're playing their game. With some exceptions, you're better off focusing on what you practiced than trying to be clever with the last-minute insight you obtained.

19.4 Miscellaneous

19.4.1 Dealing with Parents

The impact of parents on the program varies significantly by the age of the participants. For middle schoolers, parents will still be driving them to practice. For high schoolers, mom and dad may think the student needs to focus more on academics or get a job. Or they might tell you that their child deserves a larger role. For parents that appear to be overinvolved, try to set boundaries early on. If not addressed, this problem gets worse over time.

For middle and high school, communicating early and often is key. Email out the practice schedule in addition to sending it home with students as hard copies. When the schedule changes, provide as much notice as possible. Invite parents to practice so they can see the hard work paying off. For college and law school, generally keep parents on the sidelines, but encourage students to invite parents to competitions.

At any level, involved parents can be extremely helpful. Many coaches rely on a Team Mom or Team Dad to handle logistics. Parents can drive to competitions, pick up lunches when you're on a tight schedule, and help recruit guest judges.

19.4.2 Having Fun

The Mock Trial season is a grind. At the college level, there might be a hundred intense practices, plus travel. Without some fun built in, burnout is likely. If a team does not look happy to be at the competition, they won't score well.

Some practices can be informal, but still productive. "Objection Jeopardy" can be a good way to improve knowledge of the rules of evidence. A night where everyone swaps parts can be a good way to keep people on their toes.

Some practice nights should be used for team bonding. A team dinner or unexpected mini golf outing can go a long way toward building camaraderie and easing tension.

Remember that this is an activity that people do by *choice.* It's usually not a graduation requirement. The students (and generally the coaches) aren't getting paid for it. Thus, it has to be enjoyable for people to stick with it.

We encourage *you* to stick with it. This book has addressed the many rewards for students, but coaches will also receive immeasurable benefits.

Index

Printed by Libri Plureos GmbH in Hamburg,
Germany

9 781639 050925